UNFINISHED
Dialogue

Also by Isaiah Berlin

KARL MARX

THE HEDGEHOG AND THE FOX

THE AGE OF ENLIGHTENMENT

RUSSIAN THINKERS

CONCEPTS AND CATEGORIES

AGAINST THE CURRENT

PERSONAL IMPRESSIONS

THE CROOKED TIMBER OF HUMANITY

THE SENSE OF REALITY

THE PROPER STUDY OF MANKIND

THE ROOTS OF ROMANTICISM

THE POWER OF IDEAS

THREE CRITICS OF THE ENLIGHTENMENT

FREEDOM AND ITS BETRAYAL

LIBERTY

THE SOVIET MIND

FLOURISHING: LETTERS 1928–1946
(Published in the US as LETTERS 1928–1946)

Also by Beata Polanowska-Sygulska

FILOZOFIA WOLNOSCI ISAIAHA BERLINA
(Isaiah Berlin's Philosophy of Freedom)

OBLICZA LIBERALIZMU: ISAIAH BERLIN, JOHN GRAY, STEVEN LUKES,
JOSEPH RAZ W ROZMOWIE Z BEATA POLANOWSKA-SYGULSKA
(Visages of Liberalism: Isaiah Berlin, John Gray, Steven Lukes,
Joseph Raz in Conversation with Beata Polanowska-Sygulska)

FOREWORD BY HENRY HARDY

UNFINISHED

Dialogue

Isaiah Berlin

AND BEATA POLANOWSKA-SYGULSKA

Prometheus Books

59 John Glenn Drive
Amherst, New York 14228-2197

Published 2006 by Prometheus Books

Inquiries should be addressed to
Prometheus Books
59 John Glenn Drive
Amherst, New York 14228–2197
VOICE: 716–691–0133, ext. 207
FAX: 716–564–2711
WWW.PROMETHEUSBOOKS.COM

10 09 08 07 06   5 4 3 2 1

Library of Congress Cataloging-in-Publication Data

Berlin, Isaiah, Sir.
    Unfinished dialogue / Isaiah Berlin and Beata Polanowska-Sygulska; foreword by Henry Hardy.
        p. cm.
    Includes bibliographical references (p.   ) and index.
    ISBN 1–59102–376–9 (hardcover : alk. paper)
    1. Philosophy, Modern—20th century. I. Polanowska-Sygulska, Beata. II. Title.

B804.B455 2006
192—dc22

                                                                        2005032638

Printed in the United States of America on acid-free paper

Contents

6   Contents

Foreword

Henry Hardy

The remarkable dialogue between Isaiah Berlin and Beata Polanowska-Sygulska was conducted intermittently over the last fourteen years of Berlin's life. At times exhilarating, at times frustrating, this published record of some of their exchanges is a distinctive contribution to the exploration of Berlin's ideas. It also bears the clear stamp of both the personalities involved, and displays, often with moving immediacy, how a fruitful engagement with moral and political issues is a matter of sensibility as well as argument.

Beata grew up in Communist Poland. Living under Communism gives political ideas a special intensity and a pressing importance hard for many Western Europeans to imagine. Berlin, who witnessed the 1917 Russian Revolutions as a child, knew this very well; indeed, some of his own principal intellectual preoccupations were largely driven by the visceral antipathy to all forms of totalitarianism permanently laid down in him by that early experience. Conversations with sensitive and intelligent people who knew Communism's iron repression of freedom at first hand were especially poignant for him, and he always went out of his way to be available to those among them who saw his ideas as a lifeline, as an antidote to the mendacious ideology under which they were compelled to exist.[1] Beata was one such: as she wrote to Berlin in April 1997, 'For a person from my part of the world the issue of the philosophical foundations of liberalism is a vital one.'[2] And again the following month:

---

1. For the same reason he always stipulated that no charge should be made for the translation of his work into the languages of the Communist bloc.

2. 90 below (page references are given in these notes without the prefix 'p.' or 'pp.').

7

The problem itself still haunts me; especially in the context of the heated political discourse in my country (just tomorrow there will be a constitutional referendum in Poland). Is a liberal democratic State our only reasonable choice, or do we have any other equally sensible alternatives? If not, why? Because (as John Gray would say) of our particular historical tradition? Or because liberalism has a claim to universal authority, as it recognises the value of liberty, without which there is no choice and therefore no possibility of remaining human as we understand the word?[1]

The direct link between Berlin's ideas and the live political questions Beata faced in Poland gave their discussions a particular importance for him, as he makes clear more than once in his letters and conversations. It also brings their dialogue to life.

This link also explains Beata's decision to write her doctoral thesis (completed in 1988) on controversies about the concept of liberty, with special reference to Berlin's ideas. She soon had questions to ask, and so the dialogue began—by letter in 1983, and then in person in 1986, as she relates. Once the thesis was done, Beata began to plan a book on Berlin's philosophy of freedom, and her enquiries continued until the end of Berlin's life (the book appeared in 1998). She asked central, searching questions, as Berlin recognises in a letter of November 1986: 'believe me, I profited greatly from your very pointed questions. I think you are the best (oral) critic I have had, and the most constructive.'[2]

Beata persisted tenaciously when she did not feel she had been answered in the way she needed. Her doggedness is much to her credit. Anyone who has made a serious attempt to ask Berlin to clarify his ideas viva voce is familiar with the struggle to keep him to the point, to overcome his tendency to disappear into digressions which, marvellous as they often were, took him away from the issue on which his interlocutor wished to concentrate. Especially at the beginning, Beata was overawed, shy, and unsure of her untested English, but she bravely stuck to her guns as Berlin darted like a dragonfly from topic to topic, often following his own agenda rather than hers, jumping into her unfinished sentences as she struggled to express the question she wanted him to answer. Much of this maddening failure of communication has been skilfully edited out, but I have seen the raw transcripts, and I can bear witness that the cutting-room floor is littered with false starts and cross purposes.

Beata continued to correspond with Berlin throughout, which is fortunate, since his letters tended to be more reliably focused than his conversa-

---

1. 94 below.
2. 50 below.

tion. Some of them were splendidly lucid statements of his views, at times clearer than the treatments of the same topics in his published work. Indeed one of these letters, on the concept of human nature, was for this reason published in the *New York Review of Books* in 2004. Beata also wrote a number of articles on Berlin's ideas, some included here (together with later pieces), which she showed to Berlin in draft and discussed with him, and which played their part in stimulating him to explain himself where she felt explanation was needed. These articles will doubtless provoke further discussion of the issues they address. The last one in particular, which distils the results of Beata's exchanges with Berlin about the relationship between pluralism and liberalism, will be much referred to, if I am not mistaken, as the important debate as this topic continues.

Beata's main topic was liberty, but like many scholars in more recent years she was also challenged and absorbed by the value pluralism[1] that Berlin closely links to his liberalism, even if the nature of the link is controversial. Indeed her wish to clarify exactly what this link amounts to is one of the leading themes of her conversations with Berlin. Does pluralism entail liberalism? If so, in what sense of 'entail'? Or does it undermine liberalism, at any rate as a universal thesis about the best political order for mankind, as John Gray contends? Or are the two positions unconnected? Berlin's published remarks on the relationship between pluralism and liberalism seem equivocal at best,[2] and this is one of the main cruces he leaves unresolved in print; indeed, he never really addresses it seriously or systematically at all. So the light shed upon it in this book, even if fitful, does genuinely take us further.

The same applies to another crux, namely the question of whether there is a common human nature. On this, too, Berlin seems to say inconsistent things, at one time stressing the enormous cultural variety we see through time and across the world, at another insisting on a shared core of needs and values that enables us to empathise even with people situated at a great cultural or historical distance from us. This dilemma is not quite resolved here, but once more Beata's insistence on clarification of ostensible contradiction causes light to be shed. I greedily wish that she had also pressed him on the question of whether the objectivity of values in which he believes is best seen

---

1. The thesis that ultimate human values (those pursued for their own sake rather than as a means to some higher end) are, as a matter of objective empirical observation, irreducibly different from one another; from which it follows that they cannot be compared with one another on the scale of some allegedly higher-order value such as utility, or (another way of saying the same thing) translated into some common value-currency. From this 'incommensurability', as it is called, it follows in turn that, when in real situations incompatible values clash, the decision that has to be made between them will entail a sometimes tragic loss in terms of the value decided against or given lower priority.

2. See 82, 211, 287, 290 below.

as a matter of such values being widely held (his usual account), or of their being beneficial to mankind (which would allow us to reject values that are wrong-headed even if ubiquitous). Clearly the two criteria are related, but how, exactly?

One of the frustrations the reader may experience arises from the unfortunate delay between Berlin's first clear enunciation of his pluralism, in 1958, and the sustained investigation by others of this radically disturbing view, which began to gather momentum only some thirty years later—partly, perhaps, as a result of the publication of a series of collections of his previously scattered essays, some of which had more to say about pluralism. Why it took so long for the subversive implications of this idea to dawn on philosophers remains something of a mystery. Beata suitably quotes Charles Taylor:

> Isaiah's plurality thesis was not only a blow to various totalitarian theories of positive liberty, it was also deeply unsettling to the moral theories dominant in his own milieu. It is one of the paradoxes of our intellectual world, which will be increasingly discussed in the future, why this latter point was not realised. The bomb was planted in the academy, but somehow failed to go off.[1]

However that may be, it has certainly well and truly gone off now, at a time when pluralism's relevance to the contemporary world is even greater than it was at the end of the 1950s. Indeed, the increased applicability of Berlin's crucial idea today is surely one of the main reasons for the vigour of the discussion that has centred upon it. All the issues that gather round the question of the proper limits to tolerance of difference—multiculturalism, nationalism, fundamentalist terrorism, cultural imperialism—turn on whether pluralism is true, and, if so, what its implications are for our conduct in particular circumstances.

By the time this discussion was fully under way, Berlin was well into his retirement, and not actively working on what is now thought by many to be his main contribution to moral and political thought. He did not add significantly to the ballooning literature on the topic. This made those who hoped for clarification and extension of his brief 1958 statement regret that the spotlight had not been turned upon it when it was made—that is, at a time when he would have been more willing, more able, to take things further. I remember asking him once whether he did not feel the desire, on reading some of the mass of writing on the topic, to leap in and put straight those who had misunderstood him, to rule on the disputes between rival interpreters, to

---

1. 266 below.

answer his critics, especially John Gray, whose book *Isaiah Berlin* took the reader down paths where its subject would certainly not wish to follow. Berlin replied that what was happening was all perfectly normal and natural: one published one's ideas, and then others made use of them, adapted them, criticised them, rejected them. He was not unduly exercised about misunderstanding and misrepresentation—'What can I do?'—and declared himself content to let matters take their course.

This was the predicament in which Beata found herself. But she nevertheless made a good deal of headway. Her patient perseverance, her personal grace and moral charm, her origins and background, her obvious integrity, her clarity and directness (so unlike the unnecessary abstraction and defensive periphrasis so often encountered in academics and their publications) all worked together to elicit from Berlin a good deal of useful clarification, and some new thinking. Sometimes, certainly, this takes the form of hints that need some unpacking; there is also a certain amount of muddle, inconsistency and equivocation,[1] and some plain error; but my guess is that, added together, and viewed from an empathetic rather than a captious stance, the expansions and explanations recorded in this volume will be judged a permanent and valuable addition to our understanding of Berlin's thought.

What is beyond doubt is that the reader will encounter between these covers two people of evident goodness and goodwill—a young Polish Berlinophile and mother, and an old Anglophile Russian Jew—together addressing questions many of which really matter, and addressing them in a way that will surely stimulate others to continue the unfinished dialogue for themselves.

---

1. Much but not all of this derives from the spontaneous nature of the remarks published in this volume, for which, as Beata rightly observes, allowance should be made. But the confusions are still worth clearing up. Let me give two examples.

First, Berlin usually uses 'pluralism' as a descriptive term, to refer to what he believes is the irreducible incommensurability of certain values; but occasionally (see, e.g., 202 below) he seems to use it prescriptively, to mean a moral or political standpoint committed to encouraging the pursuit of a variety of values. Unless this is borne in mind, some of his remarks seem paradoxical at best. In addition, on 72 below he conflates pluralism as the belief that other moralities may be as valid as your own with pluralism as the capacity to empathise with those who entertain a morality different from yours. Though Berlin rightly believed that we should not oversimplify reality, we should not undersimplify it either, and a more precisely defined terminology, wearing these and other distinctions on its sleeve, would at times have been useful to him. For Berlin, the first of these four meanings of 'pluralism' is primary, and other uses should ideally be flagged or avoided.

Secondly, Berlin usually maintains that the shared human nature that makes communication and understanding possible between people of different times and cultures is, as he sometimes puts it, 'quasi-universal' (the modifier signalling that whatever degree of universality exists is contingent, not a priori). But sometimes he appears to exclude exotic cultures from this comprehensibility-base (see, e.g., 222 below)—a more cautious position which would undermine what seems to me his truer, more considered and more fruitful view of the extent of possible human empathy.

*He is sometimes in a muddle, but it's an honourable muddle because
everyone is in a muddle!*

Steven Lukes

Statement made at a conference,
'The Value of Liberty: The Challenge of Isaiah Berlin',
Riga, Latvia, September 1998

*I have no opinion of my works, nor of other people's either [chuckles].
Words, words, words.*

Isaiah Berlin

In conversation with Beata Polanowska-Sygulska,
All Souls College, 13 October 1991

Preface

Recent months have made me realise that Isaiah Berlin's ideas may be more alive than ever. There was a moment when there were four of us simultaneously working on this book: Henry Hardy, Berlin's editor and his closest collaborator of over thirty years; James Chappel, a graduate of Haverford College, Pennsylvania, the author of a most interesting thesis on Berlin's Jewish identity; Joshua Cherniss, a graduate of Yale, doing a PhD on the development of Berlin's political thought at Oxford; and myself. At one point our stress levels reached such heights that when one of our computers, working at that moment in Florida, ceased to function, it seemed that it had downed tools in sympathy.

The part of the book that required such intense teamwork was my conversations with Berlin: chaotic, hopelessly bitty, poorly recorded and barely intelligible. Out of the four members of the team, two were very sceptical as to the value of the rough material: Henry and myself. There were moments when we nearly gave up, paralysed by the difficulty of the task and the fear that, apart from the amount of the work involved, I should in the end do a disservice to Berlin. But the two youthful Berlinophiles were absolutely convinced that we should continue the work. They were teenagers when Berlin died, so they did not have the privilege of knowing him in person as we did. They are young Americans, so they have been brought up in a different reality, and share with Berlin neither his British nor his Slavonic cultural and historical background. And yet it was mostly their vivid interest and their youthful belief in the usefulness of our joint efforts that made us complete the task.

James once commented on his impressions of the Glastonbury music festival in Somerset, England, quoting a remark of Berlin's from my recordings. I thought, 'It's worth it, even for this one quote.' Berlin's remark concerned the historic Polish anarchy-prone institution of unanimity of votes, and it read: 'It was mad and it was wonderful.'

I tell the story of my long-lasting contact with the late philosopher in a memoir, 'Memories of Isaiah Berlin', written after his death for the *Oxford Magazine* and included in this volume. Most of the fruit of those fourteen years I had kept in a drawer. It consisted of twenty letters to me, two interviews given for Polish periodicals, several articles of mine and a heap of outdated, ancient cassettes. When the proposal for the publication of a book was made, I instantly decided to include almost all of Berlin's letters and those of my own that are relevant to the replies. Some of Berlin's letters to me are simply informal notes, but there are also whole essays written just for my sake. Both kinds tell much about the personality of their author. Some passages sound prophetic today, like the following one taken from a letter written nearly a decade ago:

> If the values of [. . .] other cultures threaten my own, if they are not only incompatible with the values of my society but actively seek to undermine it, then—even though I may understand perfectly what led people (sociologically or psychologically or religiously) to such beliefs—then I wish to defend myself against these values, and regard myself as justified in doing so; and if they are truly dangerous and threaten the compromise on the basis of which my society exists, then I may have to attack this other culture, and go to war.[1]

I have also included the original English version of the interviews, and those of my articles which (in a way) constitute an illustration of our long-lasting discussion. What remained highly dubious were the conversations. I recorded our meetings on the advice of Dr Zbigniew Pelczynski, the originator of the Oxford hospitality programme for Polish scholars.[2] They were neither planned interviews nor cohesive conversations. We met over twenty times in the years 1986 to 1995 while I was working on my PhD dissertation, and then on a book on Berlin's philosophy of freedom. These were just working meet-

---

1. Letter of 18 February 1997, 85 below.
2. Fellow of Pembroke College; author of, among other works, *The State and Civil Society: Studies in Hegel's Political Philosophy* (1984); and tutor to Bill Clinton. The official name of the programme read: 'The Oxford Colleges Hospitality Scheme for Polish Scholars' (the meaning of the word 'scheme' in British English is different from that in American English; it has no pejorative connotation).

ings, which Berlin very generously agreed to during my four stays in Oxford. I recorded them to make it possible for me to come back to Berlin's answers to my questions. I asked these questions again and again, because my interlocutor kept side-stepping them; so several themes inevitably recurred. Moreover, we discussed such thrilling topics as the articles that I had written, and although Berlin's comments were invaluable to my work and greatly improved the quality of the pieces we discussed, one could not expect those parts of our conversations to be particularly captivating. Again, when a conversation happened to drift away from the main vein, I turned the tape recorder off. I did so out of courtesy; Berlin did not like 'that machine', and when it was not likely that I would quote his words, I had no justification for recording his monologues. On top of everything there were later exchanges recorded over the previous discussions. All in all, then, the unedited material, by its very nature, *could not* be attractive.

The amount of work involved in turning the recordings into a readable text was unimaginable. To cut a long story short, while working on the transcripts we developed a whole nomenclature, inspired by gardening. There were 'weeded', 'thinned' and 'raked' versions, precisely defined by Henry. Incidentally, James's youthful unruliness and my rebellious Polish instinct stimulated our happy creativity in inventing new categories of scripts, this time related to farming. We freely introduced 'ploughed', 'sown', 'fertilised' and 'harvested' versions, duly frowned upon by our regulator. Though there were playful moments, the whole experience had much in common with fighting together during war. If it were not for Henry's utter professionalism backed with his extensive expertise, James's devotion and contagious enthusiasm, and Josh's encouragement, I would have had to give up at the very beginning. My 'brothers in arms' insisted that I take the decisions; that's why I alone bear the responsibility for the result of the battle.

Our iron rule was to preserve the sense of what Berlin said as far as possible. We allowed ourselves to introduce only tiny modifications, such as substituting pronouns for nouns, transforming the passive voice into the active, and the like. Some of Berlin's characteristically very long sentences needed stylistic tweaking. Only exceptionally did we have to insert a missing word or phrase; but such cases were meticulously thought about and discussed. This policy did not apply to my own utterances. On the whole I stuck to the outline of my enquiries, but I allowed myself to reformulate and sometimes to develop them. Oddly enough, after all these years I still remember much of what I had in mind, and what I did not say because of language problems, stress, and Berlin's extremely speedy way of speaking. I also took advantage of my old notes, which have luckily survived. My strategy towards cutting and shifting parts of the text was totally different. Here I allowed myself considerable license.

The subject-matter of the conversations was neither very wide-ranging in terms of the coverage of topics, nor breathtaking as to the originality of the views that emerged. It would not be very reasonable to expect an elderly philosopher to put forward revolutionary theses at working meetings with a student of his ideas. However, there are subjects that are hard to find treated adequately elsewhere, such as 'basic liberty' and the pluralism–liberalism nexus. And there are also two unique motifs.

During our first series of meetings I happened to refer to a quote from Friedrich Waismann about a cat growing to unnatural size.[1] Berlin knew Waismann personally, but either had forgotten the example or hadn't known it. Anyway, he evidently found it inspiring, because, I believe, of its fairy-tale ring. After nearly twenty years I perfectly remember the circumstances in which our little private myth originated. It was an early summer evening; the lights in Berlin's room in All Souls were not yet on. We sat in the dusk and the atmosphere felt a bit unreal. My interlocutor tapped his green telephone, which he always kept under his elbow on the arm of the sofa, and said: 'Supposing a telephone suddenly changes into a cat.' Reflections on the philosophy of language followed. From then on this fairy-tale transformation used to crop up regularly in our conversations. As the years went by, the green telephone tended to stop changing into a cat but, strangely, chose to turn into a goose. Submitting myself to the fairly-tale atmosphere, I was hardly surprised to hear the following remark while recording an interview for a Polish periodical in 1991: 'Supposing, to take a well-known philosophical example — supposing a telephone is suddenly changed into a goose.'[2]

A well-known example indeed! But only to me (and I had it by heart). Nothing else could possibly illustrate the climate of our meetings better than the protean transformations of the magic green telephone. Our recurring discussions of these, reflecting the current state of play, have been preserved in the consecutive conversations with proper respect.

The other new vein, unique to these discussions, was our exchanges concerning my experience of living under a totalitarian regime. Those were sometimes quite personal talks, which I was at the beginning rather reluctant to reveal. Nevertheless, I eventually did not cut them, persuaded by my 'brothers in arms', who found them moving, and insisted on their inclusion.

---

1. See 136 below, note 1.
2. Included in this volume under the title 'I Don't Want the Universe To Be Too Tidy'.

James once asked me in an email if I had not found it a bit annoying when Berlin had given me advice about living under a totalitarian regime, when he had spent those decades sitting in comfortable chairs in Oxford. Not in the least. On the contrary, he seemed to be one of the few Westerners to whom I talked in those years who was willing to listen and prepared to accept the burden of the truth, however uncomfortable it might have felt. Having been privileged to meet him in person, I realised that he interpreted the ideas of past thinkers such as Machiavelli, Mill, Herder or Herzen as well as those of his contemporaries—even simple people like myself. He was the ultimate master of empathetic understanding.

Acknowledgements

The varied material which makes up this book has mostly existed in one form or another for more than two decades. It would never have emerged in this new form if it had not been for the support and help of many people and institutions. I owe a great debt of gratitude to Zbigniew Pelczynski, the originator of a scholarship programme for Polish scholars, subsidised by George Soros, under which I came to Oxford twice, in 1986 and 1995. I wish to thank the British Council, the Wolfson Foundation, the Humanitarian Trust and the Liberty Fund for having made it possible for me to visit Oxford in 1988 and 1991. I am immensely grateful to three Oxford Colleges—St John's, Wolfson and Mansfield—for generously hosting me during those visits. I would also like to thank the State University of New York at Buffalo for the kind invitation extended to me in 2004, thanks to which I once spoke on the telephone to Professor Paul Kurtz, the president of Prometheus Books, who, after having read some of my material, offered me publication of this volume.

I am grateful to the Isaiah Berlin Literary Trust for granting me permission to include the letters from Berlin, the interviews, and the extracts of my conversations with him. I am also greatly indebted to John Gray for kindly having allowed me to incorporate the conversation in which he took part, and for the encouragement that gave me the impetus to complete the project.

It surpasses my abilities properly to thank Berlin's editor (also one of his literary trustees), Henry Hardy. This book simply would not have been written without his invaluable support. Though the responsibility for the form of the conversations is solely mine, I could not even have dreamt of preparing them for publication without Henry's aid, and that of his collaborators. Henry helped me to get parts of the text ready, especially the toughest part of the 1995 tape, and offered me expert advice at all stages of work on the conversations. He also edited both interviews. At the final stage of preparing the typescript he spent many hours re-reading it, correcting my English and drawing my attention to points which needed further clarification. His contribution to the whole project cannot be overstated: the amount of support he has given me has surpassed anything that one could possibly expect from the publisher's editor responsible for the book (which he was not), or even from the closest friend.

I wish to thank Esther Johnson and Serena Moore for transcribing the recordings, and Jennifer Holmes for checking part of the transcribed material against the tape. I owe an immense debt of gratitude to James Chappel, who performed a Herculean labour on the transcripts, checking all of them for fidelity to the tapes and giving me massive editorial aid.

I am also very grateful to Joshua Cherniss, George Crowder, Milowit Kuninski and Jan Wolenski for their comments on early drafts of the scripts.

My thanks go to all the other people who gave me substantial and linguistic advice while I was working on the interviews and articles included in this volume: John Gray, Carolyn Korsmeyer, Leslie Macfarlane, Katherine Morris, James Reed, Kenneth Fincham, John Muir, and Mary and Guy Coughlan.

I am also grateful to Camilla Hornby, literary agent to the Isaiah Berlin Literary Trust, for the legal advice which she kindly gave me. I express my special thanks to my lifelong, reliable friends Bozena Jawien and Barbara Krajewska, who generously helped me with time-consuming technical matters.

I owe a profound debt to my superiors in the Department of Theory and Philosophy of Law at the Jagiellonian University in Krakow, Professors Jerzy Stelmach and Tomasz Gizbert-Studnicki, who supported my applications for scholarships and kindly gave me leave from my duties.

No words could express my deepest gratitude to the main author of this volume, the late Isaiah Berlin. He changed my life and filled it with a meaning that helped me survive the hard times I have experienced. Whatever I say will not do justice to my appreciation of the privilege of meeting and corresponding with him. This book is an attempt to pay at least a part of my enormous debt. I very much hope that my audacious decision to revive and prolong our unfinished dialogue will not do a disservice to my great benefactor.

Some of the material included in this volume has been published before. I am indebted to the publications mentioned below for granting me permission to reprint it. I have made some small changes in the texts, and have cut some passages that would have been repetitious in this context.

A selection of the letters from Berlin appeared as an appendix to my book *Filozofia wolnosci Isaiaha Berlina* [*Isaiah Berlin's Philosophy of Freedom*] (Krakow: Znak, 1998), 168–206. Excerpts from the letter of 24 February 1986 appeared under the title 'A Letter on Human Nature' in the *New York Review of Books*, 23 September 2004, 26.

The two interviews were originally given for Polish periodicals. 'Nil Desperandum' appeared in Polish in *Odra* 6 (1994), 12–17, and 'I Don't Want the Universe To Be Too Tidy' in *Znak* 10 (1994), 114–21. Both were reprinted in a collection of my interviews, *Oblicza liberalizmu: Isaiah Berlin, John Gray, Steven Lukes, Joseph Raz w rozmowie z Beata Polanowska-Sygulska* [*Visages of Liberalism: Isaiah Berlin, John Gray, Steven Lukes, Joseph Raz in Conversation with Beata Polanowska-Sygulska*] (Krakow: Ksiegarnia Akademicka, 2003), 17–27, 29–39. 'Nil Desperandum' was recently published in its original English version, under the title 'Hottentots and Phobias: A Conversation with Sir Isaiah Berlin', in *Salmagundi* 146–7 (Spring/Summer 2005), 170–83.

Three of my articles have been previously published, as follows: 'One More Voice on Berlin's Doctrine of Liberty' in *Political Studies* 37 (1989), 123–7, reprinted in *Twentieth-Century Literary Criticism* 105 (May 2001), 67–70; 'Two Visions of Liberty: Berlin and Hayek' in *Reports on Philosophy* 13 (1989), 61–72; 'Memories of Isaiah Berlin' (under the title 'Isaiah: A Deeper Truth') in the *Oxford Magazine*, Eighth Week, Trinity Term 1998, 6–8. 'Pluralism and Tragedy' was presented at the Twenty-first World Congress of the Internationale Vereinigung für Rechts- und Sozialphilosophie [International Society for Philosophy of Law and Social Philosophy] (IVR), Lund, Sweden, August 2003, and has been accepted for publication in a *Beiheft* (supplement) to *Archiv für Rechts- und Sozialphilosophie*, published by Franz Steiner Verlag, Stuttgart. 'Value-Pluralism and Liberalism: Connection or Exclusion?' was presented at the Twenty-second World Congress of the IVR, Granada, Spain, May 2005.

Beata Polanowska-Sygulska
Jagiellonian University, Krakow
September 2005

Memories of Isaiah Berlin

When one of my Oxford friends called me on a November night to pass on the mournful news of Sir Isaiah Berlin's death, I only half believed. Next morning the Polish newspapers brought the same sad information. While going over the headlines announcing the passing away of 'one of the giants of our century'.[1] I could not help thinking how exceptionally privileged I had been, having corresponded with Sir Isaiah for years and having met him many times during my stays on scholarships in Oxford. I also reflected upon the peculiarity of official obituaries, which hardly ever reveal the deepest truth about the deceased. Though I am fully aware of the intellectual range of Sir Isaiah's achievement, I shall remember him as one of the most generous and warmest persons I have ever met. Just imagine the intellectual 'giant of our century' writing the following words to an unknown Polish graduate student (at the end of a six-page letter):

> Let me now say how grateful I am to you for taking my work seriously and for writing to me the letter that you have. I should love to talk to you about these things, which I am sure would be very useful to me and may be of some use to you. I enclose, therefore, a kind of annexe[2] to this letter, which explains the machinery whereby you might be able to come to Oxford for a month or longer, in which case I could talk to you 'freely' (in the negative sense) from time to time, and you could also meet other philosophers who might be of even greater interest and profit to you.[3]

---

1. This phrase was used by Leszek Kolakowski: see 'Jeden z olbrzymow stulecia' ['One of the Giants of Our Century'], *Gazeta Wyborcza*, 7 November 1997, 1.
2. Not reproduced here.
3. Letter of 24 February 1986, 43 below.

I needed only to show the letter to Dr Zbigniew Pelczynski, then visiting Poland, to be accepted for a two-month stay at St John's under the Oxford Colleges Hospitality Scheme. I can still recollect in detail the first meeting at All Souls. How could I expect then that there were going to be over twenty of them? I introduced myself (in a trembling voice) to the porter, who made a short phone call and told me to wait. In a moment an elderly gentleman in a brown three-piece suit and a brown hat rushed towards the lodge especially to meet me. I kept glancing at the face so familiar to me from the books' covers and suddenly felt completely unreal. He greeted me as if he had known me for years and bombarded me with questions. It was hardly possible to keep up with the answers. We climbed up the stairs; large black letters over my host's door, forming the label 'Isaiah Berlin', made me feel still less real.

What happened next surpassed my highest expectations. I had sent Sir Isaiah my first article,[1] published in Poland two years before my arrival in Oxford. The offprint was supposed to be, as I wrote in the dedication, an exotic gift never to be made use of. What I saw in my host's hands was, to my horror, an English translation of that text! A thought crossed my mind that Sir Isaiah, like myself, had prepared for our first meeting. I was so stunned that I could not utter a word. After so many years I still find it difficult to confess what followed. Sir Isaiah, as a master of empathetic understanding, instantly deciphered my state of mind. 'Why have you lost your voice?' he asked. 'This is one of the most intelligent texts on my concept of liberty I have ever read!' What he said had much less to do with the merit of my humble paper than with his own generosity. I did not delude myself for a moment into thinking that he was serious; and yet the 'opinion' I heard helped me to find my voice, at that meeting and all the following ones, when one of the greatest of contemporary intellectuals, with characteristic subtlety, did his best to create the impression that he was talking—it feels ridiculous to write these words—to his equal.

I was eventually able to ask Berlin hundreds of questions that had tormented me while reading his writings. Our conversations during my first stay in Oxford mostly concerned the questions that I posed. Following the good Oxford habit, I made the effort to prepare essays in advance of each appointment. My hosts at St John's were astonished—how very demanding Professor Berlin was!—but writing essays was my own idea. I conceived them as a way to bridle the incredible intellectual vivacity of my interlocutor: to steer the monologues, articulated at breathtaking speed, towards topics that I thought important for the doctoral thesis I was working on at that time. Two

---

1. Beata Polanowska-Sygulska, 'Krytyka koncepcji wolnosci pozytywnej w ujeciu Isaiaha Berlina' ['Isaiah Berlin's Critique of the Positive Concept of Freedom'], *Studia Nauk Politycznych* 3 (1984), 49–65.

years later, after the defence of my PhD, I was privileged to have more meetings at All Souls. During my second stay in Oxford I gave up tormenting Sir Isaiah with my essays; I just listened. Some threads from our earlier conversations kept coming back. This was unbelievable—he remembered problems I had posed two years before.

Sometimes our conversations developed in completely unforeseeable directions. I once happened to admit having spent a sleepless night devouring Nabokov's *Lolita* in Wolfson College library. To make things worse, I sat within the range of vision of a large portrait of Sir Isaiah, hanging on the back wall. 'One of the giants of our century' shook his finger at me and then spoke for nearly two hours about his fascination with Russian literature—about Turgenev, Herzen, Akhmatova, Pasternak. Another time I communicated my great anxiety after having heard from home that my father was seriously ill. Sir Isaiah showed deep understanding and subtlety. He told me he had had a similar experience when he was staying in America—his father also fell seriously ill. We then talked about death for over an hour. I remember that he invoked the ancient argument—there is no death as long as I am here; when there is death, there is no me. He told me he was not at all afraid of his own death. Some of the things I heard I shall keep only to myself. The reflections I remember best are those which their author would probably never agree to publish.

Fragments of conversations, utterances of import and valuable reflections intertwine in my recollections with funny episodes, which I retain in my memory equally scrupulously. After our meetings at All Souls the Berlins' driver usually came to take Sir Isaiah home. He used to offer me a lift to Wolfson College, completely out of his way. I was embarrassed by such kindness. 'I can go by bus,' I protested. 'I can go by bus, too,' with a twinkle in his eye and with great seriousness Sir Isaiah would reply.

He always insisted that I should treat him in an informal way. I found it too difficult to overcome my reservations; for instance I never dared just telephone him, so I used to write letters, during my first scholarship and the following ones. Sir Isaiah commented playfully on this inhibition of mine: 'I am delighted you are here, and wish to inform you that I think it absurd that you do not telephone me! Still, if you would rather not I shall accept that—what else can I do?'[1]

I visited Oxford four times altogether. Sir Isaiah was always willing to spare me his time. Our last meeting took place at Headington at the end of May 1995. We continued our unfinished conversation in a taxi, driving in the rain. Sir Isaiah was going to a reception and, true to his habit, was giving me

---

1. Not reproduced here.

a lift, that time to St John's again. We were talking about Max Weber and his famous differentiation between the ethics of responsibility and the ethics of conscience. Suddenly a well-known feeling of utter unreality overwhelmed me. 'What am I doing here?' I thought. A typical English taxi, typical English weather, Max Weber and this great intellectual, thoroughly unreasonably regarded by me as a close person. Unexpectedly I heard him say: 'This is all real, this is actually going on. And we'll meet again. You'll come back here one day.' And yet it was to be a farewell.

What is left is correspondence. The first letter was written on 3 May 1983 and the last on 17 July 1997. So much generosity, warmth and personal interest that it is difficult to quote certain passages without embarrassment. Like the letters of 20 May 1989 and 29 May 1990, in which Sir Isaiah referred to my articles, published in succession in *Political Studies* and in *Reports on Philosophy*:

> Dear Beata,
>
> I received your article with great pleasure, thank you for defending me against all those terrible people [. . .]. I fear that being about to reach the age of 80 (thank you very much for your congratulations, by which I am deeply touched), I doubt if I shall ever turn into a communitarian. I don't think I am an isolated island, but I think that relationships in an archipelago are more human and morally and politically preferable to coral reefs with little organisms squeezed all together. [. . .]
>
> Best wishes to you and your youngest daughter, I am not at all sure about the world she will live in. [. . .][1]

> Dear Beata (if I may?),
>
> You cannot imagine how delighted I was to receive from Claude Galipeau your article, but above all your letter. I read the article with pleasure and pride. [. . .] Your letter was deeply touching and went to my heart. If you ever feel inclined to write to me again, do—I wish to assure you that your letters mean a good deal to me, more, perhaps, than mine mean to you. As I am getting on in years, as you know, now almost 81, do not leave it too long—do write to me again whenever you feel you have something to say to me, I should be delighted to receive and shall certainly reply.[2]

As far as I can remember this second letter was a reply to my description of the process of transformation in Poland. These matters deeply interested my correspondent and he often referred to them:

---

1. Letter of 20 May 1989, 66 below.
2. Letter of 29 May 1990, 70 below.

[L]et me tell you that I never predicted the recent events any more than anyone else succeeded in doing: whatever may happen to Gorbachev in the Soviet Union, there is no doubt that statues should be put up to him in Poland, Czechoslovakia, even Romania—without him, the collapse of the old system could, in my opinion, not have occurred so soon. I realise only too well what you mean by saying that you and others are 'too tired' to glory in the fruits of this situation, welcome as it must be, with all its dangers and deficiencies.[1]

Poland of the early 1990s provided a perfect experimental plot for those engaged in social studies. Certain developments infused new life into long-lasting theoretical discussions. One of the totally new phenomena was a sudden invasion of advertisements, mostly on TV. These were almost unknown under Communism, because of the permanent scarcity of goods. What made me think about the impact of persuasive techniques upon individual liberty was the reaction of my five-and-a-half-year-old daughter to virtually the first professional advertisement she had seen in Poland for a washing powder. The poor child literally begged me for the advertised article and, at the same time, not being able to make head or tail of her own behaviour, she did her best to analyse the unexpected desire. 'I have no idea *why* on earth I want this washing powder; the only thing I know is that I terribly need it and just *must* have it,' she used to say. I instantly associated this purely artificial desire I had to cope with in my own home with Charles Taylor's polemics against *Two Concepts of Liberty* and the reflections of other authors, mainly S. I. Benn and W. L. Weinstein. I could not help sharing my observations and thoughts with Sir Isaiah; his reply was characteristic of his style— seemingly light, playful, and yet weighty and important for understanding his liberal theory: 'Your daughter seems to me to be gifted with an exceptional sensibility and imagination, and I do not wonder that this is so—genes are important, we are told, and she has obviously inherited excellent ones. I am glad you gave her that washing powder—once one's imagination fixes on something it is right to increase people's happiness as you have done.'[2]

In spring 1997 our correspondence became more frequent. I was intensively working on a book on Berlin's liberal doctrine and some new doubts occurred to me. His invaluable reply to my interpretations, in a letter of 19 April 1997, made me both happy and a bit confused. The last paragraph read as follows: 'If you still have questions, please address them to me: I was very stimulated by your letter—I have never expressed myself so clearly before, I

---

1. ibid.
2. ibid.

believe, so do write to me again if you feel inclined. I fully realise the central importance of the problem you put.'[1]

The issue concerned the mutual relation between ethical pluralism and liberalism. The question had originally been posed by John Gray—I tried to find answers to Gray's objections.

The typewritten part of the letter ended here—below there remained about two-thirds of the page, covered with handwriting, unfortunately absolutely unintelligible to me. The only two words that I managed to decipher were a hardly readable signature, winding towards the top of the page. Dr Henry Hardy, the editor of Berlin's writings, very kindly sent me a typewritten version of that note.

I did not manage to hand my book over to Sir Isaiah. The night call from Oxford found me working on footnotes. Several weeks later I received a moving line from Dr Hardy:

> Dear Beata,
>
> I am sure you are as desolated as I am at Isaiah's death. It is very hard to bear. I thought you would like to know that his letter to you of 17 July was the last serious intellectual letter he wrote. Five days later his final illness began, and he was not able to deal with correspondence of this level thereafter.

---

1. Letter of 19 April 1997, 93 below.

Correspondence
1983–1997

10 May 1995

Dear Beata,

    I am delighted you are here, and
wish to inform you that I think it absurd
that you do not telephone me! Still, if
you would rather not I shall accept that -
what else can I do? If you would like to
come and see me - I should like that very
much - why don't you come and have tea
with me here in Headington at about 4.30
on *Wednesday* *17th May*. If this is all right, no
need to answer - if not, do overcome your
reservations and telephone me.

        Yours,

Isaiah Berlin

The following section consists of most of the letters Berlin wrote to me and a selection of those from me to him.[1] The criterion which I applied while selecting my own letters was whether a letter of mine was necessary to provide a context for Berlin's response. Besides, while I used to preserve the post from Oxford meticulously, I was rather careless about my own, and some of my letters simply got lost. Where the correspondence concerned either personal or purely technical matters (like my scholarships or the publication of my pieces), I decided to make cuts, marking them as bracketed ellipses: [. . .]. In addition, apart from the intentional omission of ephemeral items—on both sides—there are also gaps that result either from Berlin's failure to reply to me, or from the loss of my own letters.

Sir Isaiah did not write his letters to me by hand; he used to dictate them to his secretary, Pat Utechin. So they should be read as oral statements rather than as written work. They contain the repetitions and ambiguities characteristic of spontaneous utterances. They also exhibit misunderstandings, both on my and on my correspondent's part, which I have footnoted. Readers of Berlin's books, used to his exquisite style, may sometimes feel disappointed.

I am positive that Berlin would not be enthusiastic about the publication of this correspondence. This is how he commented on it at the end of his very last letter to me of 17 July 1997, written less than four months before his death: 'I am so old, my thoughts are often so confused, that I am not sure that I can be as clear about my own opinions as perhaps in my printed work I seem to be.'

He was undoubtedly too critical. This correspondence has its weak points; and it is I who bear responsibility for some of them. But there are also gold nuggets here. Besides, there will be no more letters . . .

---

1. Berlin's letters are printed here as they were written, apart from some minor modifications made by Henry Hardy in accordance with the editorial policy he has adopted for his edition of Berlin's letters. My own letters have been largely left as they were, but where necessary some linguistic corrections have been made.

Krakow
11 April 1983

Dear Professor Berlin,[1]

May I take the liberty of writing to you with a request for your advice.

I am a lecturer-assistant at the Jagiellonian University, Krakow, Poland. I am just writing my PhD thesis on your doctrine of liberty. My interests are mostly concerned with your magnificent critique of the positive concept of freedom. I use as a basis your 'Two Concepts of Liberty' in *Four Essays on Liberty* (London: Oxford University Press, 1969) and the Introduction to this edition.

Since your views on freedom were expressed a long time ago, it would be of great importance to me to find out whether they have changed in the course of the years. I should consider it most kind if you would help me in this matter. I have encountered many difficulties in getting any of your writings in my country and none of them has been translated into Polish. There is only one analysis of your doctrine of freedom, very brief and, in my view, inadequate.

My thesis seems to be the first elaboration of this topic in Poland. Since I have no literature that could help me, it would be of great value to me to learn which thinkers you feel close to and what I should read to better understand your ideas.

I am aware that my request is troublesome, but I would be grateful for your kind reply.

Yours sincerely,
Beata Polanowska-Sygulska

---

1. Since Berlin's professorship ended in 1967, it wasn't strictly correct to address him as 'Professor'. I did so out of ignorance.

3 May 1983

Dear Mrs Polanowska-Sygulska,

Thank you for your letter. I wish I could tell you in what ways, if any, my views have changed. I am not conscious of any significant change since the controversies which I discuss in the Introduction in *Four Essays on Liberty*. But you may glean some information from the other publications which I propose to send you. In the autumn I believe that an issue of the journal *Political Studies* will contain a critique of my views by a young American, together with my rejoinder—I have asked the Editor of the journal to send you a copy when the time comes.

Yours sincerely,

Isaiah Berlin

Krakow
24 June 1983

Dear Professor Berlin,

Thank you very much for your letter. It is generous of you to show me so much consideration.

I do not know how to express my gratitude for the books you so kindly sent me. I had glanced through them all before, but they were available only in one library[1] in Warsaw. Of course it makes a great difference to have them at home. Thank you also very much for arranging for me a copy of the forthcoming *Political Studies*.

I hope that the books and the articles will help me to fulfil the great responsibility which I undertook when choosing the topic of my dissertation. [. . .]

Yours sincerely,
Beata Polanowska-Sygulska

---

1. Paradoxically enough, at the Higher School of Social Sciences, affiliated to the Central Committee of the Polish United Workers' Party. The books were *Karl Marx*, *Four Essays on Liberty*, *Russian Thinkers*, *Concepts and Categories* and *Against the Current*.

Krakow
21 January 1986

Dear Professor Berlin,

I dare write to you once again after such a long break. In the meantime my daughter was born, and the work on my thesis postponed.

Recently, while I have been writing the following chapters, I encountered serious difficulties. Among others, I have a problem with interpreting your understanding of an obstacle to freedom. At the beginning of 'Two Concepts of Liberty' you define it as an outer infringement upon liberty,[1] but later on you write about 'obsessions, fears, neuroses, irrational forces',[2] as if they also constituted obstacles. In the essay 'From Hope and Fear Set Free' you openly confirm the existence of both the 'outer' and 'inner' obstacles.[3] According to which of the two understandings should I interpret your conception of negative liberty?

One of my other crucial problems consists in the difficulties with reconstructing your views on human nature. In the essay 'John Stuart Mill and the Ends of Life' you seem to share with Mill the view that the belief in 'a basic knowable human nature', an 'unchanging substance underneath the altering appearances' is mistaken.[4] But in the Introduction to *Four Essays on Liberty* you write about 'a human being endowed with a nucleus of needs and goals [. . .] common to all men'.[5] In 'Two Concepts of Liberty' you occasionally interweave, of course in specific contexts, the following phrases and remarks with the main thread of your consideration: 'to "degrade or deny our nature"';[6] 'To threaten a man with persecution unless he submits to a life in which he exercises no choice of his goals [. . .] is to sin against the truth that he is a man';[7] 'These rules or commandments [. . .] are grounded so deeply in the actual nature of men';[8] 'our values [. . .] are bound up with our conception of man, and of the basic demands of his nature'.[9] Are these hints

---

1. 'Coercion implies the deliberate interference of other human beings within the area in which I could otherwise act.' Isaiah Berlin, 'Two Concepts of Liberty', in *Liberty*, ed. Henry Hardy (Oxford: Oxford University Press, 2002), 169. (References are to the most recent editions of Berlin's writings.)

2. ibid., 204.

3. Isaiah Berlin, 'From Hope and Fear Set Free', in *Liberty*, 270.

4. Isaiah Berlin, 'John Stuart Mill and the Ends of Life', in *Liberty*, 233–4.

5. Isaiah Berlin, Introduction to 'Five Essays on Liberty', in *Liberty*, 54.

6. Berlin, 'Two Concepts of Liberty', in *Liberty*, 173, citing Benjamin Constant, *Principes de politique*, chap. 1: Benjamin Constant, *Écrits politiques*, ed. Marcel Gauchet ([Paris]: Gallimard, 1997), 318; cf. 246 below.

7. ibid., 174–5.

8. ibid., 210.

9. ibid., 215.

intended to suggest that your standpoint is different from Mill's? Or, what is more probable, is my understanding of your ideas totally confused?

This matter is of the greatest importance to me. I am following your suggestion that our values depend on our conception of man, and trying to approach the controversy about the two concepts of liberty through the philosophy of man. In particular, I am considering the mutual relations between the two main philosophical conceptions of man, namely substantialist and activist, and the two concepts of liberty. It seems to me that one of the four configurations, i.e., negative-substantialist, provides the best safeguards for respecting individual liberty. I would be happy to know whether you consider it sensible to tackle the issue of individual liberty that way. I am having many more problems which cannot be written about in a single letter.

I am afraid that you are the only person who can help me in these matters. My first supervisor, Professor Sobolewski, to whom I owe my interest in your ideas, died of cancer two years ago. Now I can rely almost only on my own insight, in which I do not entirely trust. I am afraid that I may interpret your conception inadequately and that my ideas may turn out to be completely senseless. [. . .]

Yours sincerely,
Beata Polanowska-Sygulska

PS: I am taking the liberty of enclosing my paper concerning your doctrine of liberty. Although there is probably not much sense in sending you an article written in Polish, I would like to confirm to you that your ideas are becoming known in Poland also.[1] [. . .]

---

1. See 24 above.

24 February 1986.

Dear Mrs Polanowska-Sygulska,

Thank you very much for your most interesting letter, which I read with great pleasure and attention, and have since mislaid. Although I think I remember its contents well, having read it twice, it may be that my answer will not precisely answer any of your questions—but I shall do my best. If I find it in the meantime, I shall try to modify this letter accordingly.

First, then, let me talk about the difficult question of 'human nature'. Do I believe in a fixed and unalterable human nature?—you rightly quote me as saying that I do not, and then again rightly quote me as referring to it as the basis of human communication. What, then, do I believe? I wish I could answer this question with extreme precision, but it does not seem to me to lend itself to that. What, I think, I believe is that there are thinkers, principally believers in Natural Law, who propose that all men are created, whether by God or Nature, endowed with innate knowledge of certain truths—some 'factual', some normative—the lists differ from Aristotle, the Stoics, Isidor of Seville, Gratian, Grotius etc., but for the most part they include the existence of God, the knowledge of good and evil, right and wrong, the obligation to tell the truth, return debts, keep promises (*pacta sunt servanda*), some or all of the Biblical Ten Commandments, and so on. I do not know who first questioned this—I daresay Epicurus or Lucretius—but in modern times the main attack upon this was delivered by thinkers like Vico and Herder and Marx (and, indeed, Hegel and his followers), and, of course, the empiricists, not Locke but Hume and his followers: according to whom, whatever the status of these Natural Laws, primitive men did not possess knowledge or even awareness of them, and they came into consciousness, or, indeed, formed objects of belief or certainty, in the course of evolution, or under the influence of changes in material circumstances and the growth of culture (whatever factors enter into that); for this entails that human beings go through a process of moral or metaphysical growth and development; and this is as valid as that empirical knowledge is an onward-going process, whether one believes that it tends to progressive development towards some kind of perfection (which it may never reach) or not—that it is cumulative but possesses no identifiable structure or teleological tendency.

This is certainly what Vico and Marx believed—that is, they believed that what is called human nature varies, and differs from culture to culture, or even within cultures—that various factors play a part in the modification of human responses to nature and each other; and that therefore the idea that all men at all times in all places are endowed with actual or potential knowledge of universal, timeless, unalterable truths (whether such truths exist or not, though for the most part such people did not believe them to exist) is simply false. The belief in such a priori knowledge and such unalterable truths does form the heart of the central European tradition, from Plato and the Stoics through the Middle Ages and perhaps in the Enlightenment as well—to our own day, indeed—but if Vico and Marx etc. are right, and I think they are, this is not a valid conception: human beings differ, their values differ, their understanding of the world differs; and some kind of historical or anthropological explanation of why such differences arise is in principle possible, though that explanation itself may to some degree reflect the particular concepts and categories of the particular culture to which these students of this subject belong.

I do not think this leads to relativism of any kind; indeed, I have an essay on the alleged relativism of the eighteenth century, of which I enclose an offprint.[1] But even though there is no basic human nature in this sense[2]—in the sense in which, for example, Rousseau believed that if you strip off all the increments, all the modifications, corruption, distortion etc. (as he thought of it) brought about by society and civilisation—there will be discovered a basic natural man—sometimes identified with, say, Red Indians, who have not had the unfortunate experience of having their natures distorted by European culture. This is the position attacked, for example, by Edmund Burke, who says that the idea that there is a natural man (about whom he thinks the French revolutionaries speak, and whose rights they wish to restore) is false, that there is no such creature; that the arts, which according to Rousseau are a later and perhaps disastrous development, are, as he says, 'parts of man's nature'; that there is no central, pure, natural being who emerges after you have scraped off all the artificial beliefs, habits, values, forms of life and behaviour which have been, as it were, superimposed on this pure, natural being. That is what I mean by denying a fixed human nature: I do not believe that all men are in the relevant respects the same 'beneath the skin', i.e. I believe that variety is part of human existence and in fact—though this is quite irrelevant—that this is a valuable attribute, though that is a very late idea, probably not to be met much before the eighteenth century.

What, then, do I mean by saying that men do have a common nature? Well, I think that common ground between human beings must exist if there

---

1. 'Note on Alleged Relativism in Eighteenth Century European Thought', *British Journal for Eighteenth-Century Studies* 3 (1980); reprinted with revisions as 'Alleged Relativism in Eighteenth-Century European Thought' in Isaiah Berlin, *The Crooked Timber of Humanity: Chapters in the History of Ideas*, ed. Henry Hardy (London: John Murray, 1990).

2. The completion of (the sense of) this sentence is lost sight of until the next paragraph.

is to be any meaning in the concept of human being at all. I think that it is true to say that there are certain basic needs, for example—for food, shelter, security and, if we accept Herder, for belonging to a group of one's own—which anyone qualifying for the description of human being must be held to possess. These are only the most basic properties; one might be able to add the need for a certain minimum of liberty, for the opportunity to pursue happiness or the realisation of one's potentialities for self-expression, for creation (however elementary), for love, for worship (as religious thinkers have maintained), for communication, and for some means of conceiving and describing themselves, perhaps in highly symbolic and mythological forms, their own relationship to the environment—natural and human—in which they live. Unless there is that, communication between human beings, even within a society, let alone understanding of what others have wished to communicate in other ages and cultures, would become impossible. I believe in the permanent possibility of change, modification, variety, without being able to state that there is some central kernel which is what is being modified or changed—but there must be enough in common between all the various individuals and groups who are going through various modifications for communication to be possible; and this can be expressed by listing, almost mechanically, various basic needs—'basic' for that reason—the various forms and varieties of which belong to different persons, cultures, societies etc.

The need for food is universal, but the way I satisfy it, the particular foods I crave, the steps I take to obtain them, will vary; so with all the other basic needs—my mythology, metaphysics, religion, language, gestures will widely vary, but not the fact that these are attempted ways of trying to explain to myself, to find myself at home in, a puzzling and possibly unfriendly environment, or, indeed, world. Wittgenstein once explained the concept of 'family face'[1]—that is, among the portraits of ancestors, face A resembles face B, face B resembles face C, face C resembles face D etc., but there is not a central face, 'the family face', of which these are identifiable modifications; nevertheless, when I say 'family face' I do not mean nothing, I mean precisely that A resembles B, B resembles C and so on, in various respects, and that they form a continuum, a series, which can be attributed to family X, not to family Y. So with the various natures of various cultures, societies, groups etc.

This is what I mean—that there is not a fixed, and yet there is a common, human nature: without the latter there would be no possibility of talking about human beings, or, indeed, of intercommunication, on which all thought depends—and not only thought, but feeling, imagination, action. I do not

---

1. Usually known as 'family resemblance'.

know if I make myself clear, but that, I think, is what I believe. This may, indeed, be confused or open to criticism, and if you wish to produce such criticisms, as you have already, please feel free to do so—I should be only grateful, I do not regard anything that I think as so true as not to be totally falsifiable sooner or later—although I hope not.

Then you ask me about negative liberty: why do I define it on the one hand as the absence of external obstacles, and on the other suddenly begin talking about inner obstacles, drives, neuroses, as obstacles to free activity? The reason for it is, as I am sure I have not made clear in my writings (and as you are perfectly justified in pointing out), that in the lecture on 'Two Concepts of Liberty' I was concerned with *political* liberty; and the basic sense of political liberty, in my view, is precisely the absence of man-made obstacles, and the struggle for it is the struggle for their removal. When my critics have said that liberty is fundamentally a triadic relation—namely, that to want to be free is to want the removal of obstacle X in order to be able to perform action Y, and not simply the removal of X—I do not agree. A man who is in chains wants the striking off of those chains—what he will do when they are struck off, what he wants to do once they are removed, is another matter. His motive for wishing to remove the chains is to remove the chains which hamper his free movement, and that seems to me to apply throughout. Political liberty means the removal of obstacles created, whether deliberately or not, whether directly or indirectly, by other human beings—*not* by nature. The fact that I cannot buy an expensive wine because I lack the money with which to do so is, in ordinary usage, not an absence of political freedom, because nobody is actually stopping me from buying this wine, nobody is forbidding me, there is no law against it, no threats to me if I try to buy it; but, if socialists are right, it is a real deprivation of liberty, because my lack of money is due to a man-made system, whether brought about deliberately or by 'the forces of history', which places me among the poor and gives the rich power over me, which is in fact a removable obstacle to my free functioning—and therefore a lack of liberty in my sense, the negative sense, because it is other human beings who are preventing me; a political sense of non-liberty, because political lack of liberty is the liberty which I am prevented from having by the actions of human beings, living or dead, and preserved by living human beings. But there are thinkers, Hebrew and Christian—Jesus, who said 'Ye shall know the truth and the truth shall make you free',[1] by which I think he meant that knowledge of God frees one from the errors of idolatry—Spinoza, Kant, Freud etc.—for whom freedom *is* moral

---

1. John 8:32.

and intellectual freedom, which is blocked by fantasies or false ideas in people's heads, or biological or physiological or psychological factors. This, of course, enters deeply into the discussions of what I call positive liberty, by which the Stoic sage, once he has taught himself to ignore, not to mind, pain, poverty, oppression etc., is free, has attained to inner freedom, like Buddhists, or the martyr whose thoughts, or whose love of God and intense concentration upon all that matters spiritually, 'liberates' him from whatever might disturb or oppress or frustrate others. But whatever validity there is in this idea—and the word 'freedom' has certainly been used in this way and clearly means a great deal (neither of us, I imagine, would wish to deny that), it is not *political* freedom, which is to do only with human beings coercing other human beings, whether physically or socially, politically, through institutions, laws or however.

You would, I suspect, like to believe (at this point, I cannot recollect what you said in your letter) that there are, if not 'natural', then some kind of fundamental human rights, which all human beings are entitled to *qua* human, and the deprivation of which is a basic sense of the loss of liberty. I think I believe in that too. My only difficulty is that I do not think one can give a list of these. To say this to me means that a minimal human existence can be led only if these rights are reasonably protected, that to diminish them leads to de-humanisation, and that the real removal of them presumably leads to a reduction to the condition of animals, insanity, death. All this I also believe—that is what I mean by saying that there is a sphere in which human beings are entitled to do what they wish to do without interference; but what this sphere is, what its dimensions are, despite common human characteristics in virtue of which human beings are human, will, perhaps, differ from the natures of these beings in different cultures, circumstances, conditions. But there must be some common thread of humanity running through them, as in the Wittgenstein 'family face' example that I gave. Is this vague? obscure? unsatisfactory? Do tell me, if so—I expect it is.

Let me now say how grateful I am to you for taking my work seriously and for writing to me the letter that you have. I should love to talk to you about these things, which I am sure would be very useful to me and may be of some use to you. I enclose, therefore, a kind of annexe to this letter, which explains the machinery whereby you might be able to come to Oxford for a month or longer, in which case I could talk to you 'freely' (in the negative sense) from time to time, and you could also meet other philosophers who might be of even greater interest and profit to you.

Yours sincerely,
Isaiah Berlin

PS: I think I have now recollected something else in your letter—namely, the two main philosophical conceptions of man—inasmuch as you quite correctly say that I maintain that our values depend on our conception of human nature (I do indeed believe that at the base of ethical, political and every other normative idea is always one's notion of human nature, i.e. some kind of, usually not too empirical, conception of man). I am not quite clear what the difference between 'substantialist' and 'activist' consists in. Does the former mean some unchanging substratum, Rousseau's 'natural man'? And does the latter mean that man is to be conceived as a series, or pattern, of activities and dispositions to such activities (the word 'dispositions' is obscure enough in itself)? I am not sure that I fully understand this distinction—but the notion of a self, or human nature, is one of the most agonising problems even in contemporary philosophy, let alone in Plato and Aristotle and Hume and Kant, and the subject of the 'Cogito'. Is human nature a compound of sensations, memories, anticipations, imagination, dispositions, connected in some fashion (or, according to some thinkers, virtually identical) with physical, biological, physiological characteristics? Or do we mean something different by 'self', something, some entity, conceived in realistic terms, continuous through time, with differing characteristics but possessing an unvarying 'inner' constitution? I would rather not pronounce on that, at any rate in this letter; but if you come to Oxford, we can talk about it and about everything else, with enough time at our disposal.

I hope I have got all the points in your full letter—but perhaps I have not.

Krakow
10 April 1986

Dear Professor Berlin,

I do not know how to express my gratitude for the letter you wrote to me. I had never expected you to treat me so seriously as to write a whole treatise just for my use. Even more than ever, I feel obliged to do my best, working on your ideas.

Please forgive the awful delay in answering your letter. I learnt that Dr Zbigniew Pelczynski from Oxford, who is in charge of the whole scheme of scholarships, was going to visit Krakow during Easter. I made an appointment with him, we met twice and he was extremely kind to me. I suppose that this was because of a letter from you which I showed him. As one of the scholars already granted a scholarship happened to drop out of the scheme, Dr Pelczynski accepted me for two months in Oxford, namely July and August 1986. If everything goes well at my University (as there are some complex passport procedures), I shall be happy to visit England in the summer. I hope that you will be so kind as to spare me some of your time during this period.

I am very grateful to you for your advice and consideration; had it not been for these, I would not have been able to get the scholarship. In fact I had never thought about it seriously; it was just a dream of mine to contact you personally and ask all the questions that I have. Though I shall be terribly embarrassed, I hope that my deep interest in your ideas will help me to express myself.

The interpretation that you gave me in your letter is invaluable to my work. I was happy to find that it confirms some of my intuitions. The last of my questions that you answered at the end of your letter needs some explanation from me. I owe the differentiation between substantialist and activist conceptions of man to Professor Jozef Tischner, from the Pope's Academy, whose lectures I have attended. By the 'substantialist' orientation in the philosophy of man he meant the whole tradition coming from Aristotle and Thomas Aquinas, represented by the maxim *agere sequitur esse*; by the 'activist' the conception put forward by, among others, Leibniz, Hegel, Nietzsche, Heidegger, and all existentialists, represented by the maxim *esse sequitur agere*.[1]

This problem is certainly too complicated for me to rely on my own, very poor, insight. I have just tried to match the knowledge I had obtained from

---

1. 'Action follows being'; 'Being follows action.'

the lectures on the philosophy of man with what I learnt from 'Two Concepts of Liberty'. I am afraid that my ideas may turn out to be senseless. But I hope I shall be able to ask you for advice in Oxford.

I look forward very much to meeting you. I shall take the liberty of writing to you once again when everything is settled.

Yours sincerely,

Beata Polanowska-Sygulska

19 April 1986

Dear Mrs Polanowska-Sygulska,

Thank you very much for your delightful and interesting letter. I am so glad that Dr Pelczynski has arranged for you to come to Oxford. The only difficulty about our meetings is that I tend to leave this country for Italy in mid-July and do not return until the second week of September, so I shall be away for at least six weeks of your stay here (naturally I shall be very glad to see you at the beginning of July).

I wonder whether it would be totally impossible for you to arrange to begin your stay here in mid-June? Or alternatively, if (as I am almost sure would be the case) I could secure the necessary additional sum of money for you, to prolong your stay until the end of September (I shall be back by about the 10th or 11th). It would be best, of course, if you could come here during two months other than the holiday months of July and August, but I realise that this is probably not practicable, either from your or from this University's point of view.

My old colleague, Professor Ryle, used to say that there was nothing in the world except chaps and things (against all metaphysics, Popper's Third World etc.). Is that *esse*?

Yours sincerely,
Isaiah Berlin

Oxford
5 August 1986

Dear Sir Isaiah,[1]

I am deeply grateful to you for everything that you have done for me. The topic that I have been daring enough to take up has always meant very much to me, and our meetings left me completely enchanted; I shall never forget these days.

After your departure I met Professor Hart and then twice Dr Gray, who was extremely friendly and helpful. He entirely approved of my interpretation of Hayek. I sent the last article (the comparison between your doctrine of liberty and that of Hayek) to *Political Studies*; and the previous one (my answer to the discussion on your doctrine), as you had suggested, to Professor C. B. Macpherson. I decided not to send out the very first paper, which does not seem to me sufficiently worthwhile.

Dr Macfarlane dropped a casual hint that I could write something longer in English. This has become a kind of an *idée fixe* of mine. I would like very much to produce a small book. Dr Gray encouraged me greatly, promised his help and provided some very strong argument in support of my vague plans. In his assessment 90 per cent of the books available at Blackwell's are Marxist; and this argument seems to me very convincing, despite my lack of self-confidence.[2] [. . .] But this is for the future. I must first finish and hopefully defend my thesis.

You have encouraged me so greatly that I am afraid I shall be writing to you quite often. I shall certainly let you know how my work proceeds. I am leaving tomorrow for Poland, so much spiritually enriched and full of gratitude. Thank you for everything.

Yours, with much affection,
Beata Polanowska-Sygulska

---

1. Farewell letter, written at the end of the first scholarship in Oxford.
2. Alas, I did not succeed in realising this project. Nine years later John Gray published his influential *Isaiah Berlin* (London: HarperCollins, 1995). I eventually published a book in Polish: *Filozofia wolnosci Isaiaha Berlina* [*Isaiah Berlin's Philosophy of Freedom*] (Krakow: Znak, 1998).

Krakow
8 November 1986

Dear Sir Isaiah,

Now I am, as you said, 'in the darkness' and it has become again so hard to write. Forgive the terrible delay in writing this letter to you. I remember all the time my great stay in Oxford, our four meetings and your extreme generosity that made me behave like a silly child.[1] Now I assess that, intellectually, those two months were equal to at last three years here. I hope I shall not entirely waste the invaluable profits gained during the time that you kindly sacrificed [for] me.

As I wrote in my farewell letter I had sent out two of my papers. The one in which I discussed different critiques of your doctrine of liberty, entitled 'One More Voice on Berlin's Doctrine of Liberty', I sent, following your advice, to Professor C. B. Macpherson. I enclose a photocopy of his answer and also of the letter from the editor of *Political Theory*. They both disapproved of the article. I must say I am a bit depressed. I felt so greatly encouraged while writing these texts and now I have again lost self-confidence. I do not care so much for publication itself as for the acknowledgement that I am at all able to write sensible things. My colleagues suggest that I should try another periodical, but I have not made up my mind yet. The other article, entitled 'Two Visions of Liberty: Berlin and Hayek', was sent to *Political Studies*. The editor acknowledged receipt of the manuscript, but a decision has yet to be reached.

Let me now once again thank you for everything that you have done for me. I cannot express how much your writings and then meetings with you have meant to me. Thanks to you I am so much enriched, even if I am not able to profit from this adequately.

I am writing now the next chapter of my thesis, devoted to my critique of your doctrine of liberty. If everything goes well the whole thing should be completed by the end of the winter. I shall let you know how my work proceeds.

Yours sincerely,
Beata Polanowska-Sygulska

---

1. At our very first meeting Sir Isaiah greeted me with an English translation of the Polish article which I had sent him a couple of months before (see 26 above). I was so overwhelmed and nervous at the sight of its English translation that I could not help crying.

24 November 1986

Dear Mrs Polanowska-Sygulska,

Thank you very much for your letter of 18 November. I enjoyed our meetings at least as much as you did and do hope that you may be able to come back and resume our conversation—believe me, I profited greatly from your very pointed questions. I think you are the best (oral) critic I have had, and the most constructive.

I am not at all surprised about Macpherson's reaction—I know him well, and he is not a man who accepts criticism at all easily: he knows he is right and always has known it and is for that reason a somewhat isolated writer. He sent me his book containing the chapter of criticism of my views, but as I think I told you I mislaid it and never read it, and no one before you ever mentioned it to me. His criticism may well have substance in it—my relations with him remain quite friendly, but I would not expect him to help you in any way, nor his recommendation to *Political Theory* to be at all warm. Did I really advise you to send your piece to Macpherson?—if so, my mind must have been wandering at the time. As for *Political Theory*, I wish I had written to them myself—as I am on the Board, this might have done some good. I am very sorry about their stupidity. I fear you may get a similar disappointment with *Political Studies* (with which I am not connected), although I hope not.

I think your colleagues are right. Let me urge you to persist with your attempt to get your articles published. There must be periodicals in America which would consider your work—if you would let me know who you wish to send it to, I might be of some help.

Let me say again how very delightful and profitable I found our meetings, and how much I look forward to their renewal—do write to me whether there is any possibility of your returning here. Darkness is deeply undesirable, and, as you know, I am not mistaken about its degree.

Yours sincerely,
Isaiah Berlin

PS: I have just written to Jack Lively, the Editor of *Political Studies*, whom I do know, and suggested that he might have a look at your other piece too— the one rejected by *Political Theory*—so do please send it to him, he will be expecting it. I hope all goes well.

Krakow
10 March 1987

Dear Sir Isaiah,

Thank you very much for your letter of 24 November. [. . .]

I realise now how many questions I did not ask you during our meetings. I have recently completed a chapter on some kind of an 'outer' critique of your doctrine of liberty, from the position, among others, of K. R. Popper. I have come across only two brief remarks in your writings concerning Popper's philosophy (in 'Does Political Theory Still Exist?', 'We might take as examples Karl Popper's denunciation of Plato's political theory;'[1] and in 'Historical Inevitability' the footnote concerning Popper's critique of historicism),[2] so I am worried about the adequacy of the line of defence that I try to derive from your essays.

Your conception seems to be essentialist in Popper's terms, which is a serious objection, for he condemns essentialism as leading to insignificant and empty controversy about words. (This is my interpretation; I have not found anything on your ideas in Popper's books concerning political philosophy.) I thought that this critique should be answered on methodological grounds, so I looked for a reply mostly in your essay 'Does Political Theory Still Exist?' Incidentally, each time I read this essay, I learn quite new things, and I wonder whether I shall ever grasp it entirely. Do I interpret your (and Popper's) ideas correctly when I retort that it is impossible to avoid dispute on values in political theory, due to its metaphysical rootedness, i.e., the underlying conception of man, formed by the framework of the basic categories in terms of which we think and act? For this reason Popper's postulate of translating political theories 'into the language of demands or proposals for political actions'[3] cannot be realised. In another essay of yours, 'Political Ideas in the Twentieth Century', I have encountered an excerpt that seems to be directly addressed to Popper's chief political maxim: 'Minimise unhappiness': 'men do not live only by fighting evils. They live by positive goals, individual and collective, a vast variety of them, seldom predictable, at times incompatible.'[4] Was this statement somehow related to Popper's views or not? I would also like to ask you what you think about my own ideas on the

---

1. Isaiah Berlin, 'Does Political Theory Exist?', in *The Proper Study of Mankind*, ed. Henry Hardy (London: Chatto & Windus, 1997), 87.

2. Isaiah Berlin, 'Historical Inevitability', in *Liberty*, 101n2.

3. Karl Popper, *The Open Society and Its Enemies*, 2 vols. (London: Routledge & Kegan Paul, 1984 [1945]), 1: 112.

4. Isaiah Berlin, 'Political Ideas in the Twentieth Century', in *Liberty*, 93.

topic, namely that it seems to me that Popper is, in some way, inconsistent. In his intellectual autobiography he claims to be a pluralist:

> [W]e shall always have to live in an imperfect society. That is so not only because even very good people are very imperfect, nor is it because, obviously, we often make mistakes because we do not know enough. Even more important than either of these two reasons is the fact that there always exist irresolvable clashes of values: there are many moral problems which are insoluble because moral principles may conflict.[1]

But, at the same time, he attempts to stop the discussion on values. Returning to your ideas, Popper's technological approach would fit in with a vision of some monolithic society, which, for sure, he would not accept. Moreover, it seems to me that Popper happens to betray his own anti-essentialism. I have come across a passage in *The Open Society and Its Enemies* devoted to the critique of Plato's interpretation of the concept of justice. Popper claims that Plato distorted the meaning of the concept by having used it as a synonym for 'that which is in the interest of the best State'.[2] Popper asks a typical essentialist question: 'What do we really mean when we speak of *Justice*?' and provides an answer to it, though not without some reservation, that it amounts to his interpretation of 'the humanitarian general outlook'.[3] In this way, quite unintentionally, he acknowledges the importance of conceptual analysis, at least to the extent to which distortions are involved. Thus, Popper's methodological naturalism in the social sciences seems to me to be some sort of simplification for the sake of the unity of his philosophical system.

On the other hand, I have found some elements of methodological nominalism in your doctrine. Your definitions of positive and negative liberty satisfy Popper's methodological demands: 'The first of these political senses of freedom or liberty [. . .] *I shall call* "the negative sense" [. . .] The second *I shall call* "the positive sense".'[4] Moreover, your conception of freedom is not an insight into the meaning or nature of freedom, but a critical examination of the two main meanings that have been ascribed to it. Your thesis of the particular susceptibility to distortions of the positive doctrines of liberty seems to be testable, as far as the practical consequences of adopting each of the two concepts are concerned. Thus, your essay is less essentialist than it might seem.

---

1. Karl Popper, *Unended Quest: An Intellectual Biography* (Glasgow: Fontana/Collins, 1976), 116.
2. Popper, *The Open Society and Its Enemies*, 1: 89.
3. ibid.
4. Berlin, 'Two Concepts of Liberty', in *Liberty*, 169 (my emphasis).

I have yet another, quite different problem. At the end of my stay in Oxford I met Dr Pelczynski, who criticised your doctrine of negative liberty as devoid of any conception of the agent (either rational or empirical or any other). I must confess that I do not know whether this is a serious problem and how to answer this objection. [. . .]

Let me now once again thank you for the invaluable benefit that I gained from your writings and from our conversations. Thanks to you the work on my PhD dissertation and all that has been connected with it has become one of the most important things in my life. Even if my greatest intellectual adventure were to finish now, it will never lose its great significance for me. Please forgive my boldness and my boring you with the problems that I face. If I dare bother you it's only because there is nobody here whom I could trust intellectually so much. I shall be very grateful for your reply.

Yours sincerely,
Beata Polanowska-Sygulska

22 April 1987

Dear Mrs Polanowska-Sygulska,

Thank you very much for your letter of 10 March, which took some time to arrive here, and which I read with pleasure and interest, as I read everything that you write. I read the piece that you wrote for the *Oxford Magazine*, and I am so sorry that I embarrassed you—I shan't do it again.[1] But I should love to see you, and if it is possible for you to come here again I should welcome that warmly. [. . .]

You write about Popper. It is true that I never mentioned him much, but I don't mention anyone much unless I am specifically writing about them. I think he regards me as some kind of disciple of his, which I am not exactly, nevertheless he thinks that we have some kind of common liberal individualist standpoint—which to a certain degree is true, though he has gone far further in the direction of a kind of conservative laissez-faire liberalism than I should be disposed to or have ever embraced. I do not know what the 'outer' critique of my doctrine of liberty from Popper's position can possibly be; I should be greatly interested if you would let me know the general outlines of what you are intending—then I could tell you more precisely whether I think this truly represents my position. So do tell me what kind of thing you have in mind. You tell me that my doctrine seems to be essentialist, in Popper's terms. That I should deny flatly. Popper's essentialism, in particular as part of his attacks on Plato, Aristotle, Hegel, Marx etc., takes the form, so far as I remember it (and goodness knows how many years ago I read *The Open Society* or *The Poverty of Historicism*), of saying that these thinkers take it that there is a kind of inner structure to human beings, to their associations—tribes, societies, States—which makes it inevitable that certain courses should be pursued. In other words, that there is a kind of set libretto which people cannot help following, whether they want to or mean to or not—in other words, a form of historical inevitability, which, as you know, I am wholly opposed to. That is what

---

1. Isaiah Berlin is referring here to the following passage on the Slavonic influences in Oxford, taken from my piece on the scholarship programme for Polish scholars, written at the request of Professor James Reed, then editor of the *Oxford Magazine*: 'I happened to be kissed goodbye by a famed Oxonian scholar. I was deeply moved, a bit embarrassed, and profoundly grateful to him for his informal treatment, friendliness and encouragement. I appreciated a great man's amicability very much and mentioned it while talking to a distinguished, though much younger scholar. You can guess what happened. As this took place at our last meeting, he instantly followed the pattern, leaving me completely astonished by the widespread influence of Slavonic customs. They proved to be extremely infectious, as they had not been incited in any way.' (The two scholars were Isaiah Berlin and John Gray.) Beata Polanowska-Sygulska, 'Give Them Soothing Pills', *Oxford Magazine*, Noughth Week, Hilary Term, 1987, 3.

I take Popper's essentialism to be mainly about;[2] the proposition that history has no libretto—which, as you know, Herzen makes so much of—is precisely what I do believe, particularly with my unpopular opinion that individuals make more difference to the twists and turns of human history than is commonly supposed by the system-builders—the exact opposite of what Engels said, when he said, 'In the absence of a Napoleon, someone else would have taken his place.'[2] I am prepared to believe that men are to a large degree conditioned by the society into which they are born—see Herder—by the habits, outlook, way of life, language, beliefs, from which they can of course rebel but which nevertheless form and condition the means by which they do so and the set of their minds and emotions and hearts—nevertheless, this is not totally determined: at crucial moments, when conflicts arise within a society, particularly then, the impulse given freely by an individual acting through his own free will and not in some predictable fashion (which some psychologist or sociologist armed with sufficient data could have foretold) can send things spinning in some unforeseen and unforeseeable direction. If Alexander or Caesar had not lived, history would certainly have taken a different turn—this is true of a good many individuals, or perhaps groups of individuals, certainly of Napoleon, of Hitler, even Churchill by behaving as he did in 1939–45 prevented a situation in Europe—when Hitler's victory seemed highly probable to most rational political calculators—and things would have been exceedingly different; and the same is certainly true of 1917 in Russia—if a brick had fallen on the head of Lenin, goodness me, there might have been an upheaval, a revolution, civil war between the peasants, proletarians, landowners, officers, liberals, heaven knows what, I don't deny that—but the particular outcome could very well have been wholly different from what in fact took place. So I am a believer, more than most people, in the influence both conscious and sometimes unintended of men of unusual power—certainly not virtuous or humane, quite often—who give an impulsion which produces results quite different from those which Tolstoy, for example, insisted on in his highly determinist though in some ways ambivalent and self-contradictory theory of historical determination. That is what I take to be the heart of essentialism.

What essentialism, then, is it that you take me to hold? I remember when we met that you thought that my notion of a human nature, which makes communication possible between men in different historical situations, times, generations, countries, across vast stretches of space and time, that there is some-

---

1. Berlin here confuses Popper's essentialism with his historicism, and so misinterprets my query: cf. 60–1 below.

2. Engels to W. Borgius in Breslau, 25 January 1894. Marx and Engels, *Collected Works* (London: Lawrence & Wishart, 1975–2004), 50: 266.

thing common to men which makes for the possibility of empathy, intelligibility, explanation, interpretation—that something of that sort you took to be an essentialist thesis. But I do not see why you should say that.[1] I am far from saying that human nature 'is always the same': or that there is a kernel inside every human being, his 'essential' nature, which does not alter however much other attributes do, so that by looking into this basic nature it is possible to discover 'natural laws', true of all men everywhere at all times—*quod semper, quod ubique, quod ab omnibus [creditum est]*[2]—as held, I suppose, by Aristotle, the Christian Fathers, Isidore of Seville, Gratian, Grotius, (I suppose Spinoza,) Rousseau, Jefferson etc., and denied only by people like Vico or Hegel, who thought it was a matter of growth and development, though even they were teleological and thought that nature, God, built us to pursue certain goals which we cannot avoid or deviate from too far. None of this do I believe; only that de facto there is sufficient common ground between men at most times in most places—not, perhaps, always and everywhere—to make understanding and communication and explanation possible.

What else does Popper mean by essentialism? What are the empty controversies about words?

Let me continue. I think that I do believe 'that it is impossible to avoid dispute on values in political theory', due to the fact that these values depend on the individual thinkers' or Schools' conception of human nature. This need not be 'metaphysical'. Certainly, as people's metaphysical vision differs, so will conceptions of value: if Socrates or Plato did not believe in a metaphysical insight into what things were, they would not believe in the absoluteness of values which the citizens of Athens appeared not always to be aware of, and which only teachers who had gone through the proper discipline could impart to them—or at least to the 'Guardians' into whose hands the government of the city must be entrusted, for they alone know—so, too, all the Christian theories, where the absolute truth about what men are and what their natures inevitably crave for is founded on theological premises. So, too, with people who claim to have rational insight into true human nature, or Marxists, who also know what the drama of human history is and what part is played in it at various phases by classes, members of classes etc. But this need not be a priori, if that is what 'metaphysical' means; it is possible to say that one's

---

1. I did not in fact say this. Berlin here mistakes Popper's essentialism for a substantialist conception of man (which I did not, in fact, ascribe to him), as opposed to an activist one, a distinction we discussed during my first scholarship in Oxford. We returned to Popper during my next visit, in 1988. Somehow it was again difficult for us to communicate on this particular subject-matter. Eventually, we discussed Popper with John Gray on 6 May 1988, q.v. below.

2. 'What [is believed] everywhere, always, by all.' Vincent of Lérins, *Commonitorium* 2. 3.

empirical, however firmly held, perhaps even irrationally held but still held on empirical grounds, conception of human nature dictates moral and political judgements—that in that sense they are certainly rooted in the general conception of man and his nature—that is what I maintained and I think still believe. Why does this prevent us from 'translating political theories into the language of demands or proposals or political actions', which according to you Popper maintains; why should my rigidly fixed values, moral or political, whether Kantian or utilitarian or Christian or Marxist or whatever, prevent me from formulating demands in terms of these values? That I do not quite follow. You ask me whether my statement about minimising unhappiness is intended as pertaining to Popper's views: no, not consciously, I was not thinking of him when I said that—I said it simply because I believed it. I do not think I have said anything in conscious support or contradiction of Popper's views, save that I was influenced by *The Open Society and Its Enemies*, and not at all by *The Poverty of Historicism*, in an anti-metaphysical direction, by Popper's belief that those who know there is only one true answer to all questions and have metaphysical a priori guarantees of it are always wrong and often dangerous. That, too, I think is common to us both.

The passage you quote from Popper's autobiography about the conflict of values I do, of course, fully accept. I suspect, though I dare not say so, since he is such a fierce defender of his own total originality, that he derived this from myself: he, I think, thinks that in some telepathic way I must have derived it from him. But never mind about that. That is a position common to us. But you are quite right when you say that this is not consistent with the passage in *The Open Society* where he says that Plato is wrong about justice because the word means—'really means'—whatever it is that Popper thinks it does—'really means' is always the cloven hoof of essentialism. Of course words mean not exactly what we want them to mean, as empiricists have maintained—they have a connection with a stream of language and culture into which we are born and which we use consciously and half-consciously — we can alter their meanings but we are, as it were, educated in some definite use of words from which we can only depart by some act of will or by some accidental impact of events—revolutions, horrifying experiences, religious revelation, whatever it is that alters people's views, and to that extent the use of words. But of course the word 'really' is usually a symptom of the precise essentialism which Popper attacks and which I, too, do not accept as an a priori concept. Nor do I accept Popper's belief in the scientific nature of what are called the social sciences, what you call his 'methodological naturalism'.

I am grateful to you for acquitting me from essentialism—it is perfectly true that when I speak of negative and positive liberty I do say 'I shall call' in both cases, and I do indeed claim that the meaning or nature of freedom is not in itself a valid enquiry—all we can do is to ask what it is that the words have meant historically, or mean today, what kind of ideals or demands or situations these meanings entail; after all, the only way in which we can interpret the world is by examination of the words and concepts in terms of which we think of this world; we learn from juxtaposing dissimilar concepts, categories etc., and we discover what at least we ourselves believe, seek, and believe others to believe, seek, and suspect them, if they disagree, of confusion or self-deception (sometimes justly, sometimes not). Certainly, if I say 'Freedom is X' and someone says 'No, it isn't', we must end by arguing what the words mean—sometimes it is a mere verbal disagreement, but sometimes it is disagreement about the idea itself—this, in turn, is rooted in our general conception, view and way of life—to that extent the later Wittgenstein must be right, to that extent the doctrines of Marxist conditioning by class etc. has something to say to this. But I agree with you, that the direct magic eye, which penetrates the true essence of what things—whether material objects or justice or love or the fate of the world—might be, is something denied to me; and I suspect to everyone. And yet it is the basis of a great deal of traditional philosophical thought—it is what Hamann thought, and perhaps others, that Adam was granted in Paradise—when God taught him the use of language, the words identified the true unaltering essence, not appearance, of things. Adam before the Fall truly knew what there was; as he learnt each new word by miraculous gift of God, he knew what there is. We are not so fortunate.

Now, about Dr Pelczynski. I have no idea what he could have meant by saying that my doctrine of negative liberty was devoid of the conception of an agent. I must ask him the next time I see him—I see nothing in this at all. If he thinks that the doctrine of the absence of obstacles presupposes some kind of passive beings not engaged in deliberate will-induced activities—nothing is further from the truth. The only point of negative liberty is that it[s absence] blocks the way to active agents realising their natures in various ways; without that, the concept seems totally empty and is certainly not mine.

I am glad you are finishing your thesis, and I am very sorry that you have been ill—it is awful after Chernobyl—do you in Poland pronounce it Cher*no*byl or Cherno*byl*? In Russian, it is the latter, but on the British radio invariably the former. Why do you think it is a crazy idea of writing something on my concept of liberty? However critical, I think it would be an excellent project, and if you wanted my help with it I should, of course, give it. Dr Gray is quite right. [. . .]

I find this correspondence extremely stimulating and am grateful for it, and sincerely hope that we shall keep in touch not merely by correspondence, and that somehow you will be able to come here again. [. . .]

With my best wishes and gratitude,

Yours,

Isaiah Berlin

Krakow
17 May 1987

Dear Sir Isaiah,

Thank you ever so much for your letter of 22 April. I cannot express how much I appreciate your sacrificing so much of your time for me. Your treatises, written just for my use, are invaluable to me and I can only hope that I shall not waste the inestimable benefits which, thanks to you, I have at my disposal.

I wrote in my piece for the *Oxford Magazine* that you embarrassed me—please do not take this seriously at all, as it concerns my nicest, never to be forgotten memories from Oxford. If I was embarrassed it was only because my dream to meet and to listen to you came true in a way that surpassed anything I could have expected.

Let me start with theoretical problems. [. . .] Being aware of the number of mistakes that I have made and still may make in my interpretations of your political theory, I hope that none of them would be as unforgivable as an ascription to your ideas of 'historicism' in Popper's terms! If I properly understand your reply (of which, of course, I cannot be quite sure), what you are opposed to is what Popper calls historicism: 'I mean by "historicism" an approach to the social sciences which assumes that historical prediction is their principal aim, and which assumes that this aim is attainable by discovering the "rhythms" or the "patterns" or the "laws" or the "trends" that underlie the evolution of history.'[1] Your view on this topic is explicitly put forward in 'Historical Inevitability' and can also be read between the lines in almost everything you have written. You call your view that individuals make more difference to the twists and turns of human history than it is commonly supposed by the system-builders—'unpopular'. It is my assessment that most Poles do share your conviction. Our contemporary experience confirms it beyond any shadow of a doubt. Besides, it seems to me that I have always felt (if not consciously thought) the same. Forgive my courage, but as I see it, your political ideas so greatly appeal to me just because they so perfectly name and justify much of what I have intuitively 'sensed' ever before I got to know your writings. Having all of this in mind, how could I possibly have ascribed historicism to you? It was my fault that I did not elaborate on the problem I wanted to ask you about. That was because while writing to you I am always afraid that I shall take up too much of your time.

What I was concerned with was not historicism but essentialism in

---

1. Karl Popper, *The Poverty of Historicism* (London: Routledge & Kegan Paul, 1972), 3.

Popper's terms, which seems to be a distinct idea. (Though essentialism tends to be connected with the historicist approach, it does not necessarily have to be.) Let me now quote some excerpts to avoid misinterpretations on my part.

As Popper remembers in his autobiography, what he later called 'the problem of essentialism' arose from his 'rejection of the attitude of attributing importance to *words and their meaning* (or their *true meaning*).'[1] This then took the form of the following formulation: *'Never let yourself be goaded into taking seriously problems about words and their meanings. What must be taken seriously are questions of fact, and assertions about facts: theories and hypotheses; the problems they solve; and the problems they raise.'*[2] According to Popper the intellectual source of essentialism was 'Aristotle's method of Definitions'.[3] He comments upon the mutual relationship between the two, both criticised by him, approaches—essentialism and historicism:

> The problem of definitions and of the 'meaning of terms' does not directly bear upon historicism. But it has been an inexhaustible source of confusion and of that particular kind of verbiage which, when combined with historicism in Hegel's mind, has bred that poisonous intellectual disease of our own time which I call oracular philosophy. And it is the most important source of Aristotle's regrettably still prevailing intellectual influence, of all that verbal and empty scholasticism that haunts not only the Middle Ages, but our own contemporary philosophy; for even a philosophy as recent as that of L. Wittgenstein suffers [. . .] from this influence. The development of thought since Aristotle could, I think, be summed up by saying that every discipline, as long as it used the Aristotelian method of definition, has remained arrested in a state of empty verbiage and barren scholasticism, and that the degree to which the various sciences have been able to make any progress depended on the degree to which they have been able to get rid of this essentialist method. (This is why so much of our 'social science' still belongs to the Middle Ages.)[4]

Criticising methodological essentialism, Popper postulates methodological nominalism. He explains the difference between them in the following way:

> While we may say that the essentialist interpretation reads a definition 'normally', that is to say, from the left to the right, we can say that a definition, as it is normally used in modern science, must be read back to front, or from

---

1. Popper, *Unended Quest*, 17.
2. ibid., 19; cf. 176 (note 1) below, 256 below.
3. Karl Popper, *The Open Society and Its Enemies*, 2: 9.
4. ibid.

the right to the left; for it starts with the defining formula, and asks for a label to it. Thus the scientific view of the definition 'A puppy is a young dog' would be that it is an answer to the question: 'What shall we call a young dog?' rather than an answer to the question 'What is a puppy?' [. . .] The scientific use of definitions, characterised by the approach 'from the right to the left', may be called its nominalist interpretation, as opposed to its Aristotelian or essentialist interpretation.[1]

Popper's general condemnation of 'What is?' questions leads him to the postulate of giving up the traditional political theory. As Bryan Magee writes:

> Genuinely important questions are more like 'What should we do in these circumstances?' 'What are your proposals?' To them the answers can be fruitfully discussed and criticised, and then, if they stand up to that, tried out. Nothing that is not a proposal can ever be put into practice. So what matters in politics, as in science, is not the analysis of concepts but the critical discussion of theories, and their subjection to the tests of experience.[2]

When I wrote in my last letter that Popper's postulate of translating political theories into the 'language of demands or proposals for political actions'[3] cannot be realised, I was certainly mistaken in that I incorrectly formulated what I wanted to say. Thank you very much for your criticism. What I should have said was that reducing political theory to proposals would assume a universal agreement over political ends and values, i.e., a totally uniform society. Otherwise such a reduction would lead merely to a superficial 'silencing' of the eternal controversies.

I still think that your essay 'Two Concepts of Liberty' at first sight seems to be essentialist (as I understand this term from the passages quoted above). When you announce at the beginning that you are going to discuss two (out of over two hundred) senses of the word 'freedom' the reader cannot help associating this with Popper's critique of the preoccupation with words and their meaning. I am defending your position by partly acquitting it from essentialism, and mostly by criticising Popper's inconsistency and severe reductionism (I briefly described my discussion in the previous letter).

Let me now explain what I meant by the 'outer' critique of your doctrine. Forgive my having been so unclear—again for the sake of limiting the length of my letter. What I had in mind was the critique propounded from the posi-

---

1. ibid., 14.
2. Bryan Magee, *Popper* (London: Fontana/Collins, 1974), 106.
3. Popper, *The Open Society and Its Enemies*, 1: 112.

tion of several contemporary thinkers who, as I take it, represent different approaches to discussing the problem of liberty. According to Popper, what could be fruitfully discussed is not concepts of liberty but liberation, i.e., we should not ask, like you, which concept, negative or positive, is safer with regard to respecting individual liberty, but what we should do, under given circumstances, to minimise violations of liberty. (This is my interpretation, as Popper nowhere expresses his view on this particular question.)

I am examining also the standpoints of Raymond Aron and Ronald Dworkin in the same chapter and, again, I have many doubts. But I dare not bore you any longer—if you do not mind I shall elaborate on these problems in another letter. [. . .]

The amount of time which you have kindly spared me, your invaluable letters, and your generosity transcend anything I might possibly deserve. I shall always be deeply indebted to you.

Yours sincerely,

Beata Polanowska-Sygulska

PS: In the Polish language we always stress the last but one syllable, so we pronounce Chernobyl. (I am also afraid that your name is not pronounced in Poland as it should be.)

Krakow
22 October 1988

Dear Sir Isaiah,

I feel very ashamed that I have not written to you for such a long time. I am so grateful to you for my wonderful stay in Oxford, our most inspiring meetings and for all your precious time you generously spared me. Your philosophy has changed my life and made it more meaningful.

I have felt inhibited about writing to you, for I could not make significant progress in my work after my return. There is little to write about apart from the fact that, following your advice, I try to 'cheat as little as I can'. Surprisingly enough, I have not been dismissed from work. [. . .] Fortunately, I have the prospect of a long time of relative 'freedom from', as I am expecting a baby. I am so happy to think that, for the three following years, I shall not have to cheat at all and shall be able to do what I really want to, that is to complete my book.

Dr Taylor from Corpus Christi, who is now in Krakow, has kindly agreed to take this letter and a small present for you. I thought that you and your wife might like to have a look at some pictures from the Hermitage again.[1] Alas, the English version of this small album is unavailable.

Thank you very much indeed for everything. I shall always remember my enchanted time in Oxford and do my best not to waste the invaluable benefit I owe you.

Please send my kindest regards to your wife.

Yours sincerely,

Beata Polanowska-Sygulska

---

1. The Berlins visited the Soviet Union in 1988. To their disappointment, they did not manage to buy an album of the Hermitage, which was totally unavailable there. Funnily enough, the Russian version of such an album could easily be purchased at that time in Poland. I presented them with a copy, which they appreciated.

28 October 1988

Dear Beata (I think by now perhaps I might be allowed so to address you),

You can imagine—you are not deficient in that all-important quality without which nothing is much good—how deeply moved I was by your wonderful and funny letter. [. . .]

Your task may be tedious, but what can I say but that a decent degree of security sometimes costs even more—still, I do sympathise. I am of course glad your book is moving forward. You must not rate your own gifts too low, or my contribution too highly. Still, it is a very good thing that we met as and when we did, and nothing but good can come of it, I say with perfect confidence.

I fear that the birth of your child will mean that you cannot travel much in the near future, but life, I hope, is long, at any rate for you. So do let me know from time to time how you are getting on and whether there is any hope of meeting.

Thank you ever so much for the Hermitage—no present could have been more welcome. Aline[1] sends her warmest regards and I send my love.

Yours ever,
Isaiah B.

---

1. Berlin's wife.

20 May 1989

Dear Beata,

I received your article with great pleasure—thank you for defending me against all those terrible people. The opponents you chose are those whom I respect least (with the exception of Charles Taylor). I fear that being about to reach the age of 80 (thank you very much for your congratulations, by which I am deeply touched), I doubt if I shall ever turn into a communitarian. I don't think I am an isolated island, but I think that relationships in an archipelago are more human and morally and politically preferable to coral reefs with little organisms squeezed all together. William James once said about the Hegelian system, organicism etc. that it is like a small boarding-house in Atlantic City, where each touches each other all the time. Don't you think?

Best wishes to you and your youngest daughter, I am not at all sure about the world she will live in.

Yours ever,

Isaiah Berlin

Krakow
18 May 1990

Dear Sir Isaiah,

It has been such a long time since I last wrote to you. It has been partly because of rather vague prospects of publishing the book (which, incidentally, needs much work to be completed). Almost everything is going bankrupt in Poland nowadays. I have been told to be patient and wait. My publisher hasn't committed himself yet, as he can't even be sure about his own future. On the other hand, my daughters have contracted my sphere of negative liberty to almost nothing.

But I should not complain. You promised me four years ago the fall of Communism (you said: 'It must change, because things change'), and it has come true! We are all too tired to rejoice; but there is great relief and comparatively much hope. I myself find it all breathtaking; mostly the losing of my hump.[1]

I suppose Claude Galipeau will tell you about his impressions.[2] He was kind enough to send me his thesis (which I liked), and transcripts of his interviews with you. It was great reading. Apart from the intellectual aspect, I was so deeply touched. It was like being there with you. He wrote down the conversations with great reverence, inserting in parentheses things like 'chuckles all around', 'tapping the chair', or 'laughter'. I could feel the atmosphere which I used to know so well and, excuse my being so boldly informal, I missed you.

One thing you said in the so-called *Athenaeum Interview*[3] arrested my attention. It was about advertising. You said that people actually did want the things they bought and weren't made to want them. At first this convinced me. Then my elder daughter (aged five-and-a-half) made me think more about it. Advertising is quite a new phenomenon in Poland. Its birth coincided with the rebirth of the free market. Once we watched on TV a very clever advertisement for a certain washing powder. She had never been interested in washing before. But from then on she started begging me to buy her just this brand. I was reluctant, as I found this just a passing fad. But later on,

---

1. This was the metaphor for the condition of those living under Communism which I often used during our conversations. Berlin used it to describe the social and psychological situation of Jews and the attitudes of the 'assimilated' ones. See Isaiah Berlin, 'Jewish Slavery and Emancipation', in *The Power of Ideas*, ed. Henry Hardy (London: Chatto & Windus, 2000), 174–6.

2. The author, later, of *Isaiah Berlin's Liberalism* (Oxford: Clarendon Press, 1994). We met in Oxford in the spring 1988. In May 1990 he paid a short visit to my university.

3. Claude Galipeau, unpublished interview with Berlin, the Athenaeum Club, Pall Mall, London, 1 June 1988.

after a painful injection she had to have, I promised to do anything she wanted. She asked for the washing powder. And she was unimaginably happy! She hugged it, took it to bed with her and was most grateful to me. Obviously, she wasn't going to use it; she just possessed it. I wanted to find out what she thought about it herself. She is very self-conscious. She asks questions like: 'How is it at all possible that there is night?', and after my long explanation: 'Mummy, I understand it now, but I don't believe it at all', or: 'Do we really live or do we dream?' She thinks we dream. I asked her many questions. She really did not understand it all herself. She said: 'I have no idea what there is in my mind, but I *terribly* want this washing powder.' It seems to me that the advertisement, while appealing to a deeper need (of being a member of a light-hearted, washing family?), implanted in her a substitute need of getting hold of the means. Maybe Charles Taylor is to a certain extent right.

I enclose an offprint of a piece of mine, published recently in a Polish periodical.[1] Claude was kind enough to take a humble gift which I thought you might like. Thank you for the happy time in my life. I shall never forget you nor any single word you said to me. And I shall not give up the book.

Please send my kindest regards to your wife.

Yours, with warm affection,

Beata Polanowska-Sygulska

---

1. Beata Polanowska-Sygulska, 'Two Visions of Liberty: Berlin and Hayek', *Reports on Philosophy* 13 (1989), 61–72, included in this volume.

29 May 1990

Dear Beata (if I may?),

You cannot imagine how delighted I was to receive from Claude Gali-peau your article, your gift, but above all your letter. I read the article with pleasure and pride, but your letter really describes very vividly the conditions you are in.

First, let me tell you that I never predicted the recent events any more than anyone else succeeded in doing: whatever may happen to Gorbachev in the Soviet Union, there is no doubt that statues should be put up to him in Poland, Czechoslovakia, even Romania—without him, the collapse of the old system could, in my opinion, not have occurred so soon. I realise only too well what you mean by saying that you and others are 'too tired' to glory in the fruits of this situation, welcome as it must be, with all its dangers and deficiencies. I have just read an interesting article by Michnik—a German translation of something he had written for some organisation in Vienna—in which he says, I think with great understanding, that the alternatives before the liberated central European countries are the path of Sakharov versus the path of Solzhenitsyn—democracy, individual liberty, modernisation, use of scientific methods, the kind of liberal regimes that the Russian intelligentsia of the nineteenth century believed in—versus nationalism, anti-modernism, return to ancient values, chauvinism, authoritarianism, anti-Semitism etc., not perhaps quite so violent an overturn as recommended by really disrep-utable bodies like Pamyat or their allies, but nevertheless the kind of thing that the right wing of both the Russian emigration in the West and, evidently, many people in the Soviet Union still hanker after. I do not suppose either will come to pass, but some unsatisfactory compromise between the two, as usually happens in human affairs—I can only repeat to you what I have said to you so often, that, as Kant said, out of the crooked timber of humanity no straight thing was ever made (you must be tired of hearing or reading me quoting this—a little book of pieces by me resurrected by Henry Hardy is about to appear this autumn, under that very title, *The Crooked Timber of Humanity*, and as soon as it appears I shall send it to you).

Your daughter seems to me to be gifted with an exceptional sensibility and imagination, and I do not wonder that this is so—genes are important, we are told, and she has obviously inherited excellent ones. I am glad you gave her that washing powder—once one's imagination fixes on something it is right to increase people's happiness as you have done. About advertising: of course I would not deny that advertisements create desires which were not there previously for things which in fact may not be good for one. What I disagree with Charles Taylor about is that these artificially awakened desires are not real desires; all desires are stimulated by something, whether the depths of one's own character or one's experience—some unexpected physical, moral, emotional or intellectual event in one's mind, heart, soul. Of course the causes are many, and obscure, and difficult to trace, and the psychoanalysts may be right at any rate about some of them. What I do not think is that the desires stimulated by advertising, however dishonest and dangerous, are not real desires like all other desires—that what man desires 'truly' is something different from what he thinks he desires under the influence of these commercial or political stimuli. I take a crudely empiricist position—what one desires, one desires; it may not be a good thing to satisfy certain desires, it may do one or other people harm, but I do not think that a rigid distinction [can be maintained] between 'real' desires, which flow from one's 'true' nature and are part of the purpose (at least for Taylor) towards which one's being is directed, by God or nature or whatever directs one's life to certain individual goals, [and] these other desires which are not part of this teleological process. I think desires are desires, some good, some bad, i.e. leading to harmful consequences, and what causes them one can never quite tell, and all that is wrong with advertising is that it directs or conditions one's yearnings towards something which turns not to be as described, which is a 'false prospectus', a false description, and that is something which can justly be objected to—as against every kind of deception or manipulation—but should not be taken as leading to a distinction between 'true' and 'false' desires. If one does that, one goes back again to the two selves, one of which is entitled to dominate the other, and that, as you know, leads to my horror of the perversion of that into arguments used by every despotic regime in history.

But I must not start preaching to you. Your letter was deeply touching and went to my heart. If you ever feel inclined to write to me again, do—I wish to assure you that your letters mean a good deal to me, more, perhaps, than mine to you. As I am getting on in years, as you know, now almost 81, do not leave it too long—do write to me again whenever you feel you have something to say to me, I should be delighted to receive, and shall certainly reply.

Yours affectionately,

Isaiah Berlin

Krakow
4 October 1990

Dear Sir Isaiah,

It has been such a long time since I last wrote to you. I have very often felt the need to write but somehow I did not dare to, because of my still unpublished book on your concept of liberty. The prospects seem almost hopeless in the current economic situation in Poland. The editors have been privatised and are no longer subsidised by the State. They suffer from lack of money and do not take risks. [. . .] I am terribly sorry I took up so much of your time with such a humble result of only three articles. But I shall not give up—maybe some time the situation will improve.

There is another thing I would like to write about. Dr John Gray has kindly invited me to another seminar organised by the Liberty Fund on *Liberty, Rights, and Government in Algernon Sidney*, to be held in Oxford at the end of September (27–30 Sept.). I shall be able to prolong my stay for another two weeks, as a friend of mine from Mansfield College has arranged a temporary membership of the Senior Common Room.

If it were at all possible I would like very much to meet you. I am so happy Latvia and the other Baltic countries are independent at last. I hope I shall be able to ask you how you feel about this.

Yours sincerely,
Beata Polanowska-Sygulska

20 March 1992

Dear Beata,

Thank you very much for your letter of 14 April.[1] Please do not apologise for anything—you have committed no wrong, I do not suppose you have done a wrong thing in your life. You know how well I think of you and shall for the rest of my life, whatever you do. I am terribly sorry about your problems with your children, and I realise that you are overwhelmed with duties and family troubles. You must not blame yourself so much.

Now about your Catholic faith and pluralism. I don't think that Henry Hardy thinks that pluralism excludes all religion, e.g., Buddhism; but it is incompatible with any religion which claims to be the sole guarding and exponent of the truth, from which it must follow that all other beliefs must to some degree be false. I don't think you are being too personal at all—let me try and answer you as best I can. There is no reason why a devout Catholic should not believe that what he/she believes is the sole truth, and yet be able to understand, even sympathise with, other faiths, outlooks, beliefs, because he/she is imaginative enough to 'enter' other mentalities or spiritual conditions. Even a pluralist like me is allowed to reject views which I claim to understand, 'enter into' etc., because they are incompatible with what I believe to be the needs of life or the truth—while at the same time allowing [that], and above all understanding why, others think differently. My version of pluralism does not entail the proposition that all beliefs, moralities etc., are simply what they are—that there is no way of regarding some as better than or worse than others—indeed, [even as] wicked, perhaps. Of course my judgement is founded on what I understand and believe, I do not oscillate between many moralities, I believe what I believe, even while being able to imagine how one would think and feel if one were an ancient Roman or a follower of the Japanese Shinto religion. Consequently, Catholicism and pluralism are only incompatible to the degree that you believe what you believe, and indeed reject everything else as ghastly heresies, nonsense. [. . .] Of course you can choose, and you do not need to impose your views on others—unless you believe that they are going straight to hell and you have a duty to save them—but perhaps this is not obligatory. So what you have written is not nonsense. I do hope I have made myself clear.

Now about anti-Semitism. What I believe is very simple. You are a child of four or five, you have the Gospels read to you. You have never heard of Jews, you have no idea who or what they are. But you learn that persons

---

1. Lost.

called Jews killed God in the person of His Son made flesh. This casts a shadow on the word 'Jew', even if it is somewhat indefinite. This creates an ember, which glows less or more—and then various winds can blow it into a flame—theological, economic, social, political, nationalist, xenophobic etc. etc. etc. But if the ember had not been there, there might not have been a flame. The ember is not very dangerous as such, but the permanent possibility of a conflagration obviously is. I do not deny that many decent Christians, Catholics, Popes, have denounced anti-Semitism, stressed the fact that Jesus was a Jew (although this is not explicitly stated in the Gospels, Jew is not a favourable term in them); some Christian historians rightly emphasise that all Christians were Jews, not only at the beginning but until St Paul began to convert pagans. But still the ember glows. That is all I wanted to say. Consequently, the objection that from the 'existential quantifier' I drew a universal conclusion is not, alas, relevant.[1] I do indeed say that conflicts may arise, but not that they are necessary. [. . .]

You will have had my telegram. Let me explain that your text is somewhat confused—I am made to repeat myself endlessly (no doubt I did when speaking to you), and there are unfinished fragments and confusions for which I am sure I am mainly to blame—if one talks spontaneously, as I do, I know too well that somewhat chaotic results may follow. So I propose to send you an amended text, which I hope will correspond with the tapes and your memories. It may take me a little time to produce it—please wait and do not go on translating until you receive it. That is the greatest favour you could do me, and perhaps yourself and the readers as well.

I send you my warmest good wishes, and much love,

Yours ever,

Isaiah Berlin

---

1. Berlin refers here to the objection raised by Jozef Zycinski, then the bishop of Tarnow, Poland. Jozef Zycinski, letter to Beata Polanowska-Sygulska, 23 December 1991: '[Berlin] writes that not all ultimate values pursued by humanity are compatible, and from this existential "not all" he then draws the general conclusion that there exists a fundamental conflict between human aims, values and strivings. I find such transitions from the existential to the general quantifier ungrounded. I value Berlin as an essayist, and for his sympathetic way of formulating his thoughts, but for a philosopher a charming style is not an argument.'

10 April 1992

Dear Beata,

Thank you very much for your letter of 1 April. I didn't think you would publish the transcript of the tape as it stood,[1] but I could not resist my terrible schoolmaster's habit of correcting everything—or almost everything. I send you my version, mostly re-typed, which I have tried to make as close to what I said, and you sent me, as I could—I do hope that none of it strikes you as too new or strange or inaccurate. I have not read the corrected version because my secretary is terrified that I may start re-correcting—I hope that it reads well. If you have any problems, please write to Mrs Pat Utechin at this address and give her the page and line reference—she has a full copy of the corrected version and would be able to answer any query you might have, without consulting me (which she declines to do for fear I may start something afresh. I cannot blame her.). [. . .]

I propose to continue to call you Pani[2] unless you stop me.

I hope you and your children are reasonably well and that we may meet one day again in the not too distant future.

Yours ever,
Isaiah Berlin

---

1. Berlin refers here to the transcript, made by me, of our conversation of 11 October 1991, which provided a basis for the two interviews which I then distilled from that text: 'Nil Desperandum' and 'I Don't Want the Universe To Be Too Tidy', included in this book.

2. 'Mrs' in Polish.

Krakow
28 May 1992

Dear Sir Isaiah,

Thank you very much indeed for your letter of 10 April. Again, I do not know how to express my gratitude. The corrections, for which I am deeply indebted to you, made me realise how terribly confused the first version of the interview was! There were parts in it which I could not make out—like the passage on Latvia or on determinism. I sometimes felt desperate while transcribing from the tape, but I told myself I had to do it, and I wrote what I heard. Anyway, everything has become clear. Thank you very, very much.

I have a last query concerning the interview. I shall have to make cuts in the transcript as the text is much too long. The editor suggested it should number about 20–25 pages, while, as it stands, it numbers 45 pages. Would you like to authorise the final version or may I rely on my own judgement? I promise to do it more intelligently than the transcript. There are some parts in the interview which seem to be less substantial than the others; like my story about the film on Korczak. The part concerning your concept of liberty seems to be too difficult for a reader not thoroughly familiar with the subject; I am thinking of shortening it. On the other hand, I would like to bring into prominence especially the themes of value-pluralism, the latent danger of 'another yoke',[1] nominalism, and anti-Semitism, as they seem to be of the greatest importance to the Polish reader. I would be very grateful if you could let me know (maybe through your secretary) what your wish concerning the necessary cuts is. [. . .]

A small contribution to my redemption of the debt may be the entry on your *Four Essays on Liberty* in an encyclopaedia of philosophical works of twentieth century philosophers [*Przewodnik po literaturze filozoficznej XX wieku*] that I am working on now. The volume is being prepared by the Polish Scientific Editorial House. Though I am trying to do my best, I am nervous about the challenging task.

Thank you once again for your generosity and kindness that I shall never be able to repay.

Yours sincerely,
Beata Polanowska-Sygulska

---

1. I refer here to the following passage in the interview 'Nil Desperandum', included in this volume: 'Herzen, a socialist, warned against substituting one yoke for another. He denounced the early pre-Marxist Cabet, and others like him, and talked of the slave galleys of the commune. Some of the early communists of the 1840s wanted a complete socialisation of the whole of life—that is what Herzen called substituting one yoke for another. You strike off the yoke of Tsar Nicholas I of Russia, and you end with another yoke—exactly what happened to poor Russia. Herzen was a libertarian, and very conscious of this danger.' See 110 below.

8 June 1992

Dear Beata,

Do by all means act exactly as you say in your letter—leave out the philosophical bits as far as you can, they are bound to confuse the unphilosophical reader. Do be careful with the passage about nationalism and anti-Semitism—I need not warn you about the extreme explosiveness of this subject in eastern Europe, not only in Poland. In short, I rely upon your judgement entirely.

With my best wishes,
Yours ever,
Isaiah Berlin

Krakow
3 April 1995

Dear Sir Isaiah,

May I take the liberty of writing to you to let you know I am coming to Oxford in May 1995 for a one-month scholarship under the 'Oxford Colleges Hospitality Scheme'. I would be extremely grateful if you agreed to let me see you again.

I wonder whether you have received my letter of 8 December 1994. If not, I would like to inform you that the interview you kindly gave me was published last year, in two parts and in two different periodicals, without any cuts (I enclose copies with the letter). I am very sorry it took so much time for the conversation to be published—the terrible delay was not all my fault. Thank you very much again for giving me the interview. It is widely known in Poland, and I happened to be recognised by completely strange people as 'the happy person who has met Isaiah Berlin'.

I told you in my last letter that I received, in the end, a grant to publish a book on your concept of liberty. I am now determined to finish my work.

I would like so much to meet you again and I hope you are not totally fed up with me.

With best wishes and kindest regards,
Beata Polanowska-Sygulska

12 April 1995

Dear Beata,

Forgive me for not having replied to your last letter. I shall be delighted, as always, to see you whenever you come—please telephone me as soon as you touch British soil, and we shall make an immediate date. I am very glad that you are coming.

Yours,

Isaiah Berlin

Krakow
29 January 1997

Dear Sir Isaiah,

It has been a long time since I last wrote to you. I hope you are enjoying good health.

Last summer I took the liberty of asking you (through Henry Hardy) for permission to reproduce in my book the interview that you kindly gave me in 1991. I had planned to finish the book in the autumn, and that is why I did not write to you but to Henry Hardy, as I feared you might have already left for Italy. Unfortunately, the whole project had to be postponed till spring 1997, as my younger daughter had to have an eye operation. Your secretary, Mrs Pat Utechin, wrote to me (on 19 July 1996) that you have no objection to my reproducing the interviews in my book, provided that I send you copies before I translate them. I would like to explain that the interviews I had in mind were in fact two conversations based upon the interview you gave me on 11 October 1991. The transcript was later read and corrected by you. You introduced into it quite a lot of alterations. Using the corrected transcript, I produced two separate conversations (you gave me your permission for that). The conversations took up two basic threads: your views on nationalism, especially anti-Semitism, and your philosophy, especially value-pluralism and your concept of liberty. The former, a more popular one, was entitled 'Nil Desperandum' and was published in a monthly called *Odra* 6 (1994), 12–17; the latter, a philosophical one, was entitled 'I Don't Want the Universe To Be Too Tidy', and was published in *Znak* 10 (1994), 114–21. Both the texts were widely referred to and commented upon at the time of their publication. I would like to make them less ephemeral and still available to those who have not had access to them. Besides, I myself very often refer to the conversations in the book.

If you wish to make other corrections or alterations I will have to translate the texts back into English (they differ from the original transcript, as I rearranged the text, organising it into two separate conversations and omitting many repetitions. I am taking the liberty of enclosing copies of two letters from you in which you gave me your permission for the necessary adjustments). I shall of course comply with any requirement that you should have.[1]

I wonder if I might take up a bit more of your time and ask you two questions. The first is a technical one. In the Polish translation of *Four Essays on Liberty*, there is an incomprehensible passage which I would like to elucidate

---

1. In the end I did not include the interviews in my book, but I did include a selection of letters from Berlin.

in the book. The excerpt I mean is the counterpart of the following passage in the introduction:

> For whatever reason or cause, the notion of 'negative' liberty [. . .], however disastrous the consequences of its unbridled forms, has not historically been twisted by its theorists as often or as effectively into anything so darkly metaphysical or socially sinister or remote from its original meaning as its 'positive' counterpart. The first can be turned into its opposite and still exploit the favourable associations of its innocent origins. The second has, much more frequently, been seen, for better and for worse, for what it was; there has been no lack of emphasis, in the last hundred years, upon its more disastrous implications.[1]

There is no doubt that by 'the first' you understand the notion of positive liberty, and by 'the second'—the negative idea. Am I right when I suppose that the references have been mistaken? Or is it only in Polish that we refer to *the former* as *the first* and *the latter* as *the second*, while in English it is the other way round?[2]

The second matter is a fundamental one. I wonder whether you might remember our discussion on John Gray's book on your achievements. John's main thesis is that there are no necessary connections between value-pluralism and liberalism. He first characterises your liberalism as 'a liberalism of a distinctive and highly original kind',[3] 'the most powerfully deliberated and most powerfully defended',[4] 'by far the most formidable and plausible so far advanced, inasmuch as it acknowledges the limits of rational choice and affirms the reality of radical choice'.[5] As, according to Gray, in your thought the master-thesis of pluralism supports liberalism, he then thoroughly examines the relations between pluralism and liberalism. He analyses three strands of reasoning whereby value-pluralism might support liberal values and practices:

1. the argument that it is by the choices protected by negative freedom that we negotiate our way among incommensurable values—to which he answers that 'choice-making goes on, even in the absence of negative freedom, as it is an inescapable necessity of the human condition'.[6]

---

1. Berlin, Introduction, in *Liberty*, 39 (my emphasis).
2. This transposition has been corrected in the latest impression of *Liberty*.
3. John Gray, *Isaiah Berlin* (London: HarperCollins, 1995), 145.
4. ibid.
5. ibid.
6. ibid., 159.

2. the argument that if the radical pluralist thesis of the rational incompatibility of goods and evils is true, then the State can never have sufficient rational justification for imposing any particular ranking of values on people—this argument in John's opinion also fails, for

a particularistic illiberal regime need not claim, when it imposes a particular ranking of incommensurable values on its subjects, that this ranking is uniquely rational, or even that it is a better ranking than others that are presently found in the world. It need only claim that it is a ranking embedded in, and necessary for the survival of, a particular way of life that is itself worthwhile, and that this ranking, and the way of life it supports, would be imperilled by the unimpeded exercise of choice.[1]

3. the argument that authoritarian or illiberal societies and regimes are bound to deny the truth of value-pluralism. John agrees that it is true that value-pluralism undermines the universal claims made by illiberal societies that are Marxist, utilitarian, positivist, Platonist, Christian or Muslim at their foundations, but he insists that human history and the human prospect for the likely future abounds with illiberal cultures that are particularistic, not universalistic, in the values they claim to embody. He then gives examples of authoritarian regimes, sustained by Hindu, Shinto or Orthodox Jewish doctrine, which, in his view, seek simply to preserve a local way of life and are not committed to asserting the unique or universal authority of the ways of life which they protect, nor are they committed to denying the value of other ways of life. In John's view, just because such 'particularistic cultures' avoid universalistic reasonings, they 'would appear particularly well-placed to perceive and accept the truth of value-pluralism and its corollary, the worth and validity of radically different forms of life'.[2]

John's analysis leads him to a conclusion which forms the main thesis of his book: Liberalism is not supported by value-pluralism; pluralism is 'the deeper truth and a truth that undermines liberalism as a political ideal with a universal claim on reason'. 'What does follow from the truth of pluralism is that liberal institutions can have no universal authority. Where liberal values come into conflict with others which depend for their existence on non-liberal social or political structures and forms of life, and where these values are truly incommensurables, there can—if pluralism is true—be no argument according uni-

1. ibid., 153.
2. ibid., 152.

versal priority to liberal values.' '[T]here is no direct or universal road from the idea of man as a species whose nature is transformed through the recurrent exercise of powers of choice-making to the idea of a society in which the making of choices is conceived to be central to the human good.'[1]

When we met on 17 May 1995 I quoted John's polemics and asked you what your opinion on his argumentation was. Your first answer was (I am quoting from the tape) that although 'particularistic monism is compatible with pluralism', yet 'the Shintoists are liberal with respect to the rest of the world, otherwise they wouldn't be pluralists', and, in that sense, 'pluralism must entail liberalism'. We continued the discussion on 24 May. I referred to two important quotations taken from Ramin Jahanbegloo's *Conversations with Isaiah Berlin* which I had encountered in the meantime: 'I believe in both liberalism and pluralism, but they are not logically connected';[2] 'Pluralism entails [. . .] a minimum degree of toleration [. . .] .'[3]

You confirmed the former of the above two views, that pluralism and liberalism are not logically connected. I am quoting from the tape: 'Pluralism might be held completely fanatically. [. . .] I fully understand what [the other views are]: but they must be kept out, otherwise they're a danger to the State. Therefore I impose some kind of very rigid orthodoxy. I explain the other movements all right, I understand them [. . .], and yet I don't let them in. [. . .] I want one doctrine to prevail.'[4] You said such an attitude is purely theoretical, not very likely, but it could happen. Thus your final answer was that there is no *logical* connection between pluralism and liberalism; there is a *psychological* or a *political* connection. Yet is not a psychological link too weak a support for liberalism? Does not the example of, for instance, Machiavelli expose the weakness of the connection between pluralism and liberalism? Machiavelli having been, as you wrote, the first, though not conscious, dualist, allowed the free choice of one of the two ways of life; yet one cannot call him a liberal! Is not Gray right in the end, when he writes that 'there can be, and need be, no universal justification for liberalism. It neither possesses nor requires "foundations". It is instead best understood as a particular form of life, practised by people who have a certain self-conception, in which the activity of unfettered choice is central'[5]?

1. ibid., 146, 155, 160.
2. Ramin Jahanbegloo, *Conversations with Isaiah Berlin* (London: Peter Halban Publishers, 1992), 44; cf. 211, 225, 287, 290 below.
3. ibid.
4. See conversation of 24 May 1995, 225 below.
5. Gray, *Isaiah Berlin*, 161.

It seems to me that John's critique, more than anybody else's, touches on fundamentals.

Excuse my bothering you with such a long letter. I would be extremely grateful for any reply from you. If you do not feel like answering my demanding questions, please just let me know what I am supposed to do with the interviews.

Thank you for all the good you have done for me.

Yours, with warm affection,

Beata Polanowska-Sygulska

18 February 1997

Dear Beata,

Quod dixi, dixi.[1] I have no recollection of a single word of what I originally said, later corrected etc. Nevertheless, it cannot be too remote from what I actually think—so let it go forward in the form which you want to do it.

The passage you quote on negative liberty and positive liberty. The English you quote seems to me in order.[2] What I meant is that negative liberty, if pushed to its extreme, means total laissez-faire, e.g. little children working in coal mines in the nineteenth century because the mine-owners are at liberty to hire whomever they wish on whatever terms they wish, provided it is a free contract; the parents of these wretched children presumably receive payment; and Lord Shaftesbury had to stop this awful practice. But in theory this is a perfectly correct interpretation of negative liberty, in its extreme form, ignoring any other values or humane conditions. This does mean that, beginning with liberty in its proper form, you end with slavery. In the case of positive liberty, there is a perversion: positive liberty is an answer to the question 'Who is in charge, myself or some external agency?' If it is external, it is clearly a violation of positive liberty in its proper form, but by fiddling the notion of 'self' you identify the self not with the individual but with the Church, the Party, the class, which embody the 'higher self' that is entitled to bully the real, actual self as we understand it, now mis-named the lower self. That is what I meant and I think it is stated perhaps not as clearly as it should be.

You ask me very searching questions in the second part of your letter, and I am not sure if I can answer them all—but I will try.

I think that Gray is perfectly right in saying that a pluralist outlook need not necessarily be liberal: I have a certain set of beliefs with which I live, a certain horizon of values which are mine—perhaps those of the society to which I belong—'our civilisation'. To be a pluralist means that the choices of myself and my civilisation are not necessarily universal; there may be other civilisations, in the past or the present, which pursue values not compatible with those of my civilisation. If I am a pluralist, it means that I understand how people can come to accept these other values, whether because of their historical or geographical circumstances, or for whatever reason: the point is that I don't simply reject them as not mine and therefore nothing to me—as real relativism does—but I seek to understand what kind of world it is for those who don't share my beliefs, and how one can come to pursue values which are not mine.

---

1. 'What I have said, I have said.'
2. Berlin misses my point: see 79–80 above.

If I am a liberal I tolerate them; the mere existence of the plurality of values does not compel me to tolerate them—I tolerate them not because I am a pluralist but because I am a liberal—my civilisation happens to be a liberal one, but that is simply an isolated fact. There is a further point. If the values of these other cultures threaten my own, if they are not only incompatible with the values of my society but actively seek to undermine it, then—even though I may understand perfectly what led people (sociologically or psychologically or religiously) to such beliefs—then I wish to defend myself against these values, and regard myself as justified in doing so; and if they are truly dangerous and threaten the compromises on the basis of which my society exists, then I may have to attack this other culture, and go to war. This may not be as frequent as people suppose, basing themselves only on the horrors of the twentieth century. You must remember that not all values conflict, only some. If my society is threatened by another, physically threatened, or perhaps in extreme cases spiritually threatened—as Islam threatened, let us say, Christianity or paganism—then I am entitled to defend my culture against the hostile one, which nevertheless I am allowed to understand, and don't regard simply as an irrational force. An illiberal society is likely to try and protect itself against attempts to convert it to liberalism: and a liberal society, against attempts to make it totalitarian or theocratic (or, indeed, despotic in any way which threatens its basis). I belong to a liberal society, I preach toleration; but only to a degree. A liberal society can allow Communist or Fascist parties, religious fanaticism, fundamentalism, all kinds of other illiberal doctrines to exist provided—and only provided—they do not grow powerful enough to threaten the basis of a liberal State. That is fundamental. The old joke about German conservatives who said to German liberals, 'While you are in power, you of course have to allow us to exist and flourish, because that is your principle: but when we're in power, we shall try and suppress you because that is our doctrine and principle', is quite a significant joke: it means that self-protection on the part of a society founded on whatever principles is a basic need; basic because without it the values in which I believe (which I partly inherit, partly perhaps invent for myself, to which I am converted or [which] perhaps have been a tradition in my society—whatever the roots) are those of the only society in which I am prepared to exist. If something overcomes it, and tyrannises over it, I will—if I am a not very brave, peace-loving person—tolerate it as best I can, while hating it; if I am a bit braver, and find allies, then I try to subvert it—that is the justification of resistance to totalitarianism, to any kind of tyranny.

It is also the justification for the suppression of liberalism by tyrannies—that is what is meant by pluralism: that all these outlooks have their place, and that Herder was too optimistic when he thought that all kinds of different cultures could peacefully coexist, admire each other, not try and interfere with each other, and simply live in a garden of many flowers. Liberalism does not presuppose the existence of other cultures which it tolerates, it simply recognises them and seeks to understand them—which of course diminishes the degree of opposition which it shows, the degree of intolerance to which some societies are liable.

As I said, there are limits. Pluralism obviously allows for all kinds of illiberalisms: suppressions of negative liberty. When I defend the idea of negative liberty (and, as a matter of fact, also that of positive liberty, except in its distorted forms), I do so not as a pluralist but as a liberal—that is the society which I believe to be the best, and I can give reasons for it. But I cannot deny that a lot of other people, maybe as a result of believing in false empirical propositions, may believe the opposite. As a liberal atheist, I believe that clerical illiberal societies are due to false belief in God, in the Church, in the eternal authority of certain divine laws etc. I can give you an even stronger example. People used to say that the Nazis were simply pathological, suffering a form of dangerous lunacy. I never believed that: I thought that a German schoolboy could be taught that the only way of progress, increase of knowledge, of virtue, of decency etc., must be promoted by persons of a certain race, i.e. the Nordics; and moreover that there were creatures called sub-human, *Untermenschen*, sub-men, and that these creatures cannot help wishing to undermine, destroy the foundations of, the progressive Nordic society; then these creatures, if the good society is to survive, must be disarmed and perhaps exterminated. The propositions on which this is founded are wildly false, but evidently men can be brought to believe them. So I can say that I am fighting a war against a society which threatens the only society which has that minimum of decency which makes it tolerable to me, because it believes in these wildly false propositions, from which the rest of their behaviour quite logically and rationally follows. The Nazis were not mad, their beliefs simply rested on dangerous, destructive, lethal falsehoods, which have to be exterminated because the truth is an independent value which I, in my liberal society, think it right to pursue.

But values conflict: truth may be incompatible with happiness. The Nazis may be happier in their ongoing slaughter and conquest than I happen to be in my liberal society: no matter—I have my values, and if necessary, in a crisis, I defend them against to me intelligible values which I have a perfect right to reject, but not to misinterpret, because the truth is a value for me, political as well as every other.

One more point. Choice: there are two sorts of choice which I did not develop in the books or essays or dialogues that you have read. One is basic choice, that a human being is not fully human, not human at all, unless he can choose between A and B: I may be tied to a tree, or subject to torture, or whatever, but I can choose either to accept this or try to fight against it, to bend my little finger or not bend it, or whatever; I must have some basic powers of choice in some region—if I am deprived of choice, then I become a robot, hypnotised, to that extent not free, therefore not human. That kind of freedom, the power of basic choice, however limited, is part of what it is to be a human being, not an animal driven entirely by instinct. Then there is political choice, which is what my essay on the two freedoms was founded on: that means something different—that there are as many doors open for me to walk through as can be opened—freedom from interference, negative freedom. It is not the only value; if it conflicts with positive freedom, or with security or with other social values, needs of other members of the population, then it may have to yield to these other values—and so uncomfortable compromises have to be achieved. But this kind of liberty is political, and must not be confused with basic human liberty, which is a biological/psychological entity. There is no human culture at all, among the plural cultures, which does not entail basic liberty—suppression of that is dehumanisation of the human being who is being oppressed or tortured.

But the basic meaning of liberty is not to be tied to a tree, not to be in a prison. As you know, I don't accept the triadic conception of liberty, that it must always be from something to something else: if I am tied to a tree, I only want to be untied, if I am in prison I simply want to escape—what I shall do with that is not clear and does not need to be mentioned. That is the sense in which liberty is negative. Is there a psychological connection between pluralism and liberalism? Yes. If one of the things that I practice is to understand other cultures, how they come to be, how the differences between my culture and their kind of culture arise, what differences there are between the Homeric culture and the Roman culture, Iranian and Red Indian, or whatever—if I do that, my tendency is neither to ignore nor to suppress these cultures, nor to behave as if they didn't exist and mine was the only culture—the best, which can afford to ignore or despise the others (as the Germans sometimes felt, and the French too): that tendency is diminished by understanding itself. If you are going abroad, you may find yourself in a strange foreign culture, but you don't necessarily reject or attack it—it is not yours, but you can put up with it, you can even understand how one might live that sort of life, even though you yourself are not prepared to. That state of mind surely leads to that toleration which is at the heart of liberalism: toleration with limits, not indefinite toleration, toleration provided your culture is not in mortal danger—but still, toleration. Whereas there are cultures which are essentially intolerant, illiberal—and pluralism consists in understanding these too, however you oppose them, however much you may detest them.

I don't know if I have made myself clear—I only hope so. If not, do write to me again and we shall continue.

With all my best wishes, as always; I hope that in your case truth, happiness, knowledge, security, a good life in every way, coincide.

Yours ever,

Isaiah Berlin

PS: Two further points, about which you did not ask me.

1. Could there be a democratic illiberal society? Yes indeed—Athenian democracy was such. The majority of the electors, i.e. citizens, prevailed on all issues; they could be persuaded but not compelled to change their minds, and they could oppress, e.g. deprive of civil liberties, Socrates and one or two so-called Sophists, e.g. the man[1] who said 'The moon is as large as the Peloponnese.' There was no question of guaranteed civil liberties: freedom meant the right of universal inspection by any citizen of any other citizen's conduct.

2. Can there be a tyrannical liberal society? 'Enlightened despots' are said to have aimed at that: in Joseph's II's Empire, and even Frederick the Great's Prussia, individuals enjoyed civil rights, liberty of thought etc. far more freely than in classical Athens, under the Jacobins, in Puritan New England. Enlightened despotism, in which e.g. Voltaire believed, was strictly anti-democratic; an enlightened absolute ruler was thought to be likely to do far more social good than a prejudiced and ignorant majority. So, I fear, it is now: the great majority of the 'enlightened' English would certainly vote for the return of capital punishment, thought to be an illiberal policy.

---

1. What Anaxagoras in fact believed was that the sun was larger than the Peloponnese. G. S. Kirk, J. E. Raven and M. Schofield, *The Pre-Socratic Philosophers*, 2nd ed. (New York: Cambridge University Press, 1983), 381.

Krakow
2 April 1997

Dear Sir Isaiah,

I find it hard to express how deep my gratitude is for your invaluable letter of 18 February 1997. Henry Hardy told me the other day that you do not answer all letters you receive.[1] I fully realise how privileged I am—thank you very, very much indeed.

Thanks to your elucidation I do not have any doubts on the passage from *Four Essays* I quoted in my last letter. In fact, I had understood it properly though, as I can see now, I stupidly mistook the references in the letter! Anyway, it is all clear to me now.[2]

As to the fundamental problem of the mutual relationship between pluralism and liberalism, I still have some questions. If you agree with Gray's thesis that value-pluralism is not necessarily connected with liberalism, do you also acknowledge that there is 'no argument according universal priority to liberal values' and that 'liberalism is best understood as a particular form of life'? You do not seem to believe this, when you write in 'Two Concepts of Liberty: 'Pluralism, with the measure of "negative" liberty that it *entails*, seems to me a truer and more humane ideal than the goals of those who seek in the great, disciplined, authoritarian structures the ideal of "positive" self-mastery by classes, or peoples, or the whole of mankind.'[3] In your last letter you no longer provide the pluralist justification for liberalism, yet your liberal standpoint seems to have remained universalistic: 'When I defend the idea of negative liberty [. . .] I do so not as a pluralist but as a liberal—that is the society which I believe *to be the best* and I can give reasons for it.'[4]

In your paper written with Bernard Williams, 'Pluralism and Liberalism: A Reply',[5] you disagree with George Crowder's thesis that pluralism undermines the liberal case. Yet in your previous letter you write that 'Gray is perfectly right in saying that a pluralist outlook need not necessarily be liberal.'[6] On the other hand, you, as a liberal, do claim in your writings that freedom is to be accorded

---

1. It was very tactless of me to repeat to Berlin what Henry Hardy had told me privately to help me feel less disappointed if I didn't get a reply.

2. On further consideration I realised that Berlin had in fact missed the point: see 84 above, note 2.

3. Berlin, 'Two Concepts of Liberty', in *Liberty*, 216 (my emphasis); cf. 245, 255, 286 below.

4. Letter of 18 February 1997, 86 above (my emphasis).

5. Isaiah Berlin and Bernard Williams, 'Pluralism and Liberalism: A Reply' (to George Crowder, 'Pluralism and Liberalism', *Political Studies* 42 [1994]: 293–303), *Political Studies* 42 (1994), 306–9.

6. Letter of 18 February 1997, 84 above.

a general (though not universal) priority over other ultimate values. Why, as you say, is the liberal society the best? Is it the best because it is a part of 'your civilisation', or because there is some universal justification for it?

I am afraid there is another major question I would like to ask you. In your previous letter, in the context of discussing the phenomenon of the Nazis, you wrote the following passage: 'The Nazis were not mad, their beliefs simply rested on dangerous, destructive, lethal falsehoods, which have to be exterminated because *the truth* is an independent value which I, in my liberal society, think it right to pursue.'[1] Could a pluralist, like yourself, speak about *the truth*?[2] If so, what is the truth? Is it, like other values, that which 'has been accepted by the majority of men, during, at any rate, most of recorded history',[3] or is it that which you understand and believe in your liberal society? The following passage from your letter to me of 20 March 1992 seems to support the latter formulation:

> My version of pluralism does not entail the proposition that all beliefs, moralities etc. are simply what they are—that there is no way of regarding some as better than or worse than others—indeed, wicked perhaps. Of course my judgement is founded on what I understand and believe, I do not oscillate between many moralities, I believe what I believe, even while being able to imagine how one would think and feel if one were an ancient Roman or a follower of the Japanese Shinto religion.[4]

In your paper co-authored with Bernard Williams you criticise Crowder for 'the immensely abstract level of argument' that he has chosen. For a person from my part of the world the issue of the philosophical foundations of liberalism is a vital one. Is there a universal justification for a liberal set of values or is liberalism just a particular form of life?

Excuse my nagging questions.

I would be most truly grateful for any reply.

Yours, with warm affection,

Beata Polanowska-Sygulska

---

1. ibid., 86.

2. I completely misunderstand Berlin here. What I refer to are the Nazis' values and truth in the realm of values, while he has in mind the epistemological sense of truth. This misinterpretation of mine is referred to (and intensified) in the last passage of his letter of 28 June 1997, 102–3 below.

3. Isaiah Berlin, 'European Unity and Its Vicissitudes', in *The Crooked Timber of Humanity*, 204.

4. See the letter of 20 March 1992, 72 above.

19 April 1997

Dear Beata,

Thank you for your letter of 2 April. You ask important questions which I feel bound to try and answer. I am very glad you wrote in these terms, because it really does force me to think certain things out properly—which I may not have done so clearly before.

Let me begin again. I think that Gray is perfectly right in saying that there is no logical nexus between pluralism and liberalism, though there are all kinds of other—in a way equally important—connections, which I shall try to spell out. To begin with, we recognise 'human rights' and 'crimes against humanity'. As you know, I do not believe in a priori justification for these, or absolute values. Things would be easier if one did, but one must say what one believes—I should like to say in my case, knows—to be true. Nevertheless, there are these universal principles which can be appealed to, and which nobody has ever denounced or denied. The Nuremberg Trial was founded on these, and though one may dispute as to what they are, there is no quarter from which they are positively denied. There is no doubt that liberalism embraces these principles. Of course, torturing children for the sake of pleasure would be regarded as inhuman in that sense, contrary to the laws of humanity or natural rights; but that is not enough to establish liberal principles. Whether freedom of thought or assembly, of belief, of speech come among them can probably be disputed—I would say that they are part of the laws of humanity, in the sense intended above. Some may disagree. At any rate, these general principles, accepted by almost everyone almost everywhere at almost all times, even if not strictly, necessarily everywhere, are enough to base morality on, political as well as personal morality.

Now I come to the central point. Can one be a liberal and anti-pluralist, can one be a fanatical liberal and seek to eliminate all alternative forms of government? In theory, I suppose one can, but only in theory. Let me explain. One of the basic principles of liberalism, at least according to me, and I think to the great majority of those who talk about it in any sense, is toleration. That means toleration of views other than my own. That entails understanding what these views are, and allowing them to be expressed even if they are incompatible with my own, and perhaps sometimes hostile to my own. Without that, no liberalism, so far as I can see. Now, pluralism entails understanding the values which diverse cultures pursue, or on which they are founded. Some of these, certainly, must be among those which must be tolerated in a society that is described as liberal. Universal tolerance would entail that all these values, whether those embraced in the past, by Homeric Greeks or Red Indians or medieval Inquisitors or the Nazis, must be tolerated, even if argued against; even if, as I believe, most of these values are founded on errors which in the end are refutable by ordinary, naturalistic, empirical means—e.g. one could seek to demonstrate that Western progress, however interpreted, was not solely due to Nordic or Teutonic ascendancy, and that *Untermenschen* do not exist, that they are an evil fiction, anyway a fiction—I think these things can be shown, by ordinary, rational argument, founded on empirical observation and common reasoning. Even if I am wrong about this, even if views which I regard as intolerable, wicked, evil etc. derive from deep psychological roots which cannot be eradicated by any amount of rational or empirical argument, it follows that if a liberal society is to survive there must be certain views which are sufficiently dangerous to it not to be tolerated. Not always: if Fascism, for example, is as weak as it was in England before the Second World War, one could say that our democracy can carry this—that there is no immediate danger of subversion. So, too, with Communism, and other eccentric or vicious beliefs. But—at this point ethics turns into politics, if you see what I mean—if these views become sufficiently formidable to threaten the foundations of a liberal State, or a democracy, whether liberal or not, one can argue that at that point toleration (which is intrinsic to liberalism, and in some views intrinsic to democracy—the very idea of a party system entails it) must give way, steps must be taken in order to protect the society which is dedicated to toleration. In other words, the liberal society has a right to fight against, and indeed to suppress, any movement likely to be formidable enough to subvert the foundations of the liberal society itself. That is the principle by which you say that you can tolerate anything save that which eliminates the possibility of tolerance. [. . .]

In other words: if you are a pluralist, that commits you to the toleration of diverse views—not only to toleration, but to understanding them. Once you understand other views, you are in a position to understand the views of remote cultures (remote in time or space), cultures very different from your own (in your own time) etc. But if any of these cultures become a menace to the pluralistic society which they threaten, then that pluralistic society—in the name of the preservation of pluralism and/or liberalism, whichever you like to call it[1]—has the right to suppress, to oppose such cultures. This is why the Second World War was justified, against Fascism—and would have been justified against Communism if it had become a serious menace (nobody was sure whether it was or not) to Western liberalism. That is my view. In other

---

1. !!

words, I don't simply contemplate various types of constitution and decide on the liberal one just because I feel sympathetic towards it (though no doubt I do): I commit myself to more than that: I say to myself that toleration is a human right, a universal right as it were, or quasi-universal in my locution; if this is so, and only a liberal society can fully practice it, then that is a connection between them—it is not a logical connection, but a de facto one and none the worse for that. Toleration is the centre of the whole thing; and understanding must be presupposed in toleration. So it's a question of when one stops. There is something about a liberal society which possesses a width of understanding of different views—that is what is meant by saying the liberal society is a society in which differences of opinion exist and which is all the better for that (we choose not to have believed that in Western Europe for centuries)—a modern view, in a way, but nonetheless morally solid. I do not know if I have expressed myself properly, I hope I have.

If you still have questions, please address them to me: I was very stimulated by your letter—I have never expressed myself so clearly before, I believe, so do write to me again if you feel inclined. I fully realise the central importance of the problem you put.

I am not sure that I have made myself entirely clear: in so far as liberalism embodies as a central principle that of *tolerance*, the question is: Where should the limits of tolerance in a liberal society be drawn? I can only answer that they should stretch as far as to render the liberal society secure: one is entitled (morally) to fight against, or, in extreme situations, suppress, views and activities which seriously endanger the stability of a liberal society: i.e. the limits are those of necessary self-defence. Anti-liberal movements can be tolerated if they are not a serious menace to the society: when they are, a liberal society *can* morally resist or suppress Fascist, Communist, theocratic, intolerantly traditionalist movements. That is my belief. I do believe, unlike Bernard Williams, that political theory is the application of morality, of whatever variety, to public affairs. I showed your piece to Prof. Williams (Corpus Christi College, Oxford),[1] and he suggested I send you his enclosed article.[2] It does *not* greatly illuminate me: maybe you will find it useful.

Yours ever,
Isaiah Berlin

---

1. He means the letter to which he is replying.

2. Bernard Williams, 'Realism and Moralism in Political Theory', unpublished synopsis of his *In the Beginning Was the Deed: Realism And Moralism in Political Argument*, ed. Geoffrey Hawthorn (Princeton, NJ: Princeton University Press, 2005).

Krakow
24 May 1997

Dear Sir Isaiah,

Thank you very much indeed for your most illuminating letter of 19 April. I really appreciate your extreme generosity. Thank you also for the copy of Professor Williams's article. I found it inspiring though not helpful in my current research, as it tackles the problem of the foundations of liberalism from a different perspective.

The problem itself still haunts me; especially in the context of the heated political discourse in my country (just tomorrow there will be a constitutional referendum in Poland). Is a liberal democratic State our only reasonable choice, or do we have any other equally sensible alternatives? If not, why? Because (as John Gray would say) of our particular historical tradition? Or because liberalism has a claim to universal authority, as it recognises the value of liberty without which there is no choice and therefore no possibility of remaining human as we understand the word? (Would this be your position?)

The explanation of the mutual relationship between value-pluralism and liberalism in your political theory that you produce in your last letter [. . .] and your thesis that it is in toleration that we can recognise the key to the problem and the spanning link between pluralism and liberalism seem to provide the answer to all my doubts. Yet, what I find most distressing, there does not seem to be any failure in Gray's argumentation! Could it be that your line of reasoning should be viewed in a psychological perspective, while his in a logical one? These things are very complex and, though being theoretical, they have a clear bearing on purely practical matters! [. . .]

There is another issue I would like to ask you about. I have come across a critical review of John Gray's political theory by Ryszard Legutko[1] (professor at the Jagiellonian University, Krakow; I remember you met him at All Souls in 1986). The article comprises a chapter on your and Gray's value-pluralism. It seems to me Legutko makes intriguing points that cannot be ignored. First, he discusses the incommensurability of successively lower goods and ultimate values. Let me quote the most important passages:

> Lower incommensurables have been a part of our experience from time immemorial, and it would be odd to think that the Greeks or the medieval Christians or Jews were somehow unable to identify them. It is also mis-

---

1. Ryszard Legutko, 'On Postmodern Liberal Conservatism', *Critical Review* 8 No. 1 (Winter 1994), 1–22.

leading to speak, in this context, of 'tragic choices' and to imply that the very ancients who discovered and interpreted the notion of the tragic for us—which we moderns have been incapable of reproducing or imitating—were blind to it. Choosing between becoming a priest or a soldier—clearly two incommensurables—is no more tragic than staying at home in the summer or going on a vacation. Indeed, if anything, it is Berlin's and Gray's objective value-pluralism that seems to be devoid of the tragic in any meaningful sense of the word. Apart from the question of the religious dimension of the ultimate—an essential component of the tragic, and hardly an issue for Gray and Berlin—objective value pluralism lacks two essential ingredients for the recognition of tragedy: the notion of necessity and the notion of unity. When there is no impersonal necessity—fate or a higher moral imperative—there is no tragedy. Antigone and Creon, viewed in the light of value pluralism, are at best impractical doctrinaires, and at worst stubborn blockheads, unable to see that the only sensible solution for them was a compromise which, unaccountably, they refused to make. Similarly, there is no tragedy where there is no sense of the unity of morality, however vaguely felt. What moral loss is there for me when I become a priest instead of a soldier if they are treated as two incomparable ways of life, each having its own excellences? I would venture to maintain that moral pluralism, especially of the postmodern version, is inherently anti-tragic and was conceived as such. In a fragmented world, where there is no moral centre, but only peripheries, each periphery becomes its own disconnected centre: so many options are regarded as equally good that few may feel degraded by alternative ways of life or alternative moral outlooks. Even the fact that some forms of life are obviously unattainable to us is hardly frustrating because, given their radical incommensurability with how we live, we do not even know what we are missing: how many American university professors or TV anchormen find it tragic that they cannot experience the joys of Eskimo life, undoubtedly valuable by some non-relative standards?[1]

Then Legutko analyses value pluralism with respect to ultimate values. He agrees its message is crucial in constructing any ethical system—one cannot construct a system that would satisfy all human ideals. Nonetheless he claims that, apart from the importance of the incommensurability of ultimate values, classical philosophy remains relevant to the modern world:

First, it is not true that a recognition of incommensurability is alien to 'the Socratic founders'. Even Plato [. . .] saw the inherent incommensurability of some important values [examples from *Theaetetus* and *Laws* follow].

---

1. ibid., 6–7.

[. . .] Second, while the Socratic founders and the medieval philosophers believed in a hierarchy of goods, the highest good about which they spoke did not have an easy application to practical matters. It was more a theological or ontological concept than a moral or political one. [. . .] The fact that classical political philosophy had a theological dimension enabled its practitioners to conceive of the highest good in a non-instrumental sense [. . .]. Nothing in the concept of the highest good prohibited them from seeing the complexity of political institutions and of their evaluation. Third, objective value pluralism is not itself [. . .] free of Utopian inclinations. [. . .] Those who opt for the new world where value pluralism will be the highest principle do not differ much from the classical Utopians in the confidence they display in the beneficial character of their project. They also share a sense of political and moral finality that the classical philosophers applied to omnipotent bureaucratic structures, and with which they defend a centreless order based on foundationless epistemology and serving non-hierarchical human ideals.[1]

It seems to me that the points that Legutko makes are most original and by no means trivial. When you write in *Two Concepts of Liberty*: 'If [. . .] the ends of men are many and not all of them are in principle compatible with each other, then the possibility of conflict—and of tragedy—can never wholly be eliminated from human life, either personal or social'[2]—do you have in mind only incommensurability of ultimate values, or also of lower goods? If the latter is the case, how would you answer Legutko?

I am very sorry my letter is again so long and so full of questions. I would never dare bother you so much if these problems did not torment me as they do!

I would be very grateful for any reply.

Yours affectionately,

Beata Polanowska-Sygulska

---

1. ibid., 7–10.
2. Berlin, 'Two Concepts of Liberty', in *Liberty*, 214.

Krakow
27 June 1997

Dear Sir Isaiah,

It took me several days to make up my mind whether to write you another letter before you were able to answer the previous one. I am fully aware how terribly bold of me it has been to flood you with my letters full of demanding questions. If I dare bother you, it is only because I realise how great a responsibility I have in writing a book on your ideas.

While working on a chapter on your pluralism, I have been coming back to the texts on your ideas by other authors. It is unbelievable how many new things one encounters while re-reading writings one knows very well. While looking through a paper by Bernard Williams, I came across the following passage:

> [T]he claim that values are incommensurable [. . .] does say something true and important; or rather, it says more than one true and important thing. There are at least four important denials which the claim might be taken to involve; they are of increasing strength, so that accepting one later in the list involves accepting those earlier:
>
> 1. There is no one currency in terms of which each conflict of values can be resolved.
> 2. It is not true that for each conflict of values, there is some value, independent of any of the conflicting values, which can be appealed to in order to resolve that conflict.
> 3. It is not true that for each conflict of values, there is some value which can be appealed to (independent or not) in order rationally to resolve that conflict.
> 4. No conflict of values can ever rationally be resolved.[1]

Does this formulation account for your position? (Bernard Williams seems to think it does.) I have serious doubts on the latest claim; it seems to me to go much too far. When you say at the end of *Two Concepts of Liberty* that 'values are many, not all of them commensurable', does it not follow that some of them can be compared? Thus, isn't it the case that there are conflicts of values that *can* be rationally resolved? If one takes into consideration your example of a man who finds it pleasant to push pins into other people, would

---

1. Bernard Williams, 'Conflicts of Values', in *The Idea of Freedom: Essays in Honour of Isaiah Berlin*, ed. Alan Ryan (Oxford: Oxford University Press, 1979), 227.

not it be possible to resolve rationally the conflict between the man's pleasure and the suffering of his victims?

It always seemed to me that you point to the limits of rational judgement,
but you do not deny it altogether (you told Ramin Jahanbegloo that you are
a liberal *rationalist*). Am I right about this? Is Bernard Williams wrong?

Forgive my bothering you with another question. I promise it is going to be
the last one. If you are too busy or too fed up with me, please just ignore it.

With my best wishes for a very good rest during the summer vacation.

Yours affectionately,

Beata Polanowska-Sygulska

28 June 1997

Dear Beata,

Thank you for your letter of 24 May. You ask some searching questions which I shall do my best to deal with.

Thank you for your acceptance of my idea of toleration as a bridge between pluralism and liberalism—I am sure that is correct.

Why political democracy? Why not, for example, theocracy, or, for that matter, traditional life with blind obedience to traditional rules? Let me begin by saying that there are certain foundations on which all ethical and political beliefs rest (we have been through this before, but never mind, I'll repeat it). Men cannot do without—call it psychological, physiological, biological etc.— food, sleep, breathing, sex, security, the possibility of communication, the life of the senses. This presupposes a basic liberty of choice—do I choose to get up or lie in bed; do I rest or work? Etc. Without this, we are reduced to mere material objects, or at best animals who do everything by instinct. Hence you can say that without such conditions we are dehumanised—these are liberties that men require basically, all human beings require them; this is not an a priori statement (because I do not believe that there are a priori truths about life), but based on observation. In addition to this, men, as men, i.e. pretty universally, need society—Hobbes's solitary savages never existed (this is true even of animals in some unselfconscious way). And the need for society and communication, which all men require, presupposes certain values to be followed. For example: truth—if everyone lies, nobody can rely on anybody—in that case, society disintegrates; some sense of good and bad, what to pursue, what to avoid—this includes beauty and all the other positive values; there have to be some rules, i.e. right and wrong; promise-keeping—otherwise, again, unreliability of conduct disintegrates society. Other things too: the forbidding of murder, stealing etc.—otherwise, again, society can't survive—unless these things are forbidden, even if the rules are broken, most people must live under these rules. Hence the need for institutions, otherwise no society.

But this does not entail political liberty. Men can live under tyranny, theocracy, obedience to traditional authority. This does not dehumanise—so why liberal democracy? It is a fact, discoverable by anthropological observation, that men seek different values—negative liberty, positive liberty, equality, justice, mercy, rational organisation, family life. Some of these clash, as we know, but the question is, why seek them at all, what makes them values? The answer to this is that everything is ultimately psychological—that that is how men are made, some differing from others, and so people choose values as they do because they are so made; and if they clash, then they can compromise between them, as, for example, between traditional authority and liberty from it by means of rebellion, resistance to tyranny by—usually—minorities etc. The chief compromise, of course, is between institutions and individual liberty. Without institutions society cannot persist; if it is totally institutionalised, political liberty is extinguished. So we choose democracy, that means that governments cannot rule unless they obtain enough support from the members of society, unless the government knows that it can be turned out (by whatever the machinery may be—usually votes in elections). The government may even be despotic if enough people like that—that is still democracy, even if libertarians don't like it—but that must depend on the fact that the government is not totally safe, that there are rules under which it can be overturned, rules which they accept—that makes it democratic, that is what gives individuals so-called political rights etc. Then there is individual liberty—that is what makes the democracy liberal, the possibility of individual choice—that there are doors open. I repeat that this can clash. So we compromise to survive, and get what we can. Democracy means that the government can be turned out, liberty means that there are enough roads open for me to take, whatever the government may decide. If the government stops me from taking these roads, then I ask myself whether I want to turn out the government and start agitating under the rules— that is how societies proceed. In addition to this, there is a system of values which men widely accept or long for. Some may choose one form of life, others another, but there must be enough common values between them to make argument between them possible. I can try to convert people to my point of view, which means that I rely on a sufficient number of common values between me and everybody else to be able to argue, persuade, appeal to common values. That, again, is a fact to be anthropologically established.

Then again, why particularly liberal democracy? Not for the reason Gray gives, i.e. that all value systems are what they are and it is a non-rational toss-up between them—because we can give reasons for our choice, give reasons why we prefer this to that; whether because we cling to tradition or defy it, whether we want to live under a republic or a monarchy. We could not argue about that, and give our reasons for it, we could not try to convince slaves to rise, we could not reasonably adhere to certain general rules which may not be universally, but which are widely, accepted—none of this would be possible unless our reasons were intelligible to those who reject them. So liberal democracy is a cross between having institutions and having a degree of liberty, which we prefer—not just because we prefer it, but for reasons which we can give, although these reasons may not be convincing to others.

I don't know if I have made this clear, as against Gray. If argument between followers of different constellations of values is to be possible at all, then it is not a matter of a toss-up between them, each system being what it is, unable to condemn any of the others. Of course I can condemn systems which I hate, what I cannot do is pretend not to understand them (pluralism). I can see how one might prefer to live under some, to me odious, system, but it is odious because my life, and that of a great many other people with whom my life is bound up—my entire society in fact—chooses to live under another system. Why did they so choose?—you may say it is psychological—but in that sense everything is, nothing is logical in this region.

I shall answer your question about the concept of truth at the end of this letter, so we now come to Legutko. I think that I reject the first long quotation you give. Since I am not religious, I cannot tell how a religious person would view tragedy: but in the case which he quotes, Creon and Antigone, there is a conflict of values which is strictly speaking tragic, and is so represented by Sophocles. Antigone accepts unwritten laws which one must follow—she believes, as Creon and I do not, that there are absolute rules, discovered a priori, which one must follow—in this case the rules which tell her to bury her brother. Whereas Creon believes that the State must be obeyed, otherwise chaos ensues. Whichever solution is adopted, whether Creon or Antigone wins, there is tragedy because something has been lost: if Creon prevails, then the principles in which Antigone (rightly or wrongly) believes are violated; if she wins, then the State's authority is undermined. In either case there is a loss, and tragedy simply conveys the idea that you cannot choose both—and if you cannot choose both you lose something and it is painful, it partly destroys your peace and sometimes your whole view of life if this loss is incurred. It is very well for him to say that a man can choose to be a priest or a soldier, and if he chooses one then he doesn't regret the other—of course, there is no agony here—as he says, I go for a walk or not. The agony comes in, and with it the tragedy (for that is what tragedy is about), when both values pull strongly at you; you are deeply committed to both, you want to realise them both, they are both values under which your life is lived; and when they clash you have to sacrifice one to the other, unless you can find a compromise which is not a complete satisfaction of your desires, but prevents acute pain, in short, prevents tragedy. That is the value of compromise. In short, in my opinion he gets the Creon/Antigone situation wrong.

Let me make my view clear. Whichever side wins, the loss of the values of the other side cannot be a source of pain to the winner, who rejects the other's values. So there is no tragedy here, only a conflict. The tragedy is for the Athenian audience, who presumably believe in both sets of values, both the unwritten laws, the eternal code which Antigone obeys, and Creon's belief that the State is the ultimate source of authority. Here there is not merely a conflict, but, whichever side wins, the loss of the other side is a source of pain to the audience, which believes in both these irreconcilables. This is tragic.

Legutko's idea that Plato also believes in incommensurability of values depends on examples from *Theaetetus* and *Laws*—can I please have the quotations, otherwise I cannot judge the justice of this. He goes on that the Greek philosophers and the medieval philosophers regarded the highest good as a theological concept, not a moral or political one. I think this may be true, but what he says doesn't follow. For Plato the 'Highest Good' is something known to philosophers, who therefore can govern the city accordingly; it is opposed to democracy because there is absolute authority here which overrides the views of majorities or individuals—you can call the 'Highest Good' a theological concept if you like, but it certainly has an instrumental sense. I think Legutko is wrong. I do not know about the medievals, but God's laws after all supersede everything, and we know them: so if we do not murder because God forbids it, or if we accept the Pope's final judgement because he is the Vicar of Christ and speaks in the name of God (correctly), this is of direct relevance to political or moral behaviour. I do not understand what Legutko means by 'political and moral finality', despite the value pluralism, which he thinks they accept, on the part of classical philosophers—I do not [know] what 'a centreless order based on foundationless epistemology and serving non-hierarchical human ideals' means. Consequently, when you ask me about Legutko's originality, I do not think that he makes a case, at least, he does not for me; unless this can be further elucidated.

As for your question about whether the incompatibility of the ends of men applies to lower goods as well as ultimate values: yes, no doubt, it does occur—but the lower goods, not being ultimate, can be decided in terms of the ultimate goods; they may be incompatible, but if you solve the conflict in terms of one of the ultimate values, that would do it—even though it might leave other ultimate values unapplied. So I don't see that I need to answer Legutko in any way.

Your query about 'the truth': I am a pluralist in the realm of values, but not in epistemology.[1] Truth does not vary with cultures or societies: if true,

---

1. Berlin ascribes to me here an erroneous interpretation of his views which I actually did not make. This is a result of a piled-up misunderstanding for which I was originally responsible, having asked a misconceived question (see 90 above, note 3).

it remains so 'for ever'. While I cannot be sure that my beliefs are true—infallibility, absolute knowledge, are not, according to me, within our grasp; yet I can regard some judgements as incorrigible, and such judgements do not depend on milieu. If someone says to me that $2 + 2 = 193$, I do not say that the rules of arithmetic [that are] 'universally accepted' make this non-sense, but that in some cultures it seems acceptable: I say that it is untrue and does not make sense, and given what arithmetic is, it is nonsense—and remains nonsense whoever says it, wherever and whenever—I do not add that on the planet Venus another arithmetic may operate, unknown to us. No pluralism here.

　　With very best wishes,
　　Yours,
　　Isaiah Berlin

17 July 1997

Dear Beata,

Your letter of 27 June—forgive me for taking so long to answer it, but I have been away and could only collect myself to do this today.

You are right: Bernard Williams's formulation of my view is too extreme, your doubts are quite right. Some values do not clash, not all values are incommensurable, incompatible—that is clear. Some values clearly can be compared—we do this every day of our lives. As for rational resolution of conflicts: of course my preferences can not only be compared in some cases—for example, two pleasures of very different kinds, where I choose one in preference to the other not simply by tossing a coin (non-rationally) but because my preference can be based on argument—reasons—which are rational, even if in the end we are governed by the constellation of values by which we live; and these, in turn, are often incompatible and incommensurable with other constellations which other cultures follow. The fact that total outlooks may not be compatible, and that my outlook ultimately derives from many factors (character, experience, my society's tradition, language, habit, custom etc. etc., as well as values to which I may be converted by some preacher or thinker, or my own sudden awakening to them), means that nevertheless this total constellation is what it is, it is not just my private choice, it chooses me as much as I choose it, and it is part of the culture in which I live—in other words, part of the way of life not only of myself but of all the people I live among and communicate with, and share views, argue, disagree with. These total constellations may well be incompatible with other total outlooks—of the Romans, of the Eskimos, of whoever; but this does not mean that values always clash, or that I have no reason for preferring one particular course of conduct, or aim, to another. About this, you are absolutely right.

You ask me 'Is Bernard Williams wrong?' in denying that I am a rationalist, or rather rational. No, that is because he does not go quite so far as you make him go in denying rationality to me—I think perhaps you slightly misinterpret his interpretation of my view. Perhaps 'rational liberal' is better than 'liberal rationalist'—that would be a perfectly good description of my position.

Does this answer your questions? I do hope so. I am so old, my thoughts are often confused, that I am not sure that I can be as clear about my own opinions as perhaps in my printed works I seem to be. Nevertheless, I think I have a position, and I think you have grasped it perfectly well. So let me offer you my gratitude and hope that your work will have the success which it surely most richly deserves.

Yours ever,
Isaiah Berlin

Interviews

All Souls College, Oxford, October 1991

Nil Desperandum

BP-S: Several years ago,[1] during our first meeting, I asked you the agonising question which used to be always on my mind: 'Is there any hope?
If so, when is IT going to happen?' (it was the collapse of Communism
that I had in mind). Your answer was: 'It will happen some day because
things change. Perhaps in one hundred years.' How do you feel about the
great events that have taken place—especially about independent
Latvia?

IB: When we met and you asked me this question about Communism and
about the Soviet regime and so on, I never conceived it possible that it
would collapse so suddenly and so finally. I have a friend, an English
poet called Stephen Spender. In an interview which he gave he reported
that he asked me: 'What would you think the most wonderful thing
which could happen in the world today?' I said: 'The most wonderful
thing would be the collapse of the Soviet Union and Communism. But
of course, it will not happen in our time. We shall be long dead before it
happens, if it happens at all.'

BP-S: And yet it did happen . . .

IB: It's the sort of event which nobody predicted. The whole world was surprised. Some people were no doubt disappointed, and some people were
triumphant. Extremely pleased and glad, like me. And relieved. Pleased
that the world had become a better place. But I want to tell you this: The
only man I ever met who predicted something like this, funnily enough,

---

1. In an unrecorded conversation in July 1986.

was a British ambassador in Moscow, whose name I can't remember, about ten years ago. He and I met at some meeting in London and he said: 'The Soviet Union can't go on like this. The corruption and inefficiency are so enormous; it's bound to collapse. It can't go on. It can't. The system cannot continue.' I wish I could remember who was there at that time. But I must say I remembered it after it happened. I thought: 'He was the only man who prophesied it.' He was clearly a very good observer. No doubt it is the best thing which has happened towards the end of my life, so far as public events are concerned. I was always anti-Communist. I was not particularly anti-left-wing. In the 1930s I packed parcels for the Spanish Republic. But I saw the Russian Revolution in 1917. Anyone who has gone through it even as an innocent child, as I was at the age of eight, would have found it difficult to join the Communist Party later: I never knew anybody who was there at the time, and went abroad, and nevertheless later became a Leninist in the West. But of course there may have been such people.

BP-S: When I heard of independent Latvia I thought instantly of you . . .

IB: Well, yes, my birthplace. Riga used to be a perfectly nice little town. I last saw it in 1928. It was a republic, a little bourgeois democratic republic, provincial, not very interesting, nobody very distinguished, as far as I know, but a perfectly decent place in which people could be free and happy. It was time that the Latvians had a State of their own. Before 1910 they did not have an independent State and they had been badly treated both by Germans and by Russians. The Letts were regarded as illiterate peasants. Some were and some were not.

BP-S: Almost all contemporary doctrinal liberalisms (apart from yours) seek to formulate a theory proposing a final solution or a blueprint for a liberal society. Such liberalisms are inevitably Utopian. Yours is virtually the only exception to this. What would be your advice for a country, building up its new social order almost from scratch? People would like to know your answer.

IB: This is something about your country—I understand that. But to look to philosophers and sages to have ready answers to human problems is a mistake. The production of ideologies is not a philosopher's business— look at what Marxism has led to. Or Fichte's nationalist writings.

BP-S: But Hayek tries to produce a blueprint. Likewise Rawls . . .

IB: Well, there are certain things which you can say. You can say, for example, 'I don't know whether a market society is freer than a socialist society, I've no clear answer to it. In some ways yes, in some ways not.'

In a market society, are the poor worse off than in a planned society? Are they freer in a society where they have enough to eat, shelter, clothing, security, enough to live on, but lack political freedoms, live under rigid discipline? Of course not having to worry about where the next meal comes from is a form of liberty. But at what cost in other freedoms? I don't know. I don't know that there is a clear answer to that. All you can say is that most—not all—human beings in the world today are no longer bedevilled by an ideology which is fanatically rammed into them and their children, whether religious or political; that most of them live by values which are not all that dissimilar from one society to another. Of course there are vast differences. I don't say that the Weltanschauung of the Chinese is very like that of, let us say, the Italians. Yet I would maintain that there is enough common moral ground among most human beings in terms of which they can communicate without undue difficulty. Any society will be a good liberal society in which there is a maximum degree of genuine understanding, and consequently of toleration, of other people's views, in which the largest number of objectives can be pursued without clashing with one another too sharply; in which the greatest degree of mutual understanding occurs, between people who understand what other people want, and why, and what they need, and in what measure, and don't try to force them into a conformity which, although these others resist it, you and you alone (you and your friends, you and your party) know to be good not only for you but for everyone else. In other words, a liberal society is a society in which there is not too much paternalism, however benevolent. Not every paternalist society is Stalinist, yet even so, paternalism can do harm. Paternalist societies on the whole diminish the self-development of human beings, although in the case of a primitive or decadent society paternalism may do good.

I can't answer your question. Herzen was once asked: 'What is the purpose of life?' To which he replied: 'The purpose of life is life.' Life has no universal purpose, only individual purposes—happiness, justice, kindness, freedom, knowledge, beauty, art, love, self-expression, pleasure, amusement. All these are purposes; a general purpose of life does not exist. People do ask: What is the purpose of life? To me that is a meaningless question. I am not a teleologist, not an Aristotelian or Hegelian or Marxist or Christian, or any other kind of '-ist'. If you ask: What is my purpose? What is his purpose? Why do you do this? What are the things you would like to see in the world?, What are your ends of life? What are you ready to sacrifice your life to?—I think that these are intelligible questions. People do lament that life has no purpose, no meaning, that it depresses them. This happens often—but I've always been too stupid to understand what that means.

BP-S: John Gray's advice for Poland was a sort of 'Berlinised Popperism'. How would you comment upon this?

IB: I can't answer that. I don't know what that means. I don't know what 'Berlinised Popperism' would be like. Popper would be very, very angry at this suggestion.

BP-S: Gray's idea was that we should, in this period of transition, apply Popper's advice of the trial-and-error method.

IB: I have nothing against that. I think that the idea of social engineering, of trial and error, is a very good piece of advice, but sometimes it doesn't work. There are crises, critical situations, when you have to act in a much more decisive way. It is no use telling the people who crushed the putsch in the old Soviet Union—don't do too much all at once, use trial and error to see if you can get consensus, why don't you try a little social engineering? That would not do. What is the use of saying this to Nazis, to the Ayatollahs, to Saddam Hussein, to Stalin? I am, of course, all in favour of freedom, tolerance, reason, an open, loose texture of society; but not when you have to reconstruct a society which has been cruelly crushed, to which liberty, even relative liberty, is something comparatively new and unfamiliar. There, I think, decisive steps have to be taken, even though they may fail—but at least let us try.

There's no general rule, not even Popper's humane approach, based on the methods of the sciences, however sympathetically adjusted to particular problems and situations.

Herzen, a socialist, warned against substituting one yoke for another. He denounced the early pre-Marxist Cabet, and others like him, and talked of the slave galleys of the commune. Some of the early communists of the 1840s wanted a complete socialisation of the whole of life—that is what Herzen called substituting one yoke for another. You strike off the yoke of Tsar Nicholas I of Russia, and you end with another yoke—exactly what happened to poor Russia. Herzen was a libertarian, and very conscious of this danger.

That is why I can't say, a bit of Popper, a bit of me. There's no need to read either Popper or me. One must simply follow the normal moral instincts. On the whole, I don't believe that knowledge of what is decent has been knocked out of people by the rule of Communism. And other things have also survived: look at the Church—Stalin didn't succeed in suppressing it—he kept it down, but as soon as he disappeared, as soon as Communism lifted, it popped up again, sometimes in a reactionary guise. So, too, with nationalism: held down by Communist regimes but not destroyed. I am optimistic enough to believe that there are certain basic human needs, wishes, values, and all I ask for is the breakdown of prison houses, if need be by decisive action, and for enough opportunity to be given for at any rate some of the central values to realise themselves at some but not too much cost to other ones. It's a very dreary piece of advice. It recommends trade-offs—I talked about that in the Agnelli lecture. Alas, it is not a waving flag, not something which young men can find inspiring, by looking for radical solutions, altars to which one can courageously bring great sacrifices. But I cannot help thinking that if idle bloodshed is to be avoided, my dull solution is valid.

BP-S: You seem to be the only liberal thinker who, rejecting the concept of universal civilisation, has recognised the power of nationalist ideology. What is the source of nationalism? Is there anything we can do to moderate its expansion?

IB: First of all, nationalism is something which hasn't always existed, but tribalism always has. There's a desire to belong—Herder described this desire as basic, a deep human need. There is a basic human need to live among one's own, to be able to live among people who understand what you say without explanation, who understand your gestures, who understand the meaning of your behaviour, almost by instinct (where there is no need to explain yourself—in short, where you are among your own). I think that I said that in my lecture. I had a Montenegran friend who said, 'To be solitary means, not to be alone, but to be in a society where nobody understands what you mean.' And you want to be in a society where people know you and what you mean without you having to make it clear in so many words. That's what being at home is. Hegel said that 'Freiheit ist bei sich selbst sein'—freedom is to be at home. It seems to me a profound remark. This is not nationalism, but a sense of nationality, a national consciousness, of being part of a nation. I don't think there is anything wrong with that.

Nationalism is a pathological inflammation of national consciousness. Its symptoms are saying and believing that my nation is better than yours; and I'm going to annex you, or at least assimilate you to my pattern. I know how to live, because I belong to a nation which is full of hereditary wisdom, whereas you are a degenerate or a barbarian. I am civilised, which gives me a right to force you to lead my life, or minister to it, obey its laws, whether you like or understand them or not. It happens when I say that I act thus not because it is right but because I am a German, a Frenchman, a Zulu, and that is the German/French/Zulu way, its mission, the root of its authority. So long as there is pride, conceit, vanity, desire for power, and desire for domination—cruel wars, massacres, enslavement, humiliation, trampling on the rights of strangers, 'inferior' races, groups, individuals will continue. If you give me a recipe for teaching people not to want to dominate, not to seek power, not to believe that the superior quality of your nation or race (or Church, party, culture) entitles you to force others to obey, then there might be a solution. So long as that goes on, particularly among those groups who are reacting against their own past humiliation by other groups, the possibility of aggressive nationalism can never either be eliminated or ignored.

BP-S: When I posed the problem of nationalism I especially had in mind, as you can guess, anti-Semitism. Is there anything that distinguishes it from all other forms of nationalism?

IB: I think that anti-Semitism is an awkward problem. What well-meaning persons usually say about it is that it is due to the fact that people need a scapegoat, people need somebody to blame for their own failings or misfortunes, someone who is not one of their own. Again, it is said that Jews have always kept themselves to themselves, isolated themselves, were compelled by their religion to marry only each other, hence they were felt to be a foreign element, a cause of discomfort, at times of irritation, to the rest of society—even a threat to its integrity. Let me offer you a parable. Supposing you and I found ourselves in a society about which we knew very little, let us call it Hottentot society. We don't know the Hottentot language, customs, and we therefore feel unprotected and afraid. We are strangers among foreigners. So in order to get our bearings we learn the Hottentot language and study the customs, we do our best to understand the world in which we now live and adjust ourselves to it. We succeed. As a result of this tremendous effort to learn about these people who are not our own, we cannot help becoming experts on the Hottentots. We write Hottentot dictionaries and encyclopaedias, we explain the Hottentot soul to non-Hottentots. We do so because to survive we have to find out what is likely to occur, how the Hottentots will behave or act. They don't have to find this out. They just do what they do, are what they are, live their normal lives; whereas we have to observe and predict. All minorities have to be aware, sometimes uneasily, of what the majority do. In good times the Hottentots like us, because we have become propagandists for Hottentotology. But in bad times, because we are obliged to know the truth, because our lives depend on it, and we report this—because of this we become unpopular: people don't like to be told of faults, failures, misfortunes. Like doctors, whose diagnoses and prognoses can be unfavourable, we cause annoyance, even hatred. We feel that this is unjust: we say to them 'Why do you persecute us? We've done more for you than you've done for yourselves.' To which they reply, 'That is exactly the point—you've done things *for* us but not as part of us. Yes, you may do things for us, but you are not identical with us. You are you—you may try hard but that is because you are different.' That is the basic fate of minorities, particularly minorities whose lives depend on trying to assimilate—sometimes trying too much—to the majority—from a sense of insecurity.

Goethe was a German, a great poet who wrote about nature, love, beauty, the classical world, human life and destiny, about the spirit in all its manifestations. Because he was a German, he was a great German poet. Heine was also a great poet, a German poet, but he often thought and wrote about what it is to be a German. He was a poet of genius, and he wrote in German, but he is deeply concerned with what it is to be a German, historically, politically, spiritually—all this precisely because he is not a German among Germans, and he is very self-conscious about this. So he went to live in Paris and viewed Germany from outside.

Felix Mendelssohn was a truly devout Lutheran and a very German composer. It was he who created the Bach-Gesellschaft to revive the great Lutheran musical tradition. He was more German than the Germans—he almost overdid it. Schumann, Brahms were German composers *tout court*.

There was the German Jewish musician Hermann Levi, who was employed by Richard Wagner at Bayreuth—a pianist and conductor. Wagner, of course, was acutely anti-Semitic. Levi wrote to his father, a rabbi, to say he could not live like this, that Wagner had said awful things about Jews at lunch, and that Cosima, his wife, was even worse; but that unbearable as this was, Wagner's genius was so great that he could not bring himself to leave Bayreuth. Then he met Franz Liszt, Wagner's father-in-law, and known as a kindly man. Liszt said, 'Herr Levi, why don't you change your name?' Levi said 'Why should I change it?' Liszt replied 'Aber Herr Levi, man ist nicht Jude'—one just isn't a Jew. A Jew cannot function properly in ordinary society. That was the view of a decent man, trying to be helpful. Truly civilised people are not liable to anti-Semitism, or, at least, not to excessive feeling of it. But the number of wholly decent, civilised people is not—has never been—great.

The existence of Israel, although it saved the Jews from inferior status, has not diminished unfriendly feelings for them, especially given their behaviour towards their Arab population. Still, assimilation does work—not much, but it does. The grandchildren of intermarriages do, as a rule, cease to be, or be thought to be, Jews. But the rate of this evaporation, whatever may be thought of it, is very low. Jews can be wholly free only in Israel. Israelis are natives of a country of their own: no minority complexes, normalisation at last.

BP-S: Have you ever personally encountered cases of 'exaggerated assimilation'?

IB: I once met a German Jewish refugee, I think in 1934, in London. He'd fought in the German army in the First World War, and had been decorated. I said to him 'You got away from Germany quite early, you were lucky. Where did you go?' 'I went to Switzerland,' he replied. I said 'But didn't you find Switzerland a little dull?' 'Yes, very.' 'Then why didn't you go to Paris, surely much more interesting?' He drew himself up and said 'I would never dream of going to the country of our enemies.' He was a German patriot. Driven out by Hitler as a Jew, a pariah, a menace, he still displayed his medals—that is being a member of a minority who lived in a deep illusion.

When people try and live with another people with whom they strive to identify themselves, they tend to go too far in their zeal, to exaggerate and overdo it. People don't like apes and parrots. They don't like to be imitated, or, in the case of Heine, to be mocked. A famous American humorist, Dorothy Parker, who was Jewish, is alleged to have said 'The Jews are just like everybody else, only more so.'

Finally, the most important cause of anti-Semitism in my opinion: the Gospels, the Christian Gospels. They tell the story of the crucifixion, of the murder, of God, or the Son of God, by the Jews. You are, let us say, a little Christian child; you go to a Sunday School and you have somebody who teaches you the story of Christ. You've never met a Jew, the word may mean nothing to you. But you are told that persons called Jews perpetrated this unbelievable crime and sin, the central fact of your religion. Consequently a cloud falls over the word *Jew*. One day you meet people known as Jews. You cannot, even if only subconsciously, but have a sense in the back of your head that there is something slightly sinister about them. There is something not quite good about being a Jew, even if you don't think about the story in the Gospels. That creates an ember, a little glowing centre, which does not necessarily develop into a fire. Winds can blow it into a flame: winds, political, economic, religious, nationalistic, xenophobic—blow it into a conflagration. Without such winds it may glow without much harm being done. But my theory is that if there hadn't been an ember, there could not be a flame. Other equally passionate and often intolerant religions—Islam, Hinduism—while their followers may at times be hostile to or even persecute Jews, do not have built into them the deep, unceasing, indelible Judaeophobia characteristic of the entire Christian tradition. No matter how often Popes, bishops, churchmen of various denominations deplore this, and deny Jewish responsibility for deicide, it persists in the Church and Christian culture—and, it seems to me, is bound to continue to do so, as long as the simple, unmodified, uninterpreted message of the Gospels is taught. This is its real root. Sad but, I fear, true. Other minorities come from lands where they are a majority. The Jews are a minority everywhere, and thus unique. Everywhere, except now, at last, in Israel. That is the case for Israel, in my view. Of course anti-Semitism, which lives on, becomes acute only if certain circumstances arise—when the Church is fanatical, or if the economic situation is desperate—and those who are looking for a solution are told that it is all the Jews' fault, or, as in the Middle Ages, that Jews poison the wells; or as some modern Jew-haters, in Eastern Europe, or Muslim lands, are saying, 'The secret society of the Elders of Zion is spreading AIDS to kill Christians', and so on.

BP-S: Yet, on the other hand, do not Jews' own reactions strike you quite often as exaggerated? Andrzej Wajda once made a moving film on Janusz Korczak . . .

IB: I know about Korczak. He died in a camp. He went voluntarily with the children he looked after.

BP-S: The film was shown in Cannes, and then it was refused distribution in France.

IB: Because?

BP-S: Because it is anti-Semitic.

IB: Oh, how funny.

BP-S: The film was made by a Pole, so by definition it has to be anti-Semitic. Actually, it is the other way round.

IB: I understand. It's pro-Korczak. Korczak is a hero and a martyr.

BP-S: Prejudices and phobias pile up and up until people lose common sense. Then you've got anti-anti-Semitism.

IB: It's a terrible issue. It spoils everything. Anybody who is at all unpleasant to a Jew is immediately accused of anti-Semitism. Because of Hitler it has become a terribly sensitive and delicate issue for everybody with any human feeling. I do not, myself, react to anti-Semitism of the moderate kind. When people say that a certain person is an anti-Semite, I usually ask: 'Normal anti-Semite or more that that?' Normal anti-Semitism is no worse than irrational dislike of the French, of the Germans, what many Poles feel towards Russians, and vice versa. Ethnic hostility is a bad thing, but one can live with it. That's why I don't want to feel too strongly about this; I think there always will be people who hate the English, or the Jews, or the Arabs, or the Negroes. It can't be avoided. It's very regrettable, and does harm, but it is perhaps too optimistic to think that it could be wholly eliminated. I hope I'm wrong, I do indeed, but unfortunately I don't think I am.

BP-S: And a Polish accent at the end. In a letter to me of 29 May 1990 you refer to a paper given by Adam Michnik at a seminar in Bratislava on the relationship between ethics and politics. Michnik discusses the two cultures symbolised by two eminent Russian activists of the anti-Communist opposition—Andrei Sakharov and Igor Shafarevich. How would you comment upon Michnik's recognition of what he calls the basic contest of our time?

IB: I can't remember exactly what Michnik said, only that I greatly admired it. It was reprinted in the *New York Review of Books*. I read the article somewhere and sent it to the editor of the *New York Review of Books* and recommended it.

Sakharov is the nearest to a real saint that I have ever met in my life. Apart from his courage and his integrity, he was a very good man, and wonderful to be with. Sakharov believed in human decency. He believed in toleration. He hated nationalism. He believed in rational investigation, science. That's what the old Russian intelligentsia believed in. He believed that personal relations between people are of great importance. He was not fanatical in any way; he was not a victim of an ideology. You see, Shafarevich is a man who thinks that any foreign element in Russia is dangerous. That Jews poison wells. That Jews fundamentally are hostile to Russia, for whatever historical reason, and therefore must be removed. That is acute chauvinism. A less chauvinistic man than Sakharov I have never met in my life. But he was not a kind of, you know what I mean, amiable cosmopolitan. He was a profound Russian patriot. He thought about Russia all the time, and about the rest of the world not so much. Russia was what mattered to him. He wanted it to be a country of honourable, decent, tolerant, truth-seeking, honest people. He didn't want much more than that. Even that's asking for a great deal. What he hated was any form of fanaticism, zealotry, pursuit of one end at the expense of all others, bitter dedication to some final goal which produces blinkers that exclude from vision most of what there is in the world—something that Americans call 'tunnel vision'. As someone said of the present prime minister of Israel (a Pole, I fear), apropos of 'light at the end of the tunnel'—'At the end of the tunnel there is darkness.' Solzhenitsyn seems to me to resemble the Russian Old Believers of the seventeenth century. He knows where the truth lies. He knows what sort of Russia he seeks. He knows that there is a devil on the throne. He knows that Communism is the devil. He knows that liberalism is a form of weakness that undermines true faith. He's a religious man and a nationalist, he knows that he knows the difference between good and evil, and he does not allow any deviation from the direct march towards the clearly perceived universal goal, or at least the Russian goal. This can cause a good deal of human suffering. I think Michnik's piece was very good, particularly on modern Poland. It calls for what Russian liberals in the nineteenth century wanted, people like Herzen, like Turgenev, like Belinsky—not Tolstoy, who is another story, nor Dostoevsky, who is yet another story. But what was called the intelligentsia, a Russian word—some people say Polish, I can't tell, certainly it is a Russian idea—what the intelligentsia wanted was probably morally and politically the most humane culture imagined in the last two centuries. That's what Leninism tried to extinguish, but it survived. Just as nationalism survived Stalin, so this kind of liberalism, to my great surprise and astonishment and pleasure, has survived. If you talk to young people in Russia, and I'm sure the same is true of Poland, they are imaginative, civilised, honest, humane, spontaneous—they want to live and let live, and they've great faith in the future of human decency and goodness. Decent society is what the liberals wanted; and that is what the intelligentsia wanted and wants. They thought that the tsarist regime, the Orthodox Church and other institutions like that suppressed it. Herzen thought socialism would provide it. Well, it hasn't. The left wing, whatever its original ideas, has, to a degree, collapsed, perhaps more so than it deserves, because it was compromised by association with Soviet Communism. Even honourable, non-Communist leftists somehow believed, some of them, that while the Soviet Union was in many ways wrong and wicked, yet still, in the end, it was on the right side: they commit crimes, but still, in a sense, they're marching in our direction. That is what compromised the left everywhere. This was a terrible illusion. Now, there may be an opportunity for them to reconstitute themselves in a more honourable form. Who can say whether they can or will? Michnik's voice is the voice of Sakharov and Herzen—I can't praise anyone more than that. Herzen was exceptional in many ways, but among them in that he did not dislike the Poles—he had worked with them in London—what other Russians can one say that of?

BP-S: Coming back to hatreds among nations—if it is impossible to eliminate them entirely, can their strength be at least moderated?

IB: Germans no longer hate the French as they did, nor the French the Germans.

BP-S: What was the original source of hatred between the Germans and the French?

IB: Well, the Germans became the great power quite late in history. France was the glorious power of the seventeenth century—*Le Roi Soleil*—Louis XIV—the French had everything, everything in the world. They had all the arts, they had political power, philosophy, they were the summit of Europe. They were a top nation in every branch of human activity. They looked on the Germans in a patronising way, as beer-drinking, primitive peasants, smoking long pipes. In the end, people don't like to be patronised and despised. And there was a backlash. The Germans of the eighteenth century duly became Francophobes. After Napoleon's war this became acute. And after that, German nationalism rose as a huge resentful defensive phenomenon, aggressive—and, as we know, caused two terrible wars.

BP-S: Have the Germans and the French already got over those bad times?

IB: It seems to me that they all get on quite well—I may be wrong, but I think they do.

BP-S: So it can be done.

IB: It can be done. Don't let us despair. *Nil desperandum.*

I Don't Want the Universe to Be Too Tidy

BP-S: You have recently become widely known and read in Poland, especially since the first publication of a collection of your essays, including 'Two Concepts of Liberty'. As you told me the other day, everything else you have written is a footnote to this essay. In what way is it the culmination of the 'three strands' of your life?

IB: Ah, the three strands in my life. Yes, that's what I once said in Jerusalem, when I got a prize there. I don't think it's a culmination. If I said that, I was talking nonsense, as so often. You know—everything I've ever written is always done on commission, all done to order. I've never composed anything spontaneously.

BP-S: How is this possible? Your bibliography includes over two hundred publications . . .

IB: Once I wrote an essay on the late Professor Namier, who was a Pole. I think his name had been Bernsztajn, he changed his name to Namier. It must come from Niemirowski, something like that. . . . He was a famous historian, of some genius, who changed the way in which the eighteenth century in England was written about. A very remarkable man. I knew him and I admired him, and thought he was more like Karl Marx, as a personality, than anybody I'd ever met: formidable, rather rude, obviously brilliant, extremely intelligent, awkward, with slight paranoia. All of which I think is true of Marx. But I may well be mistaken. My book on Marx was commissioned, but the essay on Namier was not. Everything else, every single piece I've written, everything else was ordered. I'm like a taxi-cab. If I'm not summoned, I remain still. I don't move.

'Two Concepts of Liberty' is simply something I had to do when I became Professor in Oxford and had to deliver an inaugural lecture. If I could have avoided it, I should have, because I never think anything I say or write is of real interest.

However, there was no way out, and so that was the subject I chose. I can't deny that Marxist definitions of liberty, particularly in the Soviet Union, and generally behind the Iron Curtain, did influence me somewhat in my opposition towards what is called positive liberty. If I wrote this essay today I would not have been so firm about saying that negative liberty is more civilised, more important than positive liberty. I would have been much kinder to positive liberty. I thought I was kind, but most reviewers thought my lecture was simply a defence of negative liberty and, to some extent, an attack on positive liberty. That I never intended. If it is how it is read, it's a misunderstanding. I obviously didn't make myself clear enough. My fault. No, I don't think it's a culmination.

BP-S: If you do not recognise your most famous (though written under coercion) essay as the key one in your output, maybe it is the thread of liberty itself that plays the leading role in your work?

IB: Liberty has always been a subject I thought about, not only politically, but metaphysically also. I take great interest in the problem of the freedom of the will. Most philosophers are determinists. I cannot believe determinism to be valid. As I wrote in 'Historical Inevitability', I don't say that it's impossible that it should be true. For me it is an empirical proposition that everything we do is caused; that there is some cause which makes it impossible that we could act otherwise. But if this is true, and believed, people would have to alter their Weltanschauung—especially their moral ideas—in a very radical way. I'll never forget what my colleague John Austin, a famous Oxford philosopher, said to me: 'I know they say they are determinists, but have you ever met one?' There's something in this. I'm among the minority of thinkers who still think that the notion of choice is the basis of being a human being, and the idea of determined choice—choice in which the alternatives are not open, but fundamentally closed, because only one can be determined by antecedent causation—is something which most people, consciously or unconsciously, do not accept, whether it's true or not. Still, I can see that in some circumstances I would have to yield. I mean this: if somebody came into a room and said: 'Would you mind writing down everything that you think, feel, see, hear, touch, smell, taste and the like in the next twelve minutes. You can't describe everything. Do as much as you can.'

And supposing you do all this. And then he gives you a sealed envelope and you open it and it describes exactly everything you've said. Then I think I would have to say—'They've done it.' There may still be logical objections to determinism, but de facto it will have been found to be sufficiently valid not to let us go on talking about free will as we used to. I merely don't believe this could happen. I think that I still deeply believe everything that I said in that essay. But my life hasn't been a monistic development towards a single goal.

BP-S: 'Two Concepts of Liberty' brought about an effect like a stick in an ant-hill. Many of your critics accused you of a very narrow, rigid negative approach, similar to that of Bentham. On the other hand, an eminent interpreter of your ideas, Roger Hausheer, told me your views are very near to a socialist standpoint. What is your actual position?

IB: I have nothing against socialism. I don't know exactly what Hausheer meant. What do you take it to mean?

BP-S: That you are for equality; that you recognise it as a value.

IB: I am. I am for the greatest measure of equality compatible with other values. Total equality is both impossible and would produce extreme coercion. Equality for wolves would mean the death of sheep. And that's what, of course, unrestricted equality would be. Some people think equality is simply a function of rationality: that in similar circumstances similar people should be treated in a similar way. I don't think it is quite that, or that alone: I think it's an independent goal. Let me think of an example of what I mean. Supposing there is a cake. And there are five children. Then it's quite natural to give each child one-fifth of the cake. If you give one child two-fifths it's thought unfair. This is quite right, it *is* unfair, it is unequal treatment. But I do not see why it should be assumed that no rational person can want to do something unfair. He might not mind inequality. He might say: 'Life is very dull if we are to be strictly egalitarian. I want some degree of inequality; it'll make life more exciting, more interesting; élites deserve to have two slices of the cake, and fools don't deserve even one.' This would be unjust, unfair, but it is a possible view of life, a Byronic, romantic, Nietzschean view. To me unacceptable. But it is a view which does not make people who hold it necessarily irrational, only unjust, sometimes heroic. That's all I want to say. I reject this, but not because it is irrational: I believe in equality as such.

BP-S: Then the accusation of your alleged extreme negativist view on liberty was in fact a major blunder?

IB: Stick in an ant-hill . . . Or even putting one's foot in a hornets' nest? My critics simply quote Bentham and Hobbes. These thinkers said, correctly, that one of the central meanings of liberty is the absence, or removal, of obstacles. They both said this, and not many others have said it. But I'm not at all a Benthamite. I am not utilitarian. My idea of negative liberty consists in the answer to the question of how many paths, how many doors, there are through which I can enter. How many possibilities have I for doing this, that or the other. I think this is the basic sense of the concept. And when people say, 'What about moral liberty?', that is something different. For example, Spinoza's conception of freedom, derived, I suspect, from the Stoics, is based on the idea that one's liberty means that one is spiritually free, that nobody can spiritually coerce one, that one can be morally free in prison. The doctrine is that a person is spiritually free to think what he thinks and wish what he wishes even if he is physically prevented from acting freely; it is not a spiritual bond, a spiritual chain on his inner life. Well, that is true, but even here we have to say that to be free means there are no obstacles to the free functioning, to the full functioning, of the inner life. I think you asked me once about brainwashing . . .

BP-S: How would Spinoza deal with the phenomenon of brainwashing?

IB: If Spinoza had known what brainwashing was, I doubt if he could say that inner liberty alone is what counts. He may have been thinking of Epictetus, who was a slave and said that a slave can be freer than his master. But the slave is not freer in any sense if he is hypnotised, if he is made into an animal by being conditioned.

In the end, freedom, at least political freedom (which is all that I was talking about), means that human beings don't stop you from doing whatever it may be. Of course there is no such thing as being able to do everything. That's why absolute liberty is a meaningless idea. There is no structure which could prevent this or that—there is nothing else in the world except your unbridled will. That's exactly what one attributes to God, but to nobody else. That's why complete human liberty is not thinkable. But if you ask what is liberty—yes, I would say that my critics are mistaken, that my idea of liberty is the possibility of the richest imaginable life. And this is not at all Bentham's view.

BP-S: Yet, in a way, your conception of law is like Bentham's, in that you believe that every law is an infraction of liberty. Thus, your critics' searching for similarities between you and Bentham does not seem a complete misunderstanding . . .

IB: Of course, I should qualify that—there can be an infraction of my liberty which liberates other people, or even me, in some other respect. An infraction of my liberty in some respect may occur in order to make others freer—even much freer—in all sorts of ways. The law which prevents me from murdering people frees other people from being murdered. A law which stops me from carrying firearms prevents me from using them on myself, and so gives me a greater degree of liberty to live a life free from physical danger. Every law stops a liberty, but of course, it may be a means of creating greater and more numerous liberties. So that it's not mere pedantry to say that every law stops a liberty. It's simply valid against people who think that being determined by some system, being an element in some all-embracing organism, is itself liberating. It is said against people like Hegel and Marx, for whom freedom is the perception of necessity, for whom obedience, if it is of the right kind, is the same as freedom. Obedience may be necessary, it may even be harmless and it may create greater liberties than it suppresses; but it is still a suppression of something—that is what I mean.

BP-S: As I understand your writings the master idea that underpins your achievement is pluralism of aims and values. John Gray wrote that it strikes a death-blow to the central classical Western tradition. Has anybody thought of it before you?

IB: I cannot tell you the answer to that. I cannot believe that I am the first person to think of something so obvious as to say that some ultimate values conflict with others. You can't always combine mercy with justice; you can't have total liberty and complete equality. Knowledge may conflict with happiness (I am not made happier by knowing that I have an incurable disease). You can't have spontaneity with the capacity for careful planning, and so on. Therefore, somebody must have thought of this idea before me—it seems so obvious. Something of that sort was said by my colleague J. L. Austin in one of his philosophical essays; but that arose because I put it to him and he too thought it—as it is—quite obvious. So although he doesn't say so, this truism comes from me. But I'll tell you a story about that. I have a friend, a journalist called Bryan Magee. He's a very good interviewer and takes great interest in philosophy, and talks very intelligently about it. His great hero is Karl Popper. He said to Karl Popper: 'Has anyone before Berlin said something about this?' Popper said: 'Yes.' 'Who said it?' Popper said: 'I did.' I've not found it in his works. Maybe it's there, but if it is, I didn't know it. Maybe we're like Newton and Leibniz, we discovered it simultaneously.

BP-S: There is one remark in Popper's intellectual autobiography.

IB: That was written much later.

BP-S: What makes me wonder is that though he claims to be a pluralist, believing in plurality of values, he forbids discussion on values.

IB: No, because it's non-scientific and so non-objective.

BP-S: What he suggests is piecemeal social engineering and no discussion as to what aims should be realised by this engineering. All that is self-evident for him.

IB: Well, that's very different from what I say. That doesn't mean that values must clash. He is one of these people who think that all valuation is subjective; there is no test of the truth as in the physical world or mathematics. He thinks that in the sphere of values everything is relativistic, that's why he is not interested. He is interested in science. In the philosophy of science. Well, I don't accept that. That's the reason for another disagreement I have. Although I admire Popper I don't always agree with him.

I cannot believe I am the first person to have said that some ultimate values are incompatible. Maybe I am; but it's rather like the first man who said—two plus two equals four. If John Gray thinks so, he may be right. He is very learned. He knows what he is talking about. And if he is right, it is an original contribution. But I am the last person to claim it. It seems so obvious to me.

BP-S: I remember your once telling me that you don't want reality to be too tight, too tidy. To what extent is the pluralist commitment a matter of temperament?

IB: Question of temperament? I think that is true. When I say that I don't want the world to be too tidy, indeed I don't. I don't want it to be untidy, but not too tidy, not spick and span, as the English say, not screwed tight, *kruto zavincheno*, as the Communists used to say. I prefer to believe that some of the paths which occur in human life or in the rest of living nature can occasionally be broken, that occasional zigzags occur. This seems to me to contribute vitality, colour, interest, spontaneity to life. Why am I in favour of this? Because I am. It is really a question of taste in the end. I am depressed by the thought of life as a mechanism or even a biological organism. It may be so. Nietzsche may be right about the 'eternal recurrence'. But I find that suffocating. Certain critics of Hegel and Hegelianism used to talk about determinism as a kind of box which contains us, or what was called the block universe, in which there is no free movement, where despite a pattern of development there is something ultimately static. Yes, there is movement in it but the movement is entirely within the static object and controlled by it. I'd rather the world weren't like that. I can't be sure that to you it isn't, but I would be unhappy if I thought it was. I don't want the universe to be too tidy. I neither want nor believe things to be locked, that's why I believe in free will, possibilities to be open. Things might happen this way, but they also might not; this is what most probably will take place, but who knows, maybe not, miracles occur. My friend, Dr Weizmann, the first president of Israel, once said to me: 'Miracles do occur, but one has to work very hard for them!'

BP-S: When you speak of value-pluralism what do you mean by values? Let me quote some passages from your work: 'There is a world of objective values. By this I mean those ends that men pursue for their own sakes.'[1] Elsewhere you write: 'We cannot help accepting these basic principles because we are human.'[2] If we adopt, as you say, such 'empiricist dress', why not call them just anthropological modes of behaviour or sociological tendencies, instead of values?

IB: This question is very important. I don't deny that I think that people have the ends they have, the purposes they have. But they are not fixed. It's possible to have a final purpose and then, suddenly, give it up. That's how conversion occurs, when people are converted from capitalism to Communism, or from Communism to capitalism; values change; conversion to religion is like that. Artists sometimes go through tremendous crises, moral, aesthetic, spiritual. They suddenly see the universe in a different fashion. So I can't say that values are there, fixed like stars in heaven. But within an ordinary lifetime most people live according to a constellation, horizons in which certain values are embedded. Now, if you ask, is this an empirical statement? Yes—because everything we know is given by either experience or logic. The network of values, principles, beliefs which men live by are not formal structures like logic, or chess, or other non-empirical disciplines. I don't think there is anything outside or in between. To say that this is empirical is not to say that it is contingent. Let me add something. Supposing we ask: Is the existence of the three dimensions of ordinary, normal space—length, breadth, depth—an empirical fact or not? Physicists conceive of nineteen dimensions, or n dimensions—infinity—and work out all the implications. But we can't imagine this—we are space-ordinary, space-bound. Maybe, with a great effort, we can imagine a fourth dimension. For example, if

---

1. Isaiah Berlin, 'The Pursuit of the Ideal', in *The Proper Study of Mankind*, 9.
2. Berlin, 'European Unity and Its Vicissitudes', in *The Crooked Timber of Humanity*, 204.

we imagine a creature who says: 'You can't, but I can, see something at right angles to a cube.' You reply: 'I don't, this doesn't mean anything to me; in my world nothing is like that.' Yet they can say: 'You'll think your three-dimensional object has vanished, but I can still see it in my four-dimensional space.' This is like two-dimensional people being unable to see what three-dimensional people see. Five dimensions, six, seven, become impossible, de facto. Is this an empirical fact? This frame seems to be so unalterably presupposed in everything that we say about the external world that one ought to call this a category. Are categories metaphysical, absolute? No, I think that categories could, in principle, alter. For us, for human beings, there are certain categories which shape our experience—which are simply given, basic, we are made like that. But *to be made* is an empirical expression. There are categories not quite so basic as that, for example, material objects. Supposing, to take a well-known philosophical example, supposing a telephone is suddenly changed into a goose.

BP-S: Or a cat grows to supernatural dimensions as in Waismann.

IB: Very well, a cat. Then what follows? You have to say that the laws of physics or of biology will have to be re-formulated. The old natural science has broken down. At first you say—oh, it's an illusion, it can't be true. But if it happens frequently enough, and enough people see the transformation, you can no longer deny it. In which case our scientific laws will have to be modified to make room for this phenomenon. So this category is less basic than those of space and time. But still pretty basic as far as you and I are concerned. Telephones are not known to change into cats; and if somebody tells you that he has seen this you won't believe him and will say it's a dream, an optical illusion, or pure lunacy. Still, it could happen, you can't say a priori that it won't. Then there are categories even less stable than that. I think values come into that. They are categories that are not simply sociological generalisations about how people behave, but deeper than that, not just general propositions describing what you might call social tendencies, modes of behaviour, which sociologists and anthropologists investigate.

BP-S: I was talking about this matter with Roger Hausheer and I have to reveal we found it difficult to mark the boundary between empirically conceived values and sociological generalisations.

IB: What I am speaking about are products of careful observation; but it can never yield absolute truths. We can say: this is how most people behave, or this is what the tendency is. We notice that most people, when they see a fire, don't put their finger in it. But of course some fakirs might. Most people, when they see a tiger, tend to try and conceal themselves from it or try to escape. But some people perhaps don't. But values are much more fixed than that. They are something which determines one's life; in terms of which your behaviour can not only be described but explained. I do not say that X usually in situation Y behaves in manner Z, but that X in the situation Y is governed by—his behaviour, and his thoughts, and his feelings are determined by—the fact that these values, ends, purposes are a fixed point in his basic relationship to the world and himself. I cannot guarantee its permanence, but that's more than a sociological generalisation. It is a sociological generalisation that most people prefer warmth to cold. Most people would rather eat than not. Most people don't like being hungry—these are perfectly good psychological or sociological generalisations. A sociological generalisation might declare that most people prefer to have families than not—this is based on observations of majorities, the normal behaviour of a large number of specimens—but it is not something (relatively) fixed, from which you can deduce how a man will behave if you know what his values are. I don't know if I am making myself clear. Values resemble those categories of knowledge of the external world I've told you about, but they are far less fixed, capable of change, less rigorous—but still, *categories*. There is a difference between categories and generalisations. Categories are frameworks within which we think or feel. Sociological generalisations about behaviour are simply ways in which certain causes operate, certain reactions occur. This is quite different. Thus Kant was, I think, the first to draw a very clear difference between the right and the good—between duty and, let us say, felicific behaviour, ways of improving happiness. He made an ethical discovery. He discovered that people knew what they meant by right, duty, obligation, conscience, something they intend to obey. If you said to someone: 'Why don't you disobey?' he might say: 'I can't, my conscience told me not to. I know it's wrong; don't ask me how I know—all men know the difference between good and bad, right and wrong, true and false.' Never mind whether Kant was right or not. The difference between, let us say, good, which may be no more than what makes people happy, or doing whatever Bentham wants you to do, or painting beautiful pictures: all this is not at all the same as right, duty, moral obligation. Being generous is being good. Duty is different. If you do something from the sense of duty, it's not generosity. Kant taught us that there are secular, non-religious senses of words like ought, duty, obligation, conscience—a sense of these words based on an inward sense of what is right or wrong. That is the drawing of attention to a basic category, and not to an empirical generalisation. The identification of a basic moral category in terms of which people think and feel is a unique contribution. It is not that before Kant nobody thought in terms of moral obligation. That can't be true. I don't believe that in the fifth century BC nobody would have understood what is meant by the difference, asserted by Kant, between good and right. They didn't have words for it—that may be so; perhaps they weren't—given the Stoics—conscious of it. But if you had explained it to them they would have known what you meant. It's a basic category.

BP-S: Thank you very much for the conversation.

Conversations

All Souls College and Headington House

Oxford
1986–1995

My tape is probably very muddled. It is extremely vague. Don't take the tape to be the real Gospel!

Isaiah Berlin in conversation with Beata Polanowska-Sygulska,
All Souls College, Oxford, 5 July 1986

I shall be very glad to see you and talk to you about our agreements and differences.

Isaiah Berlin to Beata Polanowska-Sygulska, 7 March 1988

1986

During my first scholarship in Oxford I met Berlin four times. Three appoint-
ments were recorded (27 June, 5 and 13 July 1986), but, unfortunately, not
in their entirety. We discussed mainly Berlin's conception of liberty and the
debate triggered off by his famous essay. At least, this was what I attempted
to concentrate on; my interlocutor constantly digressed. Much time was
devoted to analysis of three papers I wrote during that stay in Oxford (two of
them are included in this volume).[1] These extensive sections of the recordings
are, of course, not included in the transcript, as they are too technical to be
interesting. These were very challenging discussions for me, serious and
sometimes intense. Yet, quite surprisingly, I often could not help laughing—
neither of us could.

The Intellectual Sources of 'Two Concepts of Liberty'

BP-S: May I ask you the question which was once put to me by a Polish professor, Jan Wolenski? His query was as follows, 'I would like to know
from where he took it all.' It's just a quotation; what he had in mind was
your doctrine of liberty. I am also very much interested in your answer.

IB: Where did I take it from? Or, in other words, who did I copy? Who did I
imitate? Well, I can tell you. Bentham not at all, nor Hobbes, not in the
least, though I do quote them. There are three thinkers, I think, who have

---

1. 235–52 below.

had a definite effect on me. One was Benjamin Constant. First, his famous essay on the difference of the conception of liberty of the Ancients, compared with that of the Moderns. It's about fifteen pages, perhaps shorter.[1] But I read Constant in general. He was a Swiss liberal who was terribly impressed by the brutality of the French Revolution, which he went through, and the suppression of liberty. He was the man who wrote the famous constitution for Napoleon. He draws the distinction between ancient liberty and modern liberty. Ancient liberty means nobody is protected against anybody else. In other words, anybody in the public assembly can speak against anyone; that's a liberty all right. Anybody can be expelled by the vote of the assembly. Nobody can forbid me to talk. Nobody can be forbidden to look into my life. Modern liberty, which is what I call negative, is a fence within which I can do what I like. The idea of private life is absent in Greece. The only reference to privacy is in Pericles' speech, where he says, 'We are not like Sparta, we are a loose society, we don't frown if other people say things with which we don't agree, but people who do not take part in public life are no good.' And that's where the word *idiot* comes from. It comes from *idiotes*, which means the person who is entirely dedicated to private life. We still say *idiosyncrasy, idiomatic*—all these *idio-* words mean individual, somehow. So *idiotes* means somebody who is outside the society, whether a god or a wild beast, who doesn't participate in our common life. Well, for Constant that's the heart of modern liberty. And he gives a list of things which nobody is allowed to do, whatever the law may say. For example, you must not denounce your parents to the Revolution, you must not bear false witness, and other things like that, absolute evils. I think situations can arise in which you can do these things, but very, very few. So that is Constant. There are some absolute rules, absolute values which you mustn't go against, and that's a result of the horrors of revolution.

BP-S: Like the Ten Commandments.

IB: Well, yes, there are about Four Commandments in Constant. He doesn't mention murder. He's thinking about what people did during the Revolution, such as bearing false witness, the denunciation of parents, humiliation, that sort of thing. Then Alexander Herzen influenced me. And finally John Stuart Mill. In the twentieth century, nobody.

BP-S: I had many problems investigating the origins of your doctrine of lib-

---

1. In fact it's twenty in the Cambridge University Press edition of 1988. Benjamin Constant, 'The Liberty of the Ancients Compared with That of the Moderns', in *Political Writings*, ed. Biancamaria Fontana (Cambridge: Cambridge University Press, 1988), 309–28.

erty. But now I know that it is your childhood that is the source of it. It seems to me that there are two aspects of your doctrine which should be considered while tracing its inspiration: the differentiation between the negative and positive concepts of liberty, and the critique of the positive one. The critique is entirely yours, but what about the differentiation?

IB: People have drawn that difference before me. That is not original.

BP-S: I found a suggestion in Hayek. There is a footnote in his *The Constitution of Liberty*, note 26, which I am going to remember to my death, where he says that the distinction between positive and negative liberty was popularised by Thomas Green, and through him derives ultimately from Hegel.

IB: It probably is there.

BP-S: I found in Hegel the idea of negativity as the basis of development. On the other hand, there is a quotation in *Phenomenology of Spirit* which suggests something like positive liberty: 'In thinking, I am *free*, because I am not in an *other*, but remain simply and solely in communion with myself.'[1]

IB: The definition of freedom in Hegel is *bei sich selbst sein*—to be at home, *chez soi*. What that means is that I am completely free only if there are no obstacles. So long as there is another country, so long as there is another person, I am not quite free. That's why God alone can be free. In other words, Hegel's idea is that if you absorb things into your system, into your mind, then they become yours and you are no longer oppressed by them. So what you want is to absorb, become part of, the entire harmonious world, so that the world is your home and nothing resists, because everything is rational. Everything is as it should be. When you don't want anything to be different from what it must be, then you are free.

BP-S: Yet he stresses the two meanings: freedom as negativity, as the basis of development, and the other as 'being by oneself'.

IB: I don't know what negativity is. It's not what we mean by negativity.

BP-S: Absolutely not.

IB: Negativity is an obscure concept.

BP-S: Everything is obscure in Hegel, I'm afraid. But after him, in Max Stirner there is another differentiation . . .

IB: Ah, yes.

BP-S: . . . and another in Marx and Engels, and another in Santayana.

IB: Stirner I know; he is really in some ways the original of Herzen. I sus-

---

1. Georg W. F. Hegel, *Phenomenology of Spirit*, trans. A. V. Miller (Oxford: Clarendon Press, 1977), 120.

pect there's some influence there, in Paris in the 1840s. I don't know about Santayana, and I didn't think about Stirner, and I didn't think about Hegel. It may be there.

BP-S: But do you remember from where you took the differentiation itself?

IB: Nowhere consciously. It may be imitation. I may unconsciously have borrowed it from somewhere else. The difference has been made before me, certainly. I'm not the inventor of this difference. But it was never quite so emphasised. I'm trying to think where it occurs.

BP-S: In contemporary writings this differentiation is referred to in virtually all papers tackling political liberty. And everybody ascribes different meanings to the two concepts. It's complete chaos.

IB: I am certainly not conscious of anything in Hegel like that. T. H. Green, perhaps. I probably read Green, probably remembered that. He was an English philosopher of the 1870s, 1880s.

BP-S: Yes, I know. And he was influenced by Hegel, wasn't he?

IB: Certainly; Hegel and Kant, both. I'll tell you another philosopher who influenced me. That is Immanuel Kant—the idea of being your own master, of not being influenced by outside factors. Positive liberty is Kant, absolutely. In a good sense, of course. Well, that's all. I can't give you any other sources known to me.

BP-S: What to me is most valuable in your doctrine is the critique of the positive concept of freedom, and of the rationalist metaphysics underlying it. This is entirely yours, I presume.

IB: I think that's probably new.

BP-S: Entirely new.

IB: And the idea of the clash of values. I don't know of anybody else who said that. The idea that ultimate values collide and cannot be reconciled seems obvious. I think everybody has thought it from Adam in paradise. As far as I know I didn't derive it from anyone else, though I wouldn't be surprised if William James or somebody like that says that, but I don't know it. I have a friend called Magee who asked Popper, when he wrote a book . . .

BP-S: Yes, Bryan Magee, the author of the monograph on Popper.

IB: He said to Popper, 'Has anyone before Berlin thought about the collision of values?' Popper said, 'Yes.' Magee said, 'Who?' 'I did,' said Popper, but there is no evidence of it in his writings.[1] If he thought of it, he certainly didn't say it. Everybody thought it; the idea of painful choice is not

1. See now http://berlin.wolf.ox.ac.uk, 'Pre-/non-Berlinian pluralism', compiled by Henry Hardy, s.v. Popper (accessed 31 December 2005).

new; but the idea that it's conceptually incoherent to assume that there can be a solution, I think that may be my own. But if not, at least it's true. Let me give you two very good quotations which I'm always using. One comes from C. I. Lewis, who was a famous American philosopher of this century. He said: 'There is no reason for supposing that, when the truth is found, it will prove interesting.'

BP-S: That's very deep.

IB: It's a very good remark. If a thing is true, it's enough—no need to make it interesting. Interesting is one thing, true is another. Some people like things to be true and some people like things to be interesting. I think I probably prefer things to be interesting, but I recognise that the other is better. And the other great quotation comes from Kant: 'Out of the crooked timber of humanity no straight thing was ever made.' That comes from one of his essays; it's marvellous.

BP-S: It seems very consoling to assume that some system explaining reality can be built. Yet this is probably impossible, as reality is so multi-faceted.

IB: Like Whitehead, who said, 'Seek simplicity and avoid it.' You must seek simplicity and yet be frightened of it, it mustn't be too simple. Seek systems, if you like, and be on your guard. Fichte once said, 'If you want to understand a philosophy, ask yourself what is the character of the philosopher.' I think it's all temperamental on my part. I don't want the universe to be too tidy—that's where it springs from. I want exceptions, miracles, occasional swerves. Epicurus talked about swerves: the *clinamen*. That's why you can't predict, because the atom may suddenly shoosh for no reason, as in the quantum theory, you see? And so, on the whole, I don't want things to be too tight. I want things to be loose and capable of change. The eruption of genius should be unpredictable. Genius is not part of the system, you see? It's what Herzen calls 'the luxury of nature'. Nature occasionally allows itself the luxury of producing geniuses. Normally, nature is regular, rigid and complete, and goes tidily from cause to effect. Occasionally it allows itself sudden moments of luxury—something it permits itself out of sheer exuberance. It suddenly becomes bored with too much order, so then men of genius are generated. I'd like to think that.

BP-S: And what's your opinion on the theory of essentially contestable concepts?[1] Were you influenced by it?

IB: Yes, I think there's a good deal of truth in it.

---

1. The notion of an essentially contestable concept was popularised by W. B. Gallie, 'Essentially Contested Concepts', *Proceedings of the Aristotelian Society* 56 (1956), 167–98.

BP-S: John Gray interpreted your doctrine of liberty in those terms.

IB: He's quite right. I think I had never read that essay when I wrote those things. I read it about ten years ago for the first time, so I was not affected by it. It's correct and I agree with it. I think some of these concepts are contestable. It's what's called an open texture, what the French call *poreux*.

BP-S: The notion of open texture comes from Waismann. But it is a bit different because it refers to empirical concepts.

IB: Absolutely. No, Waismann is different. I knew Waismann very well.

BP-S: I delight in his famous example of a cat.[1]

IB: What was that?

BP-S: Supposing you enter a room and there is a cat there which suddenly grows to an enormous size . . .

IB: Enormous, rather like an elephant!

BP-S: Yes, or it dies and is then resuscitated. Could we still use the same word for the cat in such a situation?

IB: Or take something else. Supposing a telephone suddenly turns into a cat. All right, that doesn't usually happen, but suppose that suddenly you find yourself in a situation where the laws of physics are abolished. A miracle. Then what do you say? Do you say, 'The telephone has become a cat' or 'A cat has become a telephone?' To which my colleague Austin said, 'We have no language for that, we are not prepared for it. Language does not attempt to cover a situation of this type.' You say about a cat that becomes as big as an elephant, 'I don't know what to call it.' It's like saying, 'When is a table not a table?' Supposing a table is half a mile long, is it still a table? Where do you draw the line? It comes from Wittgenstein, you know. He said, 'You will generally find that the line draws himself.' 'Itself,' he meant: his English was not perfect.

BP-S: By itself?

IB: No, no, draws itself. The line draws itself, suddenly you will find the line is drawn. The whole of Wittgenstein is about that. When asked, 'What time did you come in?' you can say, 'Five minutes to three.' But

---

1. 'Suppose I have to verify a statement such as "There is a cat next door"; suppose I go over to the next room, open the door, look into it and actually see a cat. Is this enough to prove my statement? Or must I, in addition to it, touch the cat, pat him and induce him to purr? And supposing that I had done all these things, can I then be absolutely certain that my statement was true? Instantly we come up against the well-known battery of sceptical arguments mustered since ancient times. What, for instance, should I say when that creature later on grew to a gigantic size? Or if it showed some queer behaviour usually not to be found with cats, say, if, under certain conditions, it could be revived from death whereas normal cats could not?' Friedrich Waismann, 'Verifiability', in Antony Flew, ed., *Logic and Language* (Oxford: Basil Blackwell, 1952), 119.

if you are asked, 'When did you become well dressed?' you can't give a precise time. You can't say, 'At half past three.' You can't even say, 'On 17 June.' You say, 'Well, I don't know, more or less, I suppose, sometime during 1983.' But I say, 'But exactly when? I must have the precise time.' You see, you can't answer precisely. Or, for example, if you dream of a table and you wake up and I say, 'How long is the table you dreamt about?' You reply, 'Well, I should say about two metres long.' I say, 'Two metres? Can you be more precise? I want an exact measurement. What do you mean, two metres? How many centimetres?' You say, 'I'm very sorry, I can't go back to the dream and I didn't have a ruler in the dream. I didn't measure it.' 'No, I must have an exact answer! Why are you so vague? What do you mean, "about"? Don't talk about "about." *Exactly.*' That's all quite interesting. That's where, so to speak, the language of 'exactly' doesn't fit. Objectively, it doesn't fit. There's nothing wrong with saying 'about'; this doesn't mean that you don't know. It means, in such cases, 'This is the best description that is in principle possible.' Waismann used to say, 'I am in Venice. I am floating along the canal, there are these beautiful Palazzi on both sides of the canal. What is the exact colour?' You can say purple or red, reddish, yellowish. 'Yes, but I want a precise answer. Exactly what colour?' You can't say. That's all very true, I accept all that, certainly. True about liberty, too.

Macpherson's and Taylor's Critique

BP-S: I would like to ask you about the discussion of the two, in my opinion, most challenging critics of your doctrine of liberty, C. B. Macpherson and Charles Taylor.

Macpherson writes that you owe your 'mechanical and inertial' concept of negative freedom to Herbert Spencer. It goes back through Bentham to Hobbes, and beyond him to Galileo. It stems from the concept of inertial motion: bodies go on moving until they are stopped by impact with other bodies. According to Macpherson, this understanding of freedom has been imported from mechanics to politics.[1] Do you agree with this?

IB: No, that's not it. It's false. Negative freedom is absence of obstacles, that is right. It is true that Hobbes and Galileo talk about bodies falling freely

---

1. See C. B. Macpherson, 'Berlin's Division of Liberty', in *Democratic Theory: Essays in Retrieval* (Oxford: Clarendon Press, 1973), 103–4.

through the air. Why it doesn't suit me is because a body falling freely, in that sense, is not free. It is not free not to fall. It can't stop if it wants to. It's too crude, that. I know what he wants to say: he wants to say this is a mechanical metaphor. He's right. All politics is metaphor. I think I've said that in print. In the end, all political talk is founded on some analogy with something else. As E. M. Forster once put it: 'Everything must be like something, so what is this like?'[1] Everything is like something. Otherwise you can't talk about it. In Plato, the metaphor is mathematical. I mean logical deduction from the idea of the good. In Aristotle, it's biological. In the sixteenth century—maybe the seventeenth century—social contract theories are legal. In the eighteenth century—Diderot—it's mechanical. For Hegel, people say it's organic. That's not quite correct. It's musical. If anything, it's aesthetic. If you read Hegel, you will find that all his language, when he talks about thesis, antithesis, *Aufhebung*, is about music.

BP-S: He compares man to a melody.

IB: Or a tune, or to different tunes. They collide with each other, they coalesce, they create a new harmony. These metaphors work beautifully for music. They do not work for life. The idea is that everything has its opposite, that these opposites invariably collide, and lead to some kind of new thing which contains them both but transcends them. What that means in politics nobody has ever understood, apart from the Germans. But in music it works beautifully, particularly in harmonic music. We really do have theme, counter-theme, harmony, counterpoint. All these things work, it's not linear, not direct, you don't have one thing after another. It's no good for melodic, medieval music. It's no good for single staves. As soon as you get polyphony in the late sixteenth century, early seventeenth, it begins. Leibniz and Hegel have something in common in that respect.

BP-S: Oh yes, there seems to be polyphony also in Leibniz!

IB: All this romantic language to which Hegel seems prone: nothing is what it is, it already contains within itself its own negation, so this negation in some way stimulates something fresh. If you apply it to music, it follows beautifully. If you apply it to life, not so beautifully. But the famous dialectical materialism—when one attempts to translate into social life, or even physics, some kind of Hegelian concept of non-linear development—well, there's something in it, no doubt, when forces collide.

BP-S: But not everything.

---

1. E. M. Forster, 'Our Diversions', 3, 'The Doll Souse' (1924): *Abinger Harvest* (London, 1936), 49.

IB: No, not all that much, I think. I have always thought it works in art, in music. I think the whole of romanticism is the application of aesthetic metaphors to life. For example, when the Germans admire Napoleon, they do not admire him for being rational. They're not admiring him for being better at winning battles than other people, which is a skill of a technical kind. It can be taught to some degree; Clausewitz tried to explain it. What they admire about Napoleon, of course, is that he is a creator of new forms of life, like an artist, which nobody else could do, because it's an imaginative and not a rational process. Napoleon created Imperial France. That's what excited Heine. As for you and I, if we can't ourselves create a new form of society, the least we can do is to offer ourselves as material for one of these political artists. Even if it causes torture for us, even death, it's worth it because a great new work of art is being created. We throw ourselves forward as material for *him*, that's the Führer.

BP-S: So it was Hegel and Napoleon that you had in mind when you were writing about inspired artists treating humanity as the raw material . . .[1]

IB: Hegel admired Napoleon more than he admired anybody else, not because the Code Napoléon was more rational than the German constitution—maybe it was, but that wasn't the point. He created a new world. You know the famous phrase: the absolute on horseback. When Hegel was writing *Phänomenologie des Geistes*, he said, 'When I saw Napoleon in Jena, history wrote me a letter. Yesterday I saw the absolute, it was on horseback.' That was the point. Terribly exciting, because he's a creator and transformer of the world, historical forces are embodied in him, he is the instrument of some tremendous cosmic movement: clash, collision and transcendence. The main thing is the aesthetic language, which is semi-biological. Things are put together and produce something new. It's like when Herzen said, 'Where is the song before it is sung? Where is the dance before it is danced?'[2] Nowhere. I create, I don't copy from nature, which other people did. It's not mimesis. Art is not holding a mirror up to nature. Art is inventive, something brand new, creation out of material supplied by nature or by man. Why am I saying all this to you? Because all political talk is ultimately founded on models, analogies, comparisons, something else. Therefore, when Macpherson says my concept is founded on a mechanical metaphor which goes from

---

1. Berlin, 'Two Concepts of Liberty', in *Liberty*, 197.
2. Paraphrase: see Alexander Herzen, *Sobranie sochinenii v tridtsati tomakh* [*Collected Writings in Thirty Volumes*] (Moscow, 1954–66), 6: 33, 335.

Spencer back to Bentham, Hobbes, Galileo, maybe it's true, but I think it's false. All he can say is, 'Produce a better model.' What model *should* I have used? Or should *he* have used? Politics is not an independent science. Every political thinker you may think of operated in terms of some kind of pattern; and the pattern always comes from somewhere else. There are no ur-political thinkers who begin with politics. Politics, in the end, is the application of ethics to society, which means there is some concept of society, mechanical, organic, aesthetic, legal etc., underlying the dominant political viewpoint that characterises any particular period. That's what I would answer. Now tell me about . . .

BP-S: . . . Charles Taylor. He writes that you follow Bentham and Hobbes and that their moral psychology is too simple or too crude for its purposes.

IB: What is Taylor's idea of freedom?

BP-S: Well, he agrees that there are two families of doctrines of liberty, yet he maintains that any defensible view of freedom must involve some degree of self-realisation.

IB: I see. Taylor is a real Hegelian. He believes that the universe is moving towards some end, and that man has a purpose in life. Men develop in accordance with goals, which God or nature has created for them; therefore freedom means development in accordance with a pattern that leads to some kind of perfection. We are more free to the extent that we are nearer to our proper goal. Aristotle says the same. For Aristotle, everything has a purpose. The purpose of a plant is to create flowers; the purpose of an embryo is to become a body. The purpose of a chrysalis is to become a butterfly. That is teleological biology. Taylor would believe in ultimate purposes; that is to say, the business of a chrysalis is to work to become a butterfly; if a chrysalis understood its nature, it would *want* to be a butterfly. If the acorn knew what it wanted, it would want to be a large tree with round leaves: an oak. This wanting is a desire for freedom. The first man to deny that was Spinoza. Spinoza was practically the first thinker who—denying teleology—said things do not have purposes. They are what they are: a tremendous move in the history of thought. For Aristotle, everything has a purpose and all the purposes fit into some kind of harmony. If everything was as it should be, it would be a harmonious world. For Hegel, the development of spirit led to terrible conflict. But in the end there is unity. Karl Marx used it to explain history. Some terrible tragedies occur, some frightful killings and slayings and wars, but in the end, of course, it all comes right. We'll all end very happily and with beautiful relations to each other.

If you believe that, then you will believe what Taylor believes. Then you have to say, freedom is not absence of obstacles. Freedom is self-realisation towards a given end which you have not created but which is created in you, which lives in you, made by something else: God, nature. That means development according to certain rules, on certain lines. The rest is not freedom. Yet I may suddenly say, 'I don't *want* to be a butterfly, I want to remain a chrysalis.' Maybe I can't, but to say that I am free in not being allowed to is wrong.

BP-S: I think he somehow connects the two concepts of liberty. He says that cutting off the idea of self-realisation results in holding a caricatural version of negative freedom.

IB: Because he believes in purpose. Because he believes that freedom consists in the fulfilment of a personality.

BP-S: He writes as follows: '"Freedom" would be modified to read: the absence of internal or external obstacles to what I truly or authentically want.'[1]

IB: Well, 'truly' is the important word. Truly is my real self, not what I want but what I *truly* want. 'Authentically', he says, does he?

BP-S: 'Authentically', yes.

IB: Same thing. You say that you want to buy an ice cream. I say, 'That's not what you *truly* want. You don't really want this; what you really want is something nobler', and I persuade you. You say you wanted love. What you wanted wasn't love; you just wanted something inferior. Now that I have taught you, that's real love. That's what you really wanted. If I want to get ice cream, ice cream is what I want. I am told by Taylor that advertisers pervert human nature because their advertisements, in the West, make people think they want something which they don't really want. If I understood what the universe was really like, I wouldn't want it. Maybe not. But if I want a drug, I want it. If you stop me having the drug, you curtail my liberty, quite rightly, because it is bad for me. You think that if you stop me having an ice cream, you could transform me in such a way that I would want all kinds of things which I don't want at present, and that those things would make me freer. Could be true. But for a moment you stopped freedom.

BP-S: Could we come back again to Macpherson's critique? The main objection raised by him seems to me a fundamental one. Having quoted

---

1. Charles Taylor, 'What's Wrong with Negative Liberty', in *The Idea of Freedom*, ed. Alan Ryan, 187.

your four assumptions of rational metaphysics,[1] he contends that the first assumption doesn't entail the other three monistic ones: 'The real monism is contained in the last three assumptions. [. . .] But they do not follow from the first assumption. [. . .] My point is that the last three assumptions are not needed in any concept of positive liberty. [. . .] It is not necessary for an advocate of positive liberty to assert or assume that there is a single universal harmonious pattern into which the ends of all rational beings must fit.'[2]

In other words, according to Macpherson, the perversions of the positive concept are not due to the logic of positive liberty. Thus it can and should be rescued from the reproach to which you subject it.[3] This is a crucial point. Other authors, like John Gray and Robert Kocis, seem to have similar objections.[4]

IB: Look, if my first assumption is correct, then to every question there has to be one true answer, I mean one only. All true answers must fit.

BP-S: Yet he writes that if we accept the first assumption, there would emerge not a pattern, but a proliferation of many ways of life. Please have a look at the appropriate passage.

IB: Wait—'if the chief impediments to men's developmental powers were removed, if, that is to say, they were allowed equal freedom, there would emerge not a pattern but a proliferation of many ways and styles of life which could not be prescribed and which would not necessarily conflict'.[5]

---

1. '[F]irst, that all men have one true purpose, and one only, that of rational self-direction; second, that the ends of all rational beings must of necessity fit into a single universal, harmonious pattern, which some men may be able to discern more clearly than others; third, that all conflict, and consequently all tragedy, is due solely to the clash of reason with the irrational or the insufficiently rational—the immature and underdeveloped elements in life, whether individual or communal—and that such clashes are, in principle, avoidable, and for wholly rational beings impossible; finally, that when all men have been made rational, they will obey the rational laws of their own natures, which are one and the same in them all, and so be at once wholly law-abiding and wholly free.' Berlin, 'Two Concepts of Liberty', in *Liberty*, 200; cf. 237 below.

2. Macpherson, *Democratic Theory*, 111.

3. ibid.

4. '[S]ome useful variant of the idea of a real or rational will may survive the demise of the rationalist metaphysics and philosophical psychology in which it has traditionally been embedded. [. . .] no viable view of liberty can fail to accommodate some of the conditions of rational choice.' John Gray, 'On Negative and Positive Liberty', in *Liberalisms: Essays in Political Philosophy* (London: Routledge, 1991), 59, 66. '[T]here are many forms of self-realisation. [. . .] Once the ground has been provided for growth, human self-realisation will carry us off in a variety of conflicting directions.' Robert A. Kocis, 'Toward a Coherent Theory of Human Moral Development: Beyond Sir Isaiah Berlin's Vision of Human Nature', *Political Studies* 31 (1983), 386–7.

5. Macpherson, *Democratic Theory*, 113.

Yes, that's absolutely correct, perfectly true. The removal of impediments could very well lead to many flowers; of course it could lead to pluralism. But the first assumption is that there is a correct answer to every problem, not simply that impediments have to be removed. The removal of impediments, for me, does not mean that you can get a correct answer to every question. If every problem has one correct solution and one only, then all the solutions must fit into a single pattern. Since that is the correct solution, the only impediments which have to be removed are the impediments to *that*.

BP-S: So you think it's all inherent in the first assumption?

IB: Yes. The first assumption is the one which I think is so false, which is that to every problem there is one objective solution and one only, and we *can* know it. We may be too weak, or too stupid, we may never know it in this life, but it exists.

BP-S: But he says that every man has his own individual way of self-realisation.

IB: Yes, you can say that, but realisation of what? Of the true purpose?

BP-S: Of himself.

IB: No, it's no good. My true realisation and yours can't conflict because my true realisation must rest on a perception of what it should be. And that's the answer to the question, 'What should I be?' To this question, there is only one true answer. And if it's true for me, it must be true for you, because we're both human beings. All problems are universal—rational philosophers always believed it.

BP-S: So this is all inherent in the idea of rationality?

IB: Of that kind of rationality, defined as the capacity for discovering the objective true answer to all questions. If there is no answer to the question, or if there are two answers to the same question, it can't be a real question. You can't tell Plato or Aristotle or Spinoza or Descartes or Diderot or Hegel that to this question there are two equally true answers. Truth is one. I don't believe that, but they did. If it is a *real* question, there must be *the* answer. You can't say there are four possible answers, all true, and all incompatible with each other. I can either, so to speak, be a lawyer, or a doctor, or a member of the Communist Party or—I don't know what—a street-sweeper. Of course I can be all these things, but there must be something which I *ought* to be. If they're all indifferent, we just say these are trivial questions, they are not questions which need answers. What would you like? Which wine shall I drink, red or white? There is no valid answer to this, but there should be, in theory. To every real question, there must be a correct answer.

BP-S: It seems to me that one should differentiate between the doctrines of positive liberty that aim at regulating relationships between men in a society, and purely internal conceptions of freedom, formulated for the sake of individuals. Maybe as long as a positive conception doesn't aim at arranging society, there is no danger involved?

IB: Well, you can't quite draw a line; everything you do obviously has some effect on other people.

BP-S: Yet it seems to me that all modern culture is relatively more concerned with the positive concept. For example, existentialism is built upon self-realisation, isn't it? One may come across the ideal of freedom as self-direction in novels, dramas . . .

IB: Yes, but look, where is the difficulty? If I realise myself in one way and you realise yourself in another way, we may wish to kill each other. So what do we do? We have to create some kind of machinery to prevent it. But that's not freedom. That's the machinery of the possibility of freedom. We're really talking about laws. My position is that of Bentham: laws are indispensable but they don't increase freedom as such. A law tells you that you mustn't do something. Of course it increases the amount of freedom you have, but the law itself is not a form of freedom. It's a form of possibility. It creates the framework in which there will be increased freedom. That is correct. So you can't divide the two. In order to create a morally satisfactory form of life for yourself, you have to protect yourself and other people from the possibility of collapse. You can't do without prisons unless everybody is completely kind and good.

BP-S: I have thought about this. If liberty is identified with self-realisation and abstracted from any universal pattern, a countless number of collisions are bound to emerge. There must be some principle structuring society.

IB: Well, Mill thought that you simply had to have the minimum degree of coercion which is needed for the maximum degree of freedom. But if two freedoms collide, of course something has to be done. That's what I mean by saying the pike will eat the carp, the wolves will eat the sheep. Wolves have to be stopped from eating sheep. Well, it diminishes the freedom of wolves, no doubt. Geniuses sometimes have to be stopped from crushing other people. Perhaps not too much—it's a painful thing. How much freedom will you give to the gifted against the ungifted? There is a famous play by Shaw called *The Doctor's Dilemma*. The hero—though nobody else knows it—is Karl Marx's son-in-law. He was a famous bad man. Aveling was his name; he married Marx's youngest daughter, Eleanor. In the end I think she committed suicide and he died of drugs, or something of the kind. A sad story. Anyway, the plot of the play is the following: he is an artist, he is very gifted, he wants to paint pictures, and he really has, we assume, genius. In order to paint these pictures, his wife and family have to starve. Gradually they're starving to death. Is it all right or isn't it all right? There's no answer. One chooses as one chooses, it depends on what your general conception of life is like, whether what you do fits into what you believe to be a minimum degree of tolerable life. If you think it's intolerable that they all should die, stop him painting. It's exactly like what I was told during the war. Suppose some marvellous city—Venice—is to be destroyed. Would you rather that a hundred people should be killed? Different people answer differently.

BP-S: In accordance with their hierarchy of values.

IB: Or collision of values. The man who asked me said, 'Even though I couldn't stop the destruction if the alternative were that a hundred people would die, the idea of Venice being destroyed is unimaginable.' I take a different view. Even one life is worth more than Venice. But that's a private judgement. That shows you the kind of person one is, one's whole moral horizon. The man who was talking to me was a distinguished literary critic, an aesthetic critic, and otherwise a very honourable man—now dead—who really dug *deep* into all the works of art of every kind. He wouldn't want to live in a universe with no art. You remember Dostoevsky's famous passage in *The Brothers Karamazov* where the man says, 'Would you buy thousands and thousands of years of happiness at the cost of the torture and death of a single child?' And Ivan Karamazov says: 'I don't want to take part in this performance, I return the ticket.'[1] At no price, whatever I am offered. If you were a utilitarian, you would say, 'It's mad. Hundreds of millions of people made happy? Well, one child—very sad. But you can't be so irresponsible as to say just that you don't want to contemplate this. It's just a piece of obstinacy, it's just a piece of something your nurse taught you, something which your priest has taught you; that's no good. Be rational!' It's a problem which has no clear solution.

---

1. A memory of the passage: 'too high a price has been placed on harmony. We cannot afford to pay so much for admission. And therefore I hasten to return my ticket of admission.' Fedor Dostoevsky, *The Brothers Karamazov*, trans. David Magarshack, 2 vols. (Harmondsworth, UK: 1958), 1: 287.

The Shift in Interests: A Biographical Theme

BP-S: Could you possibly tell me something more about your philosophical commitment?

IB: Oy-oy-oy . . . What does that mean?

BP-S: You wrote in your preface to *Concepts and Categories* about the change in your interests. You were first of all interested in . . .

IB: . . . philosophy and then the history of ideas, yes?

BP-S: How did it come about?

IB: Oh, I can tell you that, I have described it in that book.[1]

BP-S: After the conversation with . . .

IB: . . . with Sheffer.[2] That's what happened. I can tell you the story again. I was an ordinary Oxford philosopher until the war. I wasn't terribly good. I was not bad. I was not the leading philosopher in any sense. I used to correct other people's books, criticise and so on. I was quite a good teacher. Then came the war, and I went to Washington. I went to Harvard to pay a visit, and I met Sheffer, because he was a friend of a man I knew in Washington. Sheffer was a very humble, shy man who was a mathematical logician. He said to me, 'You know, philosophy's gone wrong in our day. It's all covered up in logic and positivism. If I really knew that my writings would generate this, I would never have written a word.' Then he said to me, 'Look, philosophy is not a progressive subject. There are only two things in philosophy which can make progress. One is logic. Logic is like mathematics. You can think of a new method or a new tool. In that case the old tools are abandoned. A new equation or a new method of solving something. Then there is psychology, and there of course you can make discoveries, but that's empirical and not really philosophy. There is the history of philosophy. But nobody could be called learned in ethics. Nobody can be called a scholar of epistemology; it doesn't mean anything. In other words, you don't accumulate. You think you know more than you did at the beginning, but the future will upset all this. New problems will arise, new solutions. It's not like physics, you don't build from the shoulders of your predecessors.' He said that. Then I was flying to England in 1944 in a bomber. It was not pressurised, so we had to take oxygen. It was dark and we were not allowed to sleep, because if you

---

1. 'Author's Preface', in Isaiah Berlin, *Concepts and Categories: Philosophical Essays*, ed. Henry Hardy (Oxford: Oxford University Press, 1980), vii–viii.

2. Henry M. Sheffer (1883–1964), a British logician who proved in 1913 that all the usual operators of the logical calculus could be defined using a single connective, the Sheffer stroke.

slept you might swallow the oxygen pipe which gave you air. That was dangerous. You had to keep awake and you couldn't read, so I was forced to think. It's a terrible thing. I think Descartes said that intensive thought could last only four minutes with him. Anyway, if you are forced to think, you think. And I suddenly thought, maybe I want to know more at the end of my life than at the beginning. I think I would prefer another subject. I came back to Oxford in '44 and told my colleagues, who were very shocked and displeased, that I wanted to study the history of ideas—particularly Russian ideas, because during the war I read Herzen, I read Belinsky, I read all these people and was terribly interested. I did go on teaching philosophy until 1950. Then I came back from New College, where I was teaching, to this place [All Souls] and began writing the things which you've read. Then I became Professor of Social and Political Theory, which I interpreted as the history of these theories. I always lectured historically and not analytically. I think to understand a period of philosophy is to understand it genetically—what it comes from. Not everybody has to adopt a historical approach. Someone like Kant or Wittgenstein or Descartes is not interested in the history of ideas. They were geniuses, without a doubt. But I don't understand ideas unless I see how they develop, where they come from, what kind of problem they seek to solve, and how this problem came to be faced in a particular context. For example, my idea that romanticism is the biggest single shift in European consciousness is a purely historical observation. I feel most comfortable with the history of ideas. And not narrowly of social and political ideas—ideas in general, ideas which have made a difference, ideas which meant that nothing would ever be quite the same. Those are the ideas which matter. Turning-points are what I like, turning-points when the history of consciousness takes a new direction. Critical moments after which nothing is quite the same. That's all I can answer to your question.

BP-S: 'Two Concepts of Liberty' was also a turning-point. What I admire, among other things, about your essay is that it emerged on British soil, where other scholars were interested in logical positivism and the analysis of language.

IB: They took no interest in political philosophy at all. For those scholars, it was a kind of swamp: too vague, too waterlogged, too muddy. They wanted dry, precise, clear things. They thought precision in political philosophy was impossible, and I agree with this. Yet I wish to defend my imprecision. Bertrand Russell once said, 'You know, with all philosophy, or the philosophy of the great philosophers, the basic theory is always rather simple. What is ingenious and complicated is the defence against objections. The fortress has a simple plan, what is complicated are the weapons on the walls to defend and to meet actual and possible objections. These men use tremendous ingenuity, but what you are defending is usually something comparatively simple.'[1] I believe this. To understand political philosophers you would have to understand how the world looked to them. Not the propositions they uttered, but how they fit into some kind of Weltanschauung, some kind of attitude, some kind of view of life—you have to grasp that. If you do, you understand. And with Hegel, Kant, Plato, Aristotle, all these people, you have to try to empathise, try to have an insight into what things looked like to them. Then you'll understand their arguments. But if you do it much more pedantically, as philosophers are apt to, if you are doing it proposition after proposition, you'll never quite understand why they say what they say. You must have a sense of the central pattern.

BP-S: Like music in Hegel!

IB: Like music in Hegel. You know who Hegel's favourite composer was? Do you like music?

BP-S: Yes, I love music.

IB: When Hegel went to Paris, M. Victor Cousin, who was his host, said to him, 'Would you like to go to the opera?' He said, 'Yes.' 'What composer would you like to hear?'

BP-S: Wagner?

IB: Wagner was still a child in 1827.[2]

BP-S: Oh, yes, Wagner followed Hegel. It was very stupid of me to say that. It's because the images somehow seem to fit . . .

IB: Absolutely, I agree. No, it's not stupid, Wagner is very like Hegel, you're quite right. But what Hegel said—it will astonish you, I hardly like to tell you, you'll be so shocked. Hegel said, 'What composer? Rossini.' You agree, it's surprising. Kant was totally unmusical, never

---

1. A paraphrase of: 'Every philosopher, in addition to the formal system which he offers to the world, has another, much simpler, of which he may be quite unaware. If he is aware of it, he probably realises that it won't quite do; he therefore conceals it, and sets forth something more sophisticated, which he believes because it is like his crude system, but which he asks others to accept because he thinks he has made it such as cannot be disproved. The sophistication comes in by way of refutation of refutations, but this alone will never give a positive result: it shows, at best, that a theory *may* be true, not that it *must* be. The positive result, however little the philosopher may realise it, is due to his imaginative preconceptions, or to what Santayana calls "animal faith".' Bertrand Russell, *A History of Western Philosophy* (New York: Simon and Schuster, 1945), chap. 23, 2nd para.

2. Georg W. F. Hegel (1770–1831), Richard Wagner (1813–83).

wrote a tune in his life, knew nothing about music. Schopenhauer was very musical, the only person who ever wrote well about music. Hegel had no relation to music, really. He should have said Beethoven, at least—*Fidelio*. Rossini! Just remember that as a paradox. Maybe there was something not quite genuine with Hegel, maybe there was a certain amount of inauthenticity in him. I always suspect that Hegel was half a charlatan, though brilliant and remarkable. When his publisher, Cotta,[1] said to him that he thought his last book was a little bit too short, he said, 'Oh, I can lengthen it to whatever you like', and went on, added another hundred thousand words, or whatever it was. That's not quite real. I feel it's a little bit like a religious incantation. He just goes on singing to his students, formula after formula, which can be extended to any degree. It's the opposite of Kant, who says what he says and stops. Hume, Berkeley, even Schopenhauer—what you say you say. But Hegel can go on and on, producing it for ever, like a sermon, like a theological work. Well, he started, as you know, as a theologian.

BP-S: Really? I didn't know.

IB: Yes, he wasn't a clergyman, but his first studies, in Tübingen, were theological. Certainly.

Inner Obstacles and Brainwashing : Their Effect on Liberty

BP-S: Let us come back to your 'Two Concepts of Liberty'. Could we discuss an excerpt in which you mention internal obstacles? Here it is: 'The essence of the notion of liberty, in both the 'positive' and the 'negative' senses, is the holding off of something or someone—of others who trespass on my field or assert their authority over me, or of obsessions, fears, neuroses, irrational forces—intruders and despots of one kind or another.'[2]

So the inner factors, like obsessions and fears, in your opinion also constitute obstacles to freedom?

IB: Certainly, to my positive freedom. Of course.

BP-S: To positive, not to negative. Then negative freedom can be curtailed only by external obstacles?

IB: Other people. Other people stopping me from doing certain things which I wish to do.

BP-S: How about brainwashing?

---

1. Johann Friedrich Cotta (1764–1832).
2. Berlin, 'Two Concepts of Liberty', in *Liberty*, 204.

IB: To be brainwashed or to be conditioned or to be manipulated means that your capacity for controlling yourself or determining your own actions is to some extent curtailed by tampering with your intellectual condition.

BP-S: There is no doubt that brainwashing constitutes an internal obstacle. Yet it seems to be external as well!

IB: Well, of course, that's done by other people too, but nevertheless they're not telling me not to go down that road, they're not saying 'You are forbidden', they merely manipulate me in such a way that I'll lose all desire to do it.

BP-S: So what they interfere with is my positive liberty.

IB: It's like giving me a drug. After I'm given the drug, they say, 'Now look, you still can go if you like, but you no longer want to, do you?' It's like curing me of a desire to smoke. This may be quite a good thing, but it certainly interferes with my positive liberty. If I want it to be interfered with, all right. But if I did cure you of a desire to smoke, I would certainly be curtailing your positive liberty, however desirable it is to do so for your health. I am not extending it.

BP-S: In a way this seems to me artificial. If my body belongs to my private sphere of independence, why not my mind?

IB: Oh yes, I wouldn't deny that. My only point is that the effect of being brainwashed isn't so much that it closes doors through which you might enter, but it closes your capacity for determining yourself to go through any doors. What it interferes with is your personality.

BP-S: But they oppress me! They in fact stop me from choosing as I wish!

IB: It comes to the same if it limits my possibilities. What I mean is that positive liberty is just as important as negative liberty. That I want to be quite clear about.

BP-S: However, if somebody attacks me, he interferes with my independent sphere.

IB: Yes, he curtails it.

BP-S: Isn't it strange to separate the two? Doesn't my mind belong to my independent sphere?

IB: I will tell you. It belongs to you just as much, there's no doubt about that, that's not the difference. The contrast is not between what belongs to you and what doesn't belong to you, or what is private and what is not. The contrast is between the answer to two questions: one is, what is the region within which I can do whatever I decide to do, or whatever I *can* do? And the other is, who controls this region? Well, whoever controls this region is the person who conditions me or brainwashes me. He's someone who actually interferes with my capacity of choice, not with the doors that open.

BP-S: So if they brainwash me or manipulate me, they do not all the same impede my negative liberty?

IB: No. That's, I think, technically so.

BP-S: So my negative liberty doesn't protect me from this thing. Therefore, even if I am living in a liberal society, it's quite conceivable that I am subject to brainwashing?

IB: A liberal society is not a society of negative liberty. Positive liberty has to occur in all societies. My positive liberty is just as important, that's what you haven't understood. That's what I said. Maybe I didn't make it clear. The idea of self-control, the idea of determining oneself and not being pushed about by others, the idea of initiating my own action, the idea that I do what I do for my own motives, that I'm not ordered about, that the source of my activity is myself and not somebody who controls me—that is positive liberty. The perversion comes when I begin talking about two selves: one self manipulates the other, and so on. Positive liberty is a perfectly genuine concept. The demand that you be your own master or mistress is perfectly genuine. Interference with my positive liberty is just as terrible as interference with my negative liberty. If I am hypnotised, it isn't that doors are closed to me, it is that my capacity to enter through *any* door is weakened. I am no longer a person, no longer a self. I'm no longer choosing.

BP-S: So the point at which the doctrine of positive liberty becomes dangerous is this very splitting of selves?

IB: Yes, I think so. Or even if I say, 'At my best I would do so. What I do is not really done by myself at my best, not by my true self.'

BP-S: Yet there are indeed two threats: a rationalist and an irrationalist one.

IB: Yes, equally. If I force other people to do what those others may not themselves feel inclined to do, in the name of an ideal which, if only they understood it, they would themselves follow, the ideal needn't be rational; the ideal can be any ideal, provided it's not theirs but mine. I force it on them because I speak for their *romantic* personality, not their *rational* personality—for their *creative* personality, their *artistic* personality, their *spiritual* personality. That's what the Catholic Church does. The Catholic Church makes me do certain things. Priests try to influence people, or even put them in jail sometimes, like the Inquisition. They act on behalf of my soul, not on behalf of my reason. But still they're acting on the basis of what I would do if I understood, or if I were like them, if

I had this great creative vision of what life could be. Provided they force me to do what I would do if I were like them, this destroys or curtails my liberty, both positive and negative. The excuse is, 'It expands my positive liberty.' The result certainly shuts off negative liberty, obviously, because I'm not allowed to go to the right, not allowed to go to the left. But it shuts off my positive liberty as well, because I no longer direct myself, I am directed by them. So it hurts both.

BP-S: Would you please listen to another excerpt concerning internal obstacles? There is one point there which I am not sure that I understand: 'Common sense may not be too well aware of the full variety of such obstacles: they may be physical or psychical, "inner" and "outer," or complexes compounded of both elements, difficult and perhaps conceptually impossible to unravel, due to social factors and/or individual ones. Common opinion may oversimplify the issue; but it seems to me to be right about its essence: freedom is to do with the absence of obstacles to action.'[1]

IB: The obstacles can be psychological.

BP-S: 'Obstacles to action.' That changes the whole thing. Why to *action*? Why not to my *choices*?

IB: All right, maybe it's inaccurate. Obstacles to being able to choose.

BP-S: Because I don't have to act. I might choose to be passive.

IB: Choosing is a kind of action. Action doesn't just mean getting up from the chair. If I decide, something has happened, a psychological act has occurred. Even so, it's badly put. You're quite right: I should have said 'choices', of course: 'freedom is to do with the absence of obstacles to choice'. You could say that; if you wish to quote me and say, 'For the word *action*, *choice* should be substituted', that would be perfectly valid.

BP-S: Because one doesn't have to take action, to take advantage of one's liberty . . .

IB: No, no, one doesn't. One could sit in a chair.

BP-S: It's a matter of potential.

IB: To remove obstacles to action doesn't mean that the action has to occur.

---

1. Berlin, 'From Hope and Fear Set Free', in *Liberty,* 270.

On Erich Fromm: Negative and Positive Freedom

BP-S: I would be very interested in your opinion on Erich Fromm's concept of freedom. Here are the relevant passages: 'Positive freedom consists in the spontaneous activity of the total integrated personality.'[1] 'Positive freedom also implies the principle that there is no higher power than this unique individual self, that man is the centre and purpose of his life: that the growth and realisation of man's individuality is an end that can never be subordinated to purposes which are supposed to have greater dignity.'[2]

Fromm definitely represents the positive approach, which you find more liable to perversion. What's wrong with these concrete formulations?

IB: What is wrong with Fromm's approach is that he thinks that positive liberty is enough, provided I am not internally subject to drives of an irrational kind. All Fromm wants is integration. Integration is a splendid thing, but it's not the same as freedom.

BP-S: But he doesn't use this word *rational*.

IB: I know he doesn't. But the idea is there, nevertheless. Why am I frightened of freedom? Because I'm irrational. That's only the real cause of being frightened of freedom, provided I don't have some completely irrational drive. What the psychoanalyst liberates me from is hatred of my mother, or of my father because of his relation with my mother, or hatred of the colour blue because I was raped by a man in a blue cloak when I was a child, anything you like. You see what I mean? And when I am liberated from all these pressures and drives, what I am liberated from is irrationality, even if he doesn't use the term. To be free means to determine oneself freely in whatever direction one chooses, even for Fromm. That's positive liberty. But he doesn't allow for negative liberty at all; he thinks it's unimportant. The whole point, for him, is that my soul should be at peace, as for Spinoza. Provided I'm harmonious, provided I am not torn apart by conflicts, provided I am not driven mad or driven to neurosis or psychosis for all kinds of biological or psychological reasons, I'm OK. Which means I can say: 'I am in prison but I'm rational, I'm all right. I am harmonious, I don't care if I am in prison. The tyrant is irrational. I'm all right.' A man can be happy and harmonious and fulfilled in chains because he doesn't care about chains and it's irrational to mind them. I don't care about chains, I don't care if I'm in

---

1. Erich Fromm, *Fear of Freedom* (London: Routledge & Kegan Paul, 1960), 222.
2. ibid., 228.

prison. All I mind about is my inner condition, and my inner condition is harmonious, full of love, full of hope, full of reason, full of creative capacity. What do I care if I find I have been locked up? There's a famous poem by the English poet Lovelace which says, 'Stone walls do not a prison make, / Nor iron bars a cage.'[1] That's Fromm, Spinoza, the Stoics and all. It's quite a respectable point of view, but it's not enough. Therefore you need negative freedom. If I'm in prison, I'm in prison. If you are in the grip of a totalitarian State, then you *psychologically* make yourself indifferent to your tortures.

BP-S: Yes. So do I interpret you correctly when I think that for you negative liberty is much more important than positive?

IB: No, I don't say more important. Negative freedom is ignored by people who prefer positive freedom; they pay no attention to it at all. Negative freedom is a sine qua non, without that there cannot be real freedom; nor can there be freedom without some degree of positive freedom.

BP-S: But if they clash?

IB: How can they clash? You mean, I am offered an alternative? Either seventeen open doors but I am not my own master? Or I *am* my own master, but only two doors? If there are seventeen open doors and I'm not my own master, I'm not free. I wish to defend positive freedom today. [*laughter*]

BP-S: So it seems!

IB: It's *perversion* of positive freedom which leads you to disaster. Perversion of negative freedom also, but far less. That's a historical point. To stress negative freedom is never to deny positive freedom. To stress positive freedom is often to deny negative.

BP-S: Yes. So is your whole doctrine a kind of a meta-doctrine, I mean a doctrine built upon other doctrines?

IB: Yes, you can say that. It's simply analysis of the concept, in so far as all analyses of concepts are.

BP-S: I've read many articles on you, and they criticise mainly your concept of negative freedom . . .

IB: As being too narrow. What I'm accused of is always the same, which is some kind of dry, negative individualism, which doesn't allow for social love.

BP-S: To me your conception of freedom amounts to a discussion, not to a body of doctrine like, for instance, Hayek's.

---

1. Richard Lovelace, 'To Althea from Prison', in *Lucasta: The Poems of Richard Lovelace* (Chicago: Caxton, 1921), stanza 4, lines 1–2.

IB: No, certainly not. It's not a body of doctrine. Oh no, it *is* discussion. It's simply saying, there are two senses of the word 'freedom'. Both are valid. They overlap to some extent, but they're not the same. Each has its perversions. Negative freedom has its perversion, which has been far less dangerous to human beings than the perversions of positive freedom. I don't deal with negative freedom because what I wanted to write about is perversion of positive freedom. You are quite right about that, that's why there are only eight pages about one and—whatever it is—twenty-three pages about the other.[1] That's correct. But if you asked me, 'What about positive freedom?' I would say it's an indispensable ideal, certainly. We don't want to say Fromm is wrong in saying that inner harmony is important, but that's not enough. If there is no negative freedom, then that's not freedom, that's something else. That's serenity, happiness, moral satisfaction, but not freedom.

BP-S: So if you were to build a body of doctrine like Bentham's, or Mill's, or whoever's, how would you protect both freedoms?

IB: I would have to say that without negative freedom there is no true freedom, politically. We're talking about political freedom. Without negative freedom, there is no freedom at all.

BP-S: How would you protect positive freedom?

IB: You protect positive freedom by trying not to be indoctrinated; by stopping people from operating on you—from putting pressure upon you morally. Take parents who apply moral blackmail to children, saying, 'If you do this, you'll make me very unhappy. If you do this, it's against the whole tradition of our family.' That's interfering with positive freedom. No doors are being shut, but I am made to think that it would be criminal if I do it. And I don't want to be a criminal. So negative freedom is essential, for without that there is no political freedom. Positive freedom is a moral consideration, not a political one. Positive freedom is what makes personality personality. Without that, I can't function at all as a free human being.

BP-S: But it can become political when the concept is expanded to cover supra-individual entities.

IB: Of course, yes, when pressure begins, for example when people say, 'I'm doing for you what you can't do for yourself because you don't understand it.'

---

1. A reference to what I wrote in 'One More Voice on Berlin's Doctrine of Liberty': 'Berlin devotes nine pages to understanding of the negative concept, whereas his critique of the positive concept occupies twenty-four pages.' See 236 below.

BP-S: So now the image is quite different from the one built up by most of your critics! They say, for instance, that the only doctrine which sticks to your concept of negative freedom is that of Bentham.

IB: Bentham made one statement which I quote, which is that the law is an obstacle, however wise or necessary. That's all I quote Bentham on. I'm not a utilitarian.

BP-S: They write that even Mill has a positive doctrine of some sort. So your answer is that you don't build a body of doctrine on strictly negative, very narrow premises.

IB: I think that positive freedom is fundamentally a metaphor based on the idea of negative freedom, but it's a metaphor for something absolutely genuine. And by sticking to positive freedom you can eliminate negative freedom and thus kill freedom. But by sticking to negative freedom, you will preserve a certain degree of freedom, even though your personality may be damaged.

BP-S: So you agree with my thesis that your doctrine forms a meta-theory of freedom?

IB: Absolutely. All I do is to examine the two concepts and their implications.

BP-S: This is the source of many mistakes one meets in the literature on your conception of liberty. Having interpreted your essay as a body of doctrine, your critics draw the conclusion that you hold an extreme negativist position, which is all wrong.

IB: Which is wrong. Certainly. I'm grateful to you for defending me.

BP-S: [*laughing*] That cannot be!

The Popularity of Hayek behind the Iron Curtain—Democracy

BP-S: We agreed that your study of liberty does not amount to a body of doctrine. I would be most interested to find out what your opinion is of a conception which is nowadays very popular in Poland—that of Hayek.

IB: Hayek's conception of freedom is simply economic. I have some sympathy for it, but it's too rigid and it leads to a society of people competing against each other. What I dislike in Hayek is that he's a kind of fanatical *laissez-faire* liberal, and that produces terrible perversion of what I call negative liberty. It has something to be said for it from the point of view of democracy, but it leads to complete abolition of the Welfare State.

The man who is quite interesting on that is not Hayek but Schumpeter. He's an Austrian economist who defines democracy in different ways. Democracy of the kind which he doesn't like is really majority rule. Majority rule can lead to tyranny—the crowd, the mob—and you can get at people's votes very easily. He wants to say that democracy depends on conflict between two or three candidates. Only those governments are democratic which are in danger of being replaced. And therefore they have to suck up to, as one says in English, they have to be nice to, or gain the favour of, the electorate. *How* they gain this is another matter—they may do it by very corrupt means, in which case it's a corrupt democracy, but it's still a democracy, because in the end the electors can turn them out. If they're in perpetual danger of losing power, that is democracy. If they're not, it isn't. It may be a better form of government—you may prefer it, you may say it's wiser and more stable—democracy it is not.

BP-S: I am asking about Hayek because he is widely read in Krakow. I had to wait almost a year to borrow the only copy of *The Constitution of Liberty*!

IB: I saw a Polish philosopher called Legutko this morning. He seems to be impressed by Hayek.

BP-S: Almost everybody is impressed by Hayek at the Faculty of Philosophy in Krakow. They read Hayek like the Bible.

IB: Like the Bible, yes. I attacked Hayek a bit, but he thought I was acceptable; also Ortega y Gasset, whom I don't at all like. He wrote a famous book against mass culture, *The Revolt of the Masses*. He thinks the French Revolution was a terrible evil, things went wrong after 1793, nothing has ever been good since. There are mobs and crowds and democracy, all these terrible things. I can see this in Poland—the anti-Marxist position, which clings to anything which resists mass bullying, mass control.

BP-S: Not to *anything* . . .

IB: Well, these people do.

BP-S: In order to survive, spiritually. It helps very much. Otherwise it would be really hard to live.

IB: I understand fully, of course I do. That's why Solidarnosc was such a tremendous affair.[1]

---

1. Solidarnosc (Solidarity), the social-political movement in Poland that opposed the Communist regime, took the institutional form of a trade union. Its emergence in 1980 marked the beginning of the later peaceful collapse of Communism, first in Poland and then in the whole Eastern bloc. About 10 million Poles joined Solidarnosc, while the local Communist Party (The Polish United Workers' Party) had in the 1980s at most 3 million members.

Liberty and Liberties—Rights

BP-S: What is your opinion on the standpoint in political philosophy according to which it is not liberty that should be discussed, but particular liberties? Hart, Dworkin, Rawls, Aron—all of them give up the abstract ideal of liberty and maintain that there is no point in discussing general concepts.

IB: I think there is. Yet I understand what they mean: liberties are always rights, privileges, that kind of thing. Liberties means more or less: I am free to do this, I am free to do that. In a way they're right. Nevertheless, there is something common to these liberties. You have to say it's not an accident that all these liberties are called liberties. It is not just a coincidence that economic liberty, liberty of worship, liberty of meetings, liberty of speech are all called liberties. There is something common, there is a kernel, there is some centre.

BP-S: And is there any right to liberty, a general right? Is your theory rights-based?

IB: No, no, because I never know what 'right' means. If you could explain 'right' to me, I'd be very pleased.

BP-S: No! It's the same with me.

IB: I'll tell you why I say this. You can't say it is simply 'right' in the abstract that someone should be treated in a certain way. There are rules or laws which say you should not kill people. It's also in my interest not to be killed, because I don't want to be. So I claim it as a right. Rights, for me, are simply things which, according to some code, it is right to do, and which happen to be something which I want done, which are in my interest. There are things which it is right to do which I don't want, such as to be put in prison. It is right to put me in prison if I do something terrible, so I could say I have a right to be imprisoned. But people don't say that. A right always means something which I want; so rights are simply those things which people owe me because the law says so, or the ruler says so, or the Ten Commandments say so, or God says so, or the prince says so, or I say so—it doesn't matter—and which happen to be the sort of things I need or want, or that are in my interest. What rights are in an absolute sense I've never understood. Rights can only be explained in terms of rules, and the rules simply say: this is right, this is wrong.

BP-S: I'm afraid that once we give up the old ideal of general liberty, and confine ourselves only to liberties, it becomes easier to manipulate people. Though the general concept is vague and unclear, it seems to provide better safeguards for individual freedom.

IB: When people say, 'I'm not free', one knows what they mean. When they say, 'I'm enslaved', 'I've lost my liberty', it's not meaningless. You don't say, 'Please be precise. You've not lost your liberty to breathe, you've not lost your liberty to frown, you've not lost your liberty to bend your finger. What do you mean?' What they mean is freedom to perform the kind of acts which I need to perform if I am to be fully myself. That's all you need.

BP-S: Without the old ideal of liberty it is much easier to deceive people. That's what they do under Communism. They list some rights in the constitution and say, 'You have liberties, you have rights.'

IB: You mean the right to eat, to drink?

BP-S: Oh, to education, to work, to healthcare, and so on.

IB: To vote in the way they want you to vote. You have a right to apply for membership of the Party.

BP-S: Yes, yes, exactly!

IB: You have a right to denounce somebody for being counter-revolutionary. What else have you got a right to do? You have a right to be grateful, you have a right to praise the Leader.

BP-S: How can you remember it all? It was such a long time ago that you lived under Communism!

IB: You have a right to try to increase the productivity of the factory by increasing the hours of work. You have a right to be a Stakhanovite.[1]

BP-S: It's like breathing in oxygen, listening to you . . .

IB: You have a right to be against America. [*laughter*]

BP-S: I wouldn't be surprised if this phone changed into a cat now!

IB: Quite so. I understand. Everything is different. You suddenly feel free, that's all that it is, you feel free. But it won't last, you insist on going back. You are a Pole, you wish to live with Poles. That's like people who say, 'Not only am I ready to die for my country, I am ready to die with my country.' Akhmatova said that to me, the Russian poet, 'I am not leaving, I am not going to emigrate, I am prepared to die with my country.' Very heroic. But are you sure you want to be so heroic? At least come back, please.

---

1. In 1953 A. G. Stakhanov (1905/6–77), a miner from Donbas (which produced 1475% of the planned daily coal output), initiated a competition aimed at the increase of industrial production that led to ruthless exploitation of workers.

1988

My three-month visit to Oxford in the spring of 1988 was the longest of the four. I cannot retrace the exact number of appointments with Berlin that I had, but there were about ten of them. I remember Roger Hausheer's comment on their frequency: 'We are not so privileged,' he sighed, having in mind Western students of Berlin's ideas.

The quantity and coverage of my recorded conversations of that period do not do justice to those meetings. Berlin was far from enthusiastic about my recording his utterances. He would rather I had made notes. This is why I seldom dared turn on my tape recorder. I did so only when we discussed topics relevant to my vague notion of a book on his ideas. The former official reason was no longer valid, as I had defended my PhD before my second visit. In consequence, whole conversations, unfortunately the most interesting ones, were unrecorded; among them fascinating spontaneous talks, or perhaps I should say monologues. Apart from further literature on Berlin's ideas, and my emerging article[1] and the questions it raised (concerning mainly Popper's philosophical system), we also discussed a wide range of completely unrelated topics, such as life and death, literature and music, and living under a totalitarian regime.

The Popper theme proved to be a tough nut. After our discussion on Popper some doubts still lingered, so I suggested that we meet together with John Gray to discuss the controversial points. During that event I almost refrained from talking, preferring instead to absorb the plain sailing of the

---

1. 'The Twilight of "Liberty" as an Abstract Ideal?', included below.

two philosophers. On another occasion, Berlin remembered his childhood in revolutionary Russia. Though a version of these memories has already been published elsewhere,[1] I have decided to include them, as they constitute a first-hand account.

There is one vivid recollection which I chuckle at when recalling those meetings. I was often required to read to Sir Isaiah passages from articles that discussed his ideas. This was not an easy task; from time to time, I found it difficult to pronounce correctly what I was reading. There was one haunting image which was responsible for my poor performance. When recalling his fascinating meetings with Russian writers, Berlin told me that the great poet Anna Akhmatova read Byron to him. In English. He didn't understand a word.

---

1. See Michael Ignatieff, *Isaiah Berlin: A Life* (London: Chatto & Windus, 1998), 20–32.

22 and 24 April 1988

Isaiah Berlin's Childhood

BP-S: May I put a large request to you? I expect that you will say no, but I hope to be pleasantly surprised. If I am to write a *reliable* book on your achievements I need to devote attention to the inspiration for your doctrine of liberty. You once told me that it was essentially derived from a traumatic experience which you went through as a child in revolutionary Petrograd. It was just a remark of yours, but it is really vital for me to get to know more about your early years and to record your memories. Would you agree? You would do me a great favour.

IB: All right. I will tell you of my childhood into your machine. Is it moving?

BP-S: Yes! Thank you so much.

IB: I was born in Riga, in what was then tsarist Russia, on 6 June 1909. According to the Russian calendar, that was 24 May. My parents and I were a perfectly respectable, middle-class Jewish family. Berlin was not my real name at all. I'll tell you how it happened:

Once upon a time, in Russia in the 1850s, there was a Jew called Berlin. He bought a piece of land somewhere. At that time, the Jews were allowed to buy land, which was not always the case. A railway was built on this land, so it went to twelve times its value and he became a millionaire. He had two sons. Among Jews in Russia, there were only two ways of achieving status. One was by money and the other was by learning. So the children of men of money tended to get their children to

marry the children of men of learning; that was the way in which inter-
marriage occurred between the people who were socially at the top of
that ghetto society. This man, in addition to his great wealth, was also a
follower of the Hasidic sect. So he got his son married to a grand-
daughter of a famous Hasidic Rabbi. She had no money at all, and they
did not have the children that all Jews desire. The Rabbi's son adopted
the son of his wife's sister, my great-grandmother; my grandfather was,
therefore, the rich man's nephew by marriage. The millionaire said he
would give his money to my grandfather, provided he changed his name
to Berlin, which of course he no doubt hastened to do. My father was the
great-nephew by marriage of the millionaire and conducted his business.
He owned forests in Russia. The timber was floated on the Dvina River
to Riga. It was there cut, sawn, axed, and sold to Germany, France, Italy
and England. My father, being a favourite pseudo-grandson, was responsible for all this. He learnt all these languages for business purposes:
French he knew quite well, English he knew quite well. Both he and my
mother went to a German school in Riga, so they were equally free in
German and Russian. He married my mother, who was his first cousin.
They lived in Riga and travelled a good deal: to England, to France, to
Germany. They had friends and acquaintances in all sorts of nations.

I'll tell you what the rich man was like. He lived in Riga and he spoke
nothing but Yiddish. Every winter he went to Menton in the South of
France with forty people. He lived like a Maharajah; they took two rabbis,
a kosher slaughterer, court fools, three secretaries. They occupied three
villas and they were completely isolated. It was exactly like some Indian
rajah, it was absolutely medieval. Every summer he went to Bad Hom-
burg, and in Germany it was exactly the same. But my father was what was
called *évolué*. He had evolved—he spoke languages and so on. He was
brought up in strict Jewish piety, but he lapsed, and my mother lapsed, too.

My language was German until the age of three, and then I got a
Russian governess and became a Russian speaker. When I was five, in
1914, the Great War came. The Germans were very near, wandering
about at Tannenberg. I don't think my parents particularly minded the
war. They didn't mind the Germans coming to Riga any more than the
Poles minded the Germans coming to Poland at that time, in the hope of
becoming liberated from the Russians. But they were afraid of being cut
off from their forests, so they retreated into the interior. Early in 1915,
they travelled to a little village called Andreapol, which was entirely
owned by my father's company. At the back were two thousand peasants

who cut the timber. They made lumber and little rafts on which they floated down to Riga. In front there was a little semi-town with a hundred houses containing all the clerks, the controllers, the bookkeepers, the postmen, and a few Russian Army officers. There we spent nine months, and I enjoyed it very much. There were officers there waiting to be disarmed, who used to read Russian literature to my mother in the evenings. There were soldiers who took me about in huge lorries. They used to play balalaikas. There were these bookkeepers' daughters who used to put on very wide dresses to go picking berries and mushrooms. There was a landowner who was dying, a charming old member of the gentry. There was a wild park one was allowed to walk in, picking berries and mushrooms. It really was the old, Chekhovian Russia. My governess, unfortunately, had an affair with a German who was hiding from the Russians. Once it was discovered, she was removed. Then my family went to Petrograd, where the main office was, and there I saw the Russian Revolution in 1917—both revolutions, the liberal revolution and the Bolshevik revolution, which I remember very vividly. But you don't want me to describe it to you now, it will take too long . . .

BP-S: But this is what I am most interested in!

IB: All right, I'll tell you. My parents took me to a balcony on the morning of 28 February 1917.

BP-S: In Petrograd?

IB: Yes. I was asleep and they woke me up at half-past nine. From the balcony I saw people with banners saying, 'Land and Liberty!', 'Down with the war!', 'Down with the Tsar!', 'All Power to the Duma!'—'Land and Liberty' above all. And they marched about with these banners. I could see them from the sixth floor. And then I saw the troops advancing on them. I didn't know entirely what that meant. I was seven-and-a-half at that time. The troops and the revolutionary crowds fraternised, all mixed together. There was no attack, it all became one body. That I saw with my own eyes. My parents were very pleased. They were revolutionary, like all liberals. My father had four brothers and two sisters, my mother had three sisters and a brother, and all these people went to meetings all the time and they listened to Kerensky and they were very excited. The whole thing was like a coup d'état, it was like something on the stage. I didn't go to any meetings because I was too young. I remember that there was no shooting; it was very bloodless. The only people who remained loyal to the tsarist government were the police. You will not find that in the books. The police shot into the crowds from attics and from roofs of buildings.

I used to go for little walks with my governess and a little daughter of the tsarist minister of Finnish affairs. One day, on one of my little walks, I saw a man struggling in the midst of other people who were obviously dragging him off to be killed. He was a pale man, a policeman of some sort in civilian clothes. The man was surrounded by people dragging him off to his death; he was pale, struggling, terrified. I've never forgotten it. It was the most horrible thing I ever saw with my own eyes. It gave me a distaste for violence for the rest of my life. That was the only revolutionary horror I ever saw.

Then we all went on a summer holiday at a place called Staraya Russa, which was a spa. There were a lot of children with whom I played. There were fancy-dress parties and nobody talked about the war at all. There was an Italian orchestra, which couldn't get new scores for its music. The old music was played all the time with different titles. First it was called 'Venetian March', then it was called 'Finnish March', then it was called 'American March', but it was all the same. I made friends with the conductor of the orchestra. He said he longed 'to get out of this horrible country', but he failed for some reason. It's something children remember. But I had a very happy time there. Then I came back to Petrograd, where I saw posters for the Constituent Assembly. There must have been thirty-four parties, including Zionists. If I hadn't been in Russia, I wouldn't have seen that. Every kind of socialist, every kind of liberal, endless parties, both serious and silly. Then I saw two young men who were tearing down these posters and putting up huge posters with a hammer and sickle. I was very pleased. I thought it was very amusing, tearing down these banners. When I told my father, he was not so pleased. Then came October. Nobody in my bourgeois world knew that the Revolution had happened. They knew something had happened. The lifts stopped working, there were no newspapers, there were no trams, there were no cars or buses, things stopped dead. There was a general strike against the Revolution. The railway union and the other unions went on strike; the unions were all anti-Bolshevik. People from my world thought, 'Well, there are two men called Lenin and Trotsky who are said to have something to do with it.' I knew nothing about all the earlier putsches of the Bolsheviks that didn't succeed. Lenin was thought to be a very honest man, fanatical, dangerous . . .

BP-S: Honest?

IB: Yes, a very honest fanatic. Wicked, fanatical, very dangerous, but certainly honest. He had terrible ideas. Trotsky was thought to be a total crook. They were never referred to separately; Lenin-and-Trotsky were hyphenated, like a firm. Nothing happened for about a week. I remember only newspapers. There was a newspaper called *Day*; it was removed and it came out as *Afternoon*; then it came out as *Evening*; then it came out as *Night*; then it came out as *Midnight*; then it came out as *Darkest Night*. Then it stopped. Gradually, gradually it dawned even on my family that the Revolution had occurred. By then, there were crowds marching. I did hear distant shooting at that time in Petrograd. The famous attack on the Winter Palace by the cruiser *Aurora* did not take place. That's a myth.

BP-S: Really?

IB: Technically there was a group of sailors who went to the Winter Palace, which had no real defence. The sailors went straight into the Winter Palace and found that there was a provisional government there, which they tried to arrest. Some escaped, some did not. There wasn't a great assault, a magnificent battle with machine guns.

BP-S: That's invented? Unbelievable! And I was taught as a schoolgirl of the heroic attack on the Winter Palace which signified the beginning of the brave new world. There were poems glorifying the storming which we were made to learn by heart and recite at academies! Though I was quite immune to indoctrination, I wouldn't dream of doubting a historical fact like this!

IB: There was no resistance of a serious kind. Then, gradually, life resumed. My father went on supplying timber for the Russian railways. There were sleepers on the railways. That was exactly the same, it wasn't touched. There was no food or fuel, so we all lived in one little room. There was just enough fuel to keep warm. People lived as they could. Professors of medicine used to come and bring turf or timber. All kinds of important persons suddenly became porters. And there was a thing called the House Committee, which was a committee of the proletarians living in a house, presided over by, in this case, a man who looked after the heating apparatus for the house. Well, for some reason he became quite a friend of my mother's. I don't know why, but she got on with him. We used to meet him and talk to him about heating and so on, so we weren't persecuted. But the Georgian royal princess, who lived above us, the minister of Finnish affairs, with whose daughter I used to go on little walks, and Max Steinberg, the nephew of the composer Rimsky-Korsakov, who lived with his daughter below us, were not well treated. There was a tremendous amount of real persecution. People were driven into the yard and made to clear up snow. They were made to do work that wasn't needed. It was a pure case of humiliation of the old regime.

We had a maid who was a tremendous monarchist, and when the Cheka sent the police to search our apartment, she met them at the door and cursed them, telling them to get out immediately. She was a proletarian, so they couldn't get past her. In the early months and years of the Revolution, any proletarian person could stop raids. So we were never searched. Such jewels as we had were buried in the snow on the balcony and later taken out by us illegally. So we just went on like that in late 1917 and 1918. I stood in felt boots in endless queues for food, for fuel, for anything. But we also went to the Mariinsky Theatre and heard Chaliapin sing in *Boris Godunov*. There was a cinema next door, which became a soup kitchen, but occasionally there were concerts. Life in this sense went on. In the summer of 1918, we went on a holiday in Pavlovsk. I remember the concert hall there. It was part of the railway station, so that royalty who came could be given concerts as soon as they arrived. I heard César Franck's symphony, which he conducted there. I was not sent to school. I was taught Russian literature by my father's brothers, who were students at the university. I was told about Garibaldi, Wagner's *Ring*, *Lohengrin*, *Tannhäuser*, the Niebelungs. I read a book on ancient Greece, from which I derived a lot of knowledge, and another book on ancient Egypt which my parents bought for me. I absolutely absorbed them. I read and read and read and read. The little girl with whom I used to go for walks survived. I met her in America about twelve years ago. She told me we used to go for these walks. I was very bookish and always telling her about what I'd read about Greece, about Sophocles, Pericles, about Egypt. I read all the novels of Jules Verne in Russian, I read Dumas. Later, at ten, I began reading *War and Peace,* which I quite enjoyed.

By this time it was 1920. In that year my parents returned to Riga because Latvia was made independent and they opted for Latvian nationality. They were allowed to leave, quite peacefully. We stayed in Riga for about two months, then we went to England. My father adored England; he thought it was the most marvellous country that ever existed. First I went to school in a little suburb called Surbiton and then to St Paul's School in London, where I studied Latin and Greek for six years. I was treated very nicely and lived a perfectly happy existence as a schoolboy. I never rebelled. If I had chains I still wear them. Participation is not my thing; by nature I am an observer. There was not a revolution in my life.

BP-S: Apart from the one which cast a dark shadow on my parents' life and later on my own. Thank you so much for your reminiscences.

Three Baskets—Uniformity of Nature—Empirical Categories

BP-S: I'd like to tell you about Jerzy Szacki's paper.[1] Here is a paper by him, in Polish, I am afraid, so you won't be able to understand it.

IB: Good heavens! But I can read it! [*tries to read in Polish*]

BP-S: I am afraid you can't, really . . . [*laughing*] It's one of the best papers on your study of the history of ideas. Among other things he writes very favourably of your conception of the three baskets.[2] Yet you once told me that you no longer believe in it!

IB: I think I still believe in the baskets after all. However, what shakes me is that sometimes you can't tell. Is the idea of quantum theory philosophical or is it scientific? How does one find out? In one sense, experimentation will make a certain difference, and in another sense, perhaps, it won't. So there are borderline questions, and the clear-cut view according to which every question is either empirical or formal or philosophical is too stiff. You mustn't cut quite so black and white. Grey areas occur. Take, for example, the philosophy of science. What is the philosophy of science? Is it empirical? You ask, 'What is the central concept of quantum mechanics?' Well, it's a philosophical question. But supposing a certain experiment occurs and this disproves something. That is not a philosophical event. It's a scientific event. So there is some overlap.

I will give you an example of a very difficult case. I once wrote a thing about the concept of the uniformity of nature.[3] Now there I say, or if I don't say I mean, that the question is, 'What is meant by rational methods of science?' It means that you presuppose that induction is correct, that what has happened in the past will also happen in the future.

1. Jerzy Szacki, 'Sir Isaiah Berlin: historia idei a filozofia' ['Sir Isaiah Berlin: History of Ideas and Philosophy'], *Literatura na Swiecie* 179 No. 6 (1986), 195–207.

2. 'The history of systematic human thought is largely a sustained effort to formulate all the questions that occur to mankind in such a way that the answers to them will fall into one or other of two great baskets: the empirical, i.e. questions whose answers depend, in the end, on the data of observation; and the formal, i.e. questions whose answers depend on pure calculation, untrammelled by factual knowledge. [. . .] Yet there are certain questions that do not easily fit into this simple classification. [. . .] if I ask "What is time?", "What is a number?", "What is the purpose of human life on earth?", "How can I know past facts that are no longer there—no longer where?", "Are all men truly brothers?", how do I set about looking for the answer? [. . .] They differ from the questions in the other basket in that the question itself does not seem to contain a pointer to the way in which the answer to it is to be found. [. . .] This shows that between the two baskets, the empirical and the formal, there is at least one intermediate basket, in which all those questions live which cannot easily be fitted into the other two.' Isaiah Berlin, 'The Purpose of Philosophy', in *Concepts and Categories*, 2–3.

3. Isaiah Berlin, 'Induction and Hypothesis', *Proceedings of the Aristotelian Society*, supp. vol. 16 (1937), 63–102.

There is a certain uniformity in nature; if there is causality, effects must follow their causes. But no one knows why they must follow. What kind of proposition is that? Normally it's been thought of as philosophical. My conception is that the proposition that things repeat themselves is ultimately empirical, but it is something which is, at the same time, a kind of category. Unless things are uniform, unless A is always followed by B, unless we can assume that water will flow downhill not uphill, unless we can assume that fire will burn a piece of paper and the piece of paper will not extinguish the fire, we can't predict anything. Therefore it will be impossible to make general propositions. It will be impossible to think properly. But the assumption that this is so, that rational thought can exist only in a world in which there is regularity, is in itself an empirical assumption, because it could be otherwise. It could be otherwise, but just isn't. We have to assume that it isn't, otherwise we can't say anything. We can't avoid making the assumption. That's what deduction is founded on. We can't avoid making the assumption that the future is like the past. All we have at our command is the past. How can you find out about the future? The present hardly exists, the future is not yet, so all we have is the past. That's all we can use, that's our capital. So unless the future imitates the past, we can't say anything, we can't live, we don't know what to do next, we shall be destroyed because we can't assume anything about what will happen—we'll be in complete chaos.

But that proposition is empirical. Some people would say, 'No, it's a philosophical presupposition. It's a kind of regulative idea of reason. It's some kind of category in terms of which we think.' I think exactly the same about space. Take, for example, the empirical idea that space has three dimensions. If you live in a flat territory, where there is no depth, you will not understand what I mean by saying 'deep'. In the end, categories are very unchangeable empirical properties. And not everybody believes that. Kant thought categories were eternal, unchanging, a priori.

BP-S: Yes, Szacki relates your understanding of categories to that of Kant's and stresses the differences.[1]

---

1. 'The author of *Concepts and Categories* refers to Kant, or, strictly speaking, to the Kantian differentiation between facts and categories in terms of which the agent organises the data of experience, perceives facts, forms an image of them, reflects on them. The field of philosophy is, for Berlin, just these categories, "models", "conceptual structures", "paradigms", [. . .] "spectacles", thanks to which people organise the world of their experience and monitor their practical activities. There would be no point, however, in labelling Berlin as a Kantian. As the author of *Concepts and Categories* betrays Kant in several important respects, what we really encounter in Berlin is an approach analogous (moreover, this is only a loose analogy) to the German philosopher's conception, rather than its actual implementation.' Szacki, 'Sir Isaiah Berlin: historia idei a filozofia', 199 (all translations from Polish in this volume are my own).

IB: It's really quite a bold idea. My view is that categories are of varying degrees of stability. For example, space is very stable. Time is terribly stable. We can't think in terms of two times. If we try to think of two dimensions of time we'll go mad, as Tarski once said. But some things are less stable. For example, material objects. We live in a world of material lumps in space, but things could melt. If things melted, we wouldn't have arithmetic any more because we couldn't count. You would then say, 'Well, the laws of physics have changed. We were wrong. Things can happen which we didn't dream could.' You would have to revise everything. Some things aren't stable at all; colours and so on change. Psychological facts are completely unstable. Our general propositions about how men think are completely fluid. The same is true of sociology and history. Their practitioners try to establish scientific generalisations, which are totally unstable. What stable categories exist in history? For example, industry must follow commerce and commerce must follow agriculture. Maybe, but maybe not. Supposing you had a situation in which a commercial society becomes industrial, and then destroys all its machines and becomes agricultural again? It's not likely to happen, but it's not as unlikely as space changing. The assumptions which we make, the frameworks in terms of which we work, are of differing orders of stability. But I don't accept a priori categories. Everything's empirical. It is what it is. Mathematics is not empirical, because we have invented it, but some people think that numbers are objective. Plato thought so.

BP-S: What about music?

IB: We invented it. It has no relation to nature. It's the only art which is absolutely . . .

BP-S: . . . absolutely our creation, yes. I have thought about this. Music is entirely human. Music is something we could be proud of.

IB: Yes, we made it. It does not come from nature. Nor does language come from nature. Language is not noises; it does not come from the animal sounds. Herder was right about that; it doesn't come from cries. It has something to do with the growth of the mind. It's impossible that animals should actually have language. They have means of communication.

BP-S: But think about infants. When they are completely tiny, they use a language of noises . . .

IB: Well, so do animals. Language is different from communication. Language is a framework. It has a structure and a grammar.

BP-S: Could we come back to Professor Szacki's article? Your categories, he says, are not universal even within one culture. Some of them, unlike Kant's, may refer only to a particular sphere.

IB: Well, yes and no. Some categories are universal.

BP-S: But only some of them.

IB: A category is a general way of thinking. The way in which the Polynesians think is different from the way in which you and I think. Take totemistic cultures. If you say, 'We are crocodiles', what does that mean? 'They are donkeys and we are crocodiles,' says some savage tribe in Brazil. 'We are the crocodile tribe.' We don't recognise what they mean; the categories are different. What does to 'worship' a cow mean to the Indians? One may say, 'Well, it's a sort of worship of nature.' That's something that we say, but we don't really understand. We don't really understand why the Jews should have worshipped the golden calf. Why a calf? Why not a goat? We don't know. Idolatry, where the idol stands for something else, is beyond our comprehension.

BP-S: Szacki also says that your categories, models and paradigms are always plural and intrinsically contradictory and competitive. Do you agree?

IB: It could be. One paradigm knocks out another. He's talking about political paradigms?

BP-S: Not only.

IB: No, but in particular. For example, the difference between the religious paradigm of the father and his children, as opposed to the paradigm of the social contract, as opposed to the paradigm of society as an organism, or society as a mechanism, or society as something else. These are models in terms of which we think, and one model pushes out another. They are not compatible with each other. When you have a mechanistic model and someone wrecks it, you say, 'Yes, this is much, much more like what things are like.'

BP-S: But he's got a question. I believe we discussed it in correspondence.[1] He says that, on the one hand, you're a pluralist. You affirm diversity, you believe that there is no objective standard in politics, morality, or art by which one could judge all the other competitive ideas. But, on the other hand, there is in your writings a longing for some kind of universal norm of human nature.[2] Is that true?

IB: In the end, all the differences between philosophies and outlooks boil down to different conceptions of human nature. I do say that.

---

1. Letters of 21 January and 24 February 1986, 37–41 above.

2. 'Berlin's intention consists in, so to say, reconciling historicism with some image of 'human nature', conceived of as a sort of a universal *norm*. [. . .] Yet the status of such a norm does seem to me quite clear in Berlin. [. . .] I am inclined to think that this norm, as it is conceived of by him, is revealed to the philosopher by, among other things, precisely the history of ideas.' Szacki, 'Sir Isaiah Berlin: historia idei a filozofia', 206–7.

BP-S: Yet you give an example, to which Szacki refers, of a man to whom it really makes no difference whether he kicks a pebble or kills his family. You state that in such a case we should speak of insanity, not of a different code of morality.

IB: Correct. Or take the famous example of Hume. A man comes along to you and asks whether you would destroy the universe for the sake of curing a pain in your little finger. Why not?

BP-S: So there is something universal in the human world.

IB: Yes, de facto. It's an empirical proposition that there is. Even in ethics. If a man is outside the universal framework in some way, at some point you say, 'That man is mad.' Imagine a man who says, 'I like sticking pins into people.' You say, 'Why?' and he says, 'Because it gives me pleasure.' That's a perfectly good answer. And then you say, 'But why does it give you pleasure?' He says, 'Well, I rather like the feeling of pins entering these surfaces.' You go on and say, 'Look, it causes pain.' And the man says, 'What of it?' And you say, 'But if they did it to you, you wouldn't like it.' He says, 'No, if they did it to me I wouldn't like it. But if I do it to them, I don't suffer any pain. Why should we universalise?' So you say, 'Look, supposing I gave you a rubber ball instead of a human being, would sticking pins be just as pleasant?' 'Yes, just as good.' Then you think that he's mad. He's mad because to say that pain is unimportant, that causing acute pain to human beings is not something of which one takes notice, is not quite human.[1]

Rights

IB: [*reads*] 'Dworkin claims that the idea of liberty as license is untenable and tries to argue it away. Thereby the consensus in favour of some *right to liberty* seems to him absurd. The conclusion is firm: no general right to liberty exists. We have only "distinct rights to certain liberties like the liberty of free expression and of free choice in personal and sexual relations."'[2] I don't know what the difference is between rights and liberties. They are very similar. Have I ever told you my theory about the idea of rights?

BP-S: Yes, you once roughly sketched it, but I would love to have it on my tape!

IB: I'll tell you about it for your tape. Once upon a time, people believed in nat-

---

1. The same example is given elsewhere, e.g., in 'Rationality of Value Judgments', in Carl J. Friedrich, ed., *Nomos VII: Rational Decision* (New York: Atherton Press, 1967), 222.

2. Excerpt from my 'The Twilight of "Liberty" as an Abstract Ideal?', 260–1 below.

ural law. This means that men were created for certain purposes and that they can only fulfil themselves in certain ways: serving God, not telling lies, returning debts, not killing people. A man could not fulfil himself unless he tried to behave according to these laws. If he didn't, it was because he was somewhat distorted, perverted, crippled. A normal man must want to serve himself. That's what natural laws are: *pacta sunt servanda* in the old sense. Then Spinoza appeared and said that there were no natural laws. The universe was simply a collection of people and things bound together by all kinds of metaphysical necessities. Therefore goals are made by men. The goal of a clock is to show the time because I made it so. What is my goal? My goal is to eat, my goal is to make men more free, my goal is to write a book, my goal is to serve the truth. And, of course, it is right to serve the truth and my goal is to do what is right. But it needn't have been, there might have been wicked men who said, 'My goal is to tell lies.' That is possible. If you don't believe that God made man, as Spinoza didn't, then natural law evaporates and the idea of purposes means human purposes. Now, rights are based on the fact that I will require certain things if I am to follow natural law: I require a certain degree of freedom, I require food, I require drink, I require the possibility of moving, I require love. If I don't have them, I cannot realise my God-given goal. Those are natural rights, but they disappear once you deny natural law. It's still possible to believe in them, but the reason for them has evaporated. Jefferson, in the famous preamble to the American Constitution, says that every man has a right to life, liberty and the pursuit of happiness. That's because he believes that nature has been created by God. But if you are an atheist, it's different. Then the question is, what are rights? Well, I think that there are certain things which we believe or know, if we believe in knowledge, to be right. If the things which are right are in my interest, I instruct you to do what is right, which you then have a duty to do. If I don't instruct you, in which case it is not necessary to do your duty, I don't claim it as a right. I can waive my rights, I can abjure my rights, I can lend my rights to you. I can't have rights against myself. I may have a right that you should not stop me from doing this, but you have a right to give me food or not, you have a right to demand money from me or sue me. That means that it is wrong for me not to pay, and you profit by the fact that I don't do what is wrong. That's all. That's the only sense in which I can reason about rights. Anyway, go to Gray. Give him this paper.[1] Tell him that I object and say that I'd be delighted to meet you both. We could have a discussion about Popper.

---

1. 'The Twilight of "Liberty" as an Abstract Ideal?'

6 May 1988

(with John Gray)

Three people were engaged in this conversation: Isaiah Berlin, John Gray and myself. We met at All Souls College, Oxford.

Popper's Critique of Essentialism

BP-S: There were two controversial points on which we disagreed during our last meeting. You questioned my interpretation of Popper's essentialism[1] and then his attitude towards discussing values. Dr Gray was kind enough to read my piece on that.

IB: One thing I was very shocked about were your quotations from Popper. Indeed, I was shocked at Popper. I had no idea that he objects to enquiries into meaning.

JG: Yes, he does.

IB: It's a terrible thing. I can't see how any philosopher can do without.

JG: He says that anyone who talks about the meaning of words is an essentialist.

IB: Is an *essentialist*! Well that assumes that every word pins on to an object.

JG: Yes, but, for example, Austin and Wittgenstein would both be essentialists, which is absurd.

IB: Yes, it's absurd, but in general, without knowing what words mean or how people use words, I can't even read them. It's extraordinary, it

---

1. ibid., 255–6 below.

seems to me fanatical in some curious way. It's all directed against positivism. It's against saying that the meaning of a proposition is the means of its verification. The meaning of a proposition is not the thing we want to know about. We want to know if it's true or false, we understand what it means without help.

JG: That's right, without analysis.

IB: Without help, too. We all know what these words mean, so there's no point in bothering with it. I didn't realise how far it went.

BP-S: Popper interpreted essentialism in such an extreme way only in his intellectual autobiography.[1]

IB: I'm really interested in his disciples in that respect. Do any of them have the appearance of saying the same thing?

JG: Well, he has so few disciples left anyway . . .

IB: Oh, you talk to [Bryan] Magee and he'll tell you that great congresses of Popperists meet in America, in Germany, in Italy, everywhere in the world, full of Popper disciples. But they are not philosophers, perhaps.

JG: No, that's just it. Some are scientists, some are psychologists—very few philosophers.

IB: I'll tell you who was: Lakatos was. You know what Lakatos said about him?

JG: No.

IB: I found out the other day. He thought that *The Open Society and Its Enemies* should have been called *The Open Society by One of Its Enemies*.

JG: That's very good!

IB: Lakatos was remarkable. He was a Hungarian socialist and Communist. He was very Stalinist and one of the real commissars in Hungary after 1947/8. Then in 1956 he quarrelled with the Communists and decided he couldn't go on. He was a mathematician by training. He read mathematical physics and mathematical philosophy, and he became a devoted disciple of Popper. There was a tremendous breach, and then he died. I don't know what he was in the end.

JG: He considered himself a sort of critical Popperian.

IB: He was a very clever man.

JG: Very. His essays on Popper are cleverer than Popper. Much better.

IB: But he was always a little mad. He was offered a job here, in mathematical logic. And there was a committee, attached to this College, on

---

1. '*Never let yourself be goaded into taking seriously problems about words and their meanings. What must be taken seriously are questions of fact, and assertions about facts: theories and hypotheses; the problems they solve; and the problems they raise.*' Popper, *Unended Quest*, 19; cf. 61 above, 256 below.

which I sat for some reason. He sent us a telegram saying that he went as far as Reading station for the interview, but then thought better of it and went back.

JG: He died very young, didn't he?

IB: Yes, sadly. Popper said of him, 'I cannot put his recommendation in higher terms than the following five words: he has changed my ideas.' More than that no man could hope to do. It was quite funny. I'm sorry, let's go back. First of all, essentialism.

BP-S: His understanding of it evolved.

IB: In *The Open Society* it has a clear meaning. All that essentialism means is that things have an unchanging core or nature which cannot be altered by empirical forces and which determines their development, i.e., their future or whatever they have. That's what he thinks Plato or Aristotle says.[1] And they do, he's right on that, since they do believe in essences. Kant believed that, Leibniz believed that, and quite a lot of others.

JG: Even Spinoza.

IB: Spinoza believed that. Metaphysics is the study of the nature and development of entities in the world without empirical help. Well, with empirical help, but so that empirical evidence cannot be followed. So in theory, if you have a special kind of eye, a magic eye, by looking at a chicken very, very steadily you would know that it must produce eggs, without ever seeing it happen.

JG: Yes, it is the nature of a chicken to produce eggs.

IB: The nature of a chicken is to be unable to avoid producing eggs, and you would be able to predict that it will produce eggs without anyone having ever seen an egg. That is a slight parody of it but, in a way, it's what it comes to. Man must develop in certain ways and if he does not develop in that way then he is warped, then he is twisted, then he's a failure of creation. That's what it all comes to. It is monistic because you can't have two paths which this entity is compelled metaphysically to go along.

JG: So essences can't contain inconsistencies or even complexities.

IB: Exactly. They cannot. I don't think anyone thinks they can. Essences are dialectical in Hegel. Essences do not exactly contain contradictions. They contain development, which takes the form of certain conflicts, which then result in something else. The conflicts are inevitable, the results are inevitable, the whole thing is foretold. Few people foretell it

---

1. 'I use the name *methodological essentialism* to characterise the view, held by Plato and many of his followers, that it is the task of pure knowledge or "science" to discover and to describe the true nature of things, i.e. their hidden reality or essence.' Popper, *The Open Society*, 2: 31.

because they are too stupid, or too ignorant, or too prejudiced, or haven't read Hegel. But in principle . . .

JG: So Popper's early sense of essentialism was very clear.

IB: Perfectly clear, and that's what he denies, and that's why all empiricists are in favour of Popper and that book of his. But there is the other sense, according to which the examination of words depends on thinking that words are in some metaphysical way attached to something in the universe, like caps attached to heads.

JG: He claims that the early Wittgenstein thought that.

IB: Well, the early Wittgenstein said that all words were names of atomic facts. And since the world consisted of atomic facts, if you had enough names, and the relations between the names were adjusted to the relations between the facts, then you could read off what relates to what, as if from a sheet of graph paper.

JG: Popper seems to think that anyone who's concerned about meanings must have that belief.

IB: Atomic facts are simply a private invention of Russell which Wittgenstein took over. Nobody except Russell and Wittgenstein believed in atomic facts. It was a specific belief, attached to a particular metaphysical doctrine of what the world consisted of, and it was really believed only by two philosophers and their disciples at the time.

JG: Wittgenstein said a funny thing, didn't he, when he abandoned the view . . .

IB: 'My God,' he said, 'I thought all words were names and they're not.'

JG: Yes, and then he said, 'I've never given an example of an atomic fact. I thought it was a purely empirical matter.'

IB: They were like little bits of stuff, tiny little things, little atoms. He said that they were indivisible, the ultimate constituents of the world. It's very naive in a way, but Leibniz thought the same. It was an attempt to say that mathematics can be applied to the world, and if there was a language which accurately reflected the mathematical structure of reality, you could read the structure off. So it's an old idea which comes to Russell via Leibniz, I would think.

JG: Yes, of course his first book was on Leibniz.

IB: Not his first book; his first book was on German social democracy.[1] Sorry, back to essentialism.

BP-S: You questioned what I said about Popper; that he believes in the unity of method.

---

1. Bertrand Russell, *German Social Democracy: Six Lectures* (London: Longmans, Green, 1896).

JG: I think he does, doesn't he?

IB: Well, maybe, but I have one more question. He certainly believes in the unity of method in the sciences, that's clear. He thinks that the *Logik der Forschung*, research establishing a theory in the sciences, follows a very definite formula. But I'm not so sure that he applies that to the world, and certainly not to ethics.

JG: No, certainly not to ethics.

IB: Nor to common sense. Because they're subjective, because they're not science.

JG: Nor to metaphysics.

BP-S: But how about the social sciences?

IB: Well, ideally, yes. He knows it doesn't quite work, but in principle, yes. You're quite right. He thinks that economics and sociology are capable of being sciences. Most people do.

JG: That's where his disciple Soros disagrees with him, isn't it? He says he's a methodological dualist. He says his work as a financier has convinced him that there are no laws in the social sciences.

IB: He's quite right. That's why Popper disapproved of me. The first difference I had with Popper was on what I wrote in an article entitled 'History and Theory'.[1] It was the first article of the first number of a journal called *History and Theory*; the periodical is named after that article. I never wrote for it again. There I made an attempt to show that the application of scientific method to history is bound to be a failure. I don't say that I believe everything in it, but the fundamental thesis was this: When you say about a historian, 'He's very doctrinaire', that is a reproach. Nobody says about scientists that they are doctrinaire, because doctrines are their business. Scientists can't operate without theories. Yet why do you think it is said about historians, 'He's very doctrinaire'? As a criticism. The assumption is that there is some kind of theory into which the facts can be fitted, and if some facts don't fit, you have to do something with the facts, squeeze them or squash them, rather like Marxism. There were lots of historical theorists. Hegel was one, Spengler was one, Toynbee was one.

JG: Hayek does that, too.

IB: Hayek, yes, I'm sure. He believes that there is a theory.[2] He doesn't believe it about social science, you remember. Scientism is a heresy.

JG: That's right.

---

1. 'History and Theory: The Concept of Scientific History', *History and Theory* 1 (1960), 1–31, reprinted in *Concepts and Categories*, 103–42, and in *The Proper Study of Mankind*, 17–58.

2. A reference to Hayek's idea of a spontaneous social order and so-called 'conjectural history'.

IB: Hayek says that the attempt to apply the new methods of the new sciences which came to fruition in the early nineteenth century, in France particularly, is a fatal application of the theory of the natural sciences to human events. That leads in the end to despotism, to tyranny and all the rest of it. That is very Hayek. That, I think, Popper doesn't accept.

BP-S: He says that the methods of the natural sciences and the social sciences are very close.

IB: Very close. That's an attempt to say truth is a science. Freud said, 'Science may not be able to solve all problems, but you may be sure that what science can't solve, nothing else will either.' That's virtually Popper.

BP-S: He says in *Conjectures and Refutations* that the aim of the social sciences is to trace unintended consequences.[1]

IB: Well, that's all right.

BP-S: And that this is testable empirically.

IB: Well, no doubt any given doctrine about the unintended consequences of factors A, B, C, D can be tested. If you are sure you have enough instances, well, then of course any general proposition can be tested. It's undeniable that sociologists, psychologists, and you and I make a large number of propositions beginning with the word 'any' or beginning with the word 'all', and that all these propositions, in principle, can be tested. But it doesn't follow that the methods of the sciences—experiment, observation etc.—apply to everything. Let me give you an example. When Engels said, 'In the absence of a Napoleon, someone else would have taken his place',[2] how do you test that?

JG: You can't.

IB: Or if someone says, 'A lot of what you're doing now, if there were a genius, he would have done.' Maybe, maybe not. Anyhow, I stick to my dogmatic, narrow view of the possibility of applying the methods of the natural sciences to history. What methods occur in history is another matter. My view is quite simple—it's rather like Vico. Anything which the natural sciences can do, they should do. Whatever can be done— probability calculations, examinations of the effects of climate, of the weather, examination of biological factors, physiological factors, anything which you can do in natural science—should be done. You mustn't

---

1. 'The characteristic problems of the social sciences arise only out of our wish to know the *unintended consequences*, and more especially the *unwanted consequences*, which may arise if we do certain things.' Karl R. Popper, *Conjectures and Refutations: The Growth of Scientific Knowledge* (London: Routledge, 1972), 124.

2. See 55 above, note 2.

stop, you mustn't say it's no good, it doesn't apply. But after that everything is left because . . .

BP-S: The third basket.[1]

IB: The third basket, all right. I'll tell you another thing which I believe, and about which there is disagreement between me and others, although it's never come out in the form of controversy. Take the analysis of the French Revolution. The first thing which the scientific historian, in that sense of scientific, would have to do would be to say, 'What is common to the French Revolution and all other revolutions which we know about?' Can you examine, for example, the English Revolution, or the American Revolution, or the Russian Revolution, or the 1848 revolutions, or forty-seven other revolutions? And from that you would abstract something which you regard as common to all revolutions as such. This could be done. I don't deny that you probably would get a result. There are things common to all revolutions. They occur when the previous regime was not very strong, or where indignation on the part of a large number of people is of a sufficient degree of violence, whatever. But then, after you've done all that, what people really want to know about the French Revolution is: What happened then? What is unique to that revolution, not what it has in common with others. What Danton did, what Robespierre did, what happened in this situation, who was then killed, what did they want and how was it frustrated, why didn't this happen, why didn't that happen? Karl Marx believed the opposite. He said that the French Revolution went wrong because they didn't take account of enough theories. For example, they were entirely interested in politics, or they were interested in a strong political desire for liberty, not in economics, not in sociology. If they'd attended to that, the French Revolution wouldn't have failed. Because a revolution made on the basis of strict scientific knowledge would be enabled to predict the results of certain actions. You have to take these actions, and the results follow. If you apply a match to a piece of paper, it will burn. If you know enough, you can guarantee a successful revolution.

The main thing about the French Revolution is this. The whole of social theory in the first half of the nineteenth century is concerned with

---

1. Berlin believed that questions could be separated into three categories (or 'baskets'): questions that are answered formally according to pre-arranged rules (such as those encountered in formal logic or chess), questions that are answered empirically (such as 'What colour is the sky?'), and questions, normally called 'philosophical', that do not fit easily into either of these categories. Berlin, 'The Purpose of Philosophy', in *Concepts and Categories*, 1–11, especially pp. 1–3 (see a long quotation from this article in a note to the previous conversation, 169 above, note 2).

this question: Why did the French Revolution fail? That's a question which troubles everybody. The Catholics said it was because of atheism in Paris, wickedness, because we wandered from the word of God, because we abandoned the revealed truth, we abandoned principles by which we lived. The Marxists said economic remedies were not sufficiently attended to. The Saint-Simonians said science was not sufficiently attended to. The liberals—and Saint-Simon, too—said that the Revolution failed because the masses were released and they guillotined the élite.

JG: The liberals also cited the evil influence of Rousseau, didn't they?

IB: Well, all right, but Tolstoy was much the funniest. Tolstoy was, of course, the greatest sceptic about the possibility of scientific history who's ever lived. He says: If we ask about the causes of the French Revolution, some say it was the sufferings of the French people—taxation and poverty. Some people say it was because the King betrayed the constitution, or the King was wicked, and his wife, Marie Antoinette, was even worse. Some blame the decline of religion. Others say little books had done it: Rousseau, Voltaire, all these works were evil. That's what historians claim, but you can't fuse these answers, you can't say it was books plus religion plus private character plus psychology. Or one cause is economics, one is history of ideas, one is sociology, one is whatever it may be. And the idea of lumping all these together and saying, '*These* are the causes of the French Revolution' can't be rational. That's what Tolstoy says, quite amusingly, in that epilogue to *War and Peace*. Sorry, this is all irrelevant.

BP-S: No it's not. Anyway, the last controversial thing was the status of values in Popper's system.

IB: Is he purely subjective?

JG: I think he is, yes. I think he's a subjectivist about values.

IB: I think it's just what we happen to believe. Considering the passion with which he denounces the wrong theory, you'd presume that he thinks there are certain eternal values, but he doesn't say that, because scientific method comes in first.

JG: He said, on the one occasion I met him, 'All this talk about values is in very bad taste.'

IB: That's wonderful, yes. I'll tell you, he has one disciple: Oppenheim.

JG: Felix Oppenheim? Yes, I know Felix.

BP-S: Oh, the one who wrote *Dimensions of Freedom*?[1]

IB: Yes, he is a Popperist in this respect, and that's called 'value neutrality'. He calls himself value-neutral.

---

1. Felix Oppenheim, *Dimensions of Freedom: An Analysis* (New York: St Martin's Press, 1961).

JG: Values are preferences.

IB: Well, subjective preferences of groups or of individuals. You can't say they are right or wrong, you can't say they are true or false, and you can't do anything with them, you can only fight wars against them.

JG: But I think there's another aspect of it. I remember Freud (who has much in common with Popper, I think) saying, 'To me, right and wrong have always been obvious.'

IB: Very Freudian.

JG: 'It was always obvious to me', and it's the same with Popper. The reason why he's not interested in conflicts of values is that he thinks it's easy and obvious to know what to do.

IB: Well, all right, but supposing you contradict it? Then no argument is possible.

JG: That's right.

IB: Supposing I say: You don't agree, but I think Fascism is splendid. I think it's wonderful to kill twenty million people, whether you enjoy it or not. I rather like violence, history would be very boring if there wasn't that.

JG: Like D. H. Lawrence, that sort of thing.

IB: Well, yes. There was a Russian thinker called Leontiev who was a kind of religious thinker of the 1850s and 1860s. He was a diplomat, really. He was an extreme homosexual, too, which was unusual in Russia at that time. He was a Russian Consul in the Balkans, in Tulcha, and then he became wildly religious and very mystical and quite interesting, but he hated liberalism with a blind hatred and he secretly became a monk in the end. He went and lived at Optina Pustyn, a famous monastery which I also visited. He wrote quite an interesting literary essay on the novels of Count Lev Nikolaevich Tolstoy. Now he says:

Is it not dreadful, is it not degrading to suppose that Moses climbed Mount Sinai, that the Hellenes built their magnificent Acropoleis, that the Romans fought their Punic Wars, that the brilliant, handsome Alexander crossed the Granicus in his plumed helmet and fought at Arbela, that the Apostles preached, martyrs suffered, poets sang, painters painted, and knights glittered at tournaments—and all of this so that the French, German and Russian bourgeois in his hideous and ridiculous clothing might indulge in the pleasures of life, 'individually' or 'collectively', on the ruins of all this past greatness?[1]

---

1. Konstantin Nikolaevich Leontiev, *Vostok, Rossia i Slavyanstv* [*The East, Russia and Slavdom*] (Moskva: Respublika,1996), 373 (my translation). I have substituted the original for Berlin's remembered paraphrase.

It's a Nietzschean point of view, it's in a sense rather close to nature. It wasn't to create a horrible egalitarian, modern world of dreary, middle-class bourgeois, trying to make profits, that the great Greek conquerors destroyed Oriental civilisation. 'Alexander the Great in his plumed helmet', that was the phrase.

JG: Was it Leontiev who said, 'Russia is like a piece of rotting meat, the only thing that can be done with it is to freeze it for as long as possible'?

IB: He might have, but it was Pobedonostsev who said, 'Freeze it up, don't let progress happen.' Meaning that scientists are dangerous and progress is dangerous. That was the advice given to Nicholas II, whose tutor he was. He was the procurator of the Holy Synod and a professor of inter-national law, an extremely clever man, but violently reactionary in his ideas. Even Dostoevsky was a little bit frightened of him.

JG: I remember an anecdote. Someone said to this man, 'What about public opinion?' and he spat on the floor and then ground the spittle with his heel and walked away.

IB: Yes, exactly. He also said, 'The world is something like a desert on which the evil one walks about.'

JG: Popper would think that Leontiev was mad or something.

IB: Oh, absolutely. But I don't suppose he would think that about the entire romantic movement. The romantics are people who don't like equality, who want change, excitement, differences, who want the world to be full of colour, unexpectedness. And then you say, 'Well, but a lot of people suffer', to which they answer, 'So what, what does it matter?'

JG: Perhaps better so.

IB: Well, but even if I don't want them to suffer. If they do, too bad. You remember in the film *The Third Man*, based on the novel by Graham Greene, there is this man who sells drugs and kills people, makes money in post-war Vienna; and when his friend says, 'How can you be so evil?' he says, 'In Italy for thirty years under the Borgias they had warfare, terror, murder and bloodshed, but they produced Michelangelo, Leonardo da Vinci and the Renaissance. In Switzerland they had brotherly love—they had five hundred years of democracy and peace, and what did that pro-duce? The cuckoo clock.'[1] The *condottieri*, Cesare Borgia, the Medici, they didn't mind. That was real heart, heroism. Down with mediocrity and equality and humanity, and all the old things! It's a view which you may reject, but it's perfectly European. What Popper would say, then, is just, as you say, 'I'm not interested.' That's just dogmatism.

---

1. I have substituted the original for Berlin's remembered paraphrase.

JG: Or he would say, 'It's uncivilised', or something like that.

IB: So why be civilised? It's only swapping one value for another. Wittgenstein on ethics was very obvious, you know. He thought that ethical theory was absurd because in the end it was always using ethical attributes as if they were natural, and utilitarianism was simply business speculation on what was likely to give you most pleasure, and nothing to do with ethics. Well, if it gives pleasure, why not? Ethical values to him were a question of some kind of direct mystical illumination which you can't put in words. That's the famous sentence from the *Tractatus* which says: 'Wovon man nicht sprechen kann, darüber muss man schweigen.' 'What one cannot speak of, thereof one must be silent.' That's ethics. Once you try to fit it into words, you vulgarise it. It's like Kierkegaard.

JG: It may be that Popper has some sort of whiff of that view, not of course the mystical element, but the view of ethics as consisting entirely in individual . . .

IB: No, but it isn't individual for Wittgenstein. The individual he gets rid of. Either you see these things or you don't, and you can't talk to somebody who doesn't. If someone doesn't see it, then you ignore him. I mean, it's not a question you can argue about. You can despise him, but he doesn't see it. It is the truth in a sense, but you can't speak it. It's like mystical Christianity.

JG: Interestingly as well, though, doesn't Popper deny that there's progress in the arts? I'm thinking that that is the one area where Popper thinks there's no progress.

IB: I don't think there is progress in the arts, is there?

JG: Well, probably not. Not in ethics, either. In the realm of values, there can't be, I suppose.

IB: How can there be? That's also untrue about the arts. It's true and untrue; there is a certain sense in which it's true. The theory of linear progress, which the seventeenth century believed, is of course absurd. To say that Michelangelo is a primitive Picasso is rather difficult.

JG: Or that Shakespeare was a proto-Corneille.

IB: Exactly. But within certain periods, certain schools of art, one can talk of progress. You can say that the discovery of perspective within a certain school of painting made it more possible for the artists to realise certain ideals. You can say that Leonardo is in some ways an advance on Verrocchio because the purposes, the attitudes, were sufficiently similar. One can talk about progress within schools of art, or movements. But between them, no.

JG: But if you asked Popper, 'Well, what about a culture like Russia? Supposing Leontiev's attitudes expressed something in Russian culture?' He would just have to say 'I hate it' or . . .

IB: Not exactly. No, he wouldn't say, 'I hate it', he would say 'It's monstrous.'

JG: It's monstrous, yes.

IB: 'Down with it, suppress it.' You say, 'Why?' 'Because it's obvious,' he would say.

JG: Moral simplicity. It's very morally simple, isn't it?

IB: Einstein is morally simple, you know. I'm sure that Einstein had morally simple views.

JG: Well, even Freud appears wise in his controversies with Einstein over the causes of war. Freud says they're very deep, Einstein says it's misunderstanding.

IB: I'm sure. He doesn't know any of the facts.

JG: The argument is that people don't understand each other.

IB: But they could.

JG: But they could and, if they did, they would be harmonious. And Freud says: 'Nonsense.'

IB: So Freud is right. We all know Freud is right, about everything Freud is right. People living in the twentieth century are less likely to believe that Einstein is right than anyone living in the nineteenth. To say that if Hitler or Stalin understood people they would not have done the things they did seems rather a difficult proposition. They understood quite a lot.

JG: Yes, very well, in fact.

IB: Well, more than that. Too well, in some sense.

22 and 30 May 1988

Our antepenultimate meeting in 1988 (on 16 May) had proved to be a great disappointment from the technical point of view. I had been allowed to record the conversation, but afterwards my tape-recorder turned out to have failed. During that meeting, the topic of the model political man of action somehow cropped up. Berlin gave a captivating talk on the capacity for natural integration of multiple factors which, in his view, is responsible for a talent for politics. It was not an easy task to persuade him to recapitulate the main points of the unrecorded conversation, but he eventually agreed.

The Political Man of Action

IB: In political, economic, social action of any kind there is always the difficulty that the number of factors involved is usually very large, or infinite. And although disciplines like economics, sociology, political science, psychology or history provide quite a lot of information about the way human beings behave, there are nevertheless many factors which these disciplines don't embrace and which, in any concrete situation, come into play. So one of the things which I've noticed is that revolutions very seldom succeed in producing the results for which they were planned, because they concentrate on only some particular section of human experience. Let's call it the top of the iceberg, which can be seen. But there is a large sunken part which cannot be seen, and in which the changes in the top part will cause reactions. The sunken part will then produce a reaction of its own which will trigger off unpredicted, maybe unpredictable, results. Those, in turn, will frustrate the intentions of the original planners. The most successful political men of action are those who have some kind of natural capacity for understanding, which is different from knowledge of facts. It's the kind of understanding which we have of, for example, the meaning of sentences, or human character, or the behaviour of people we know, or works of art. That sort of understanding applies to public life as well. A kind of natural integration of all the factors does occur in the same way as when you understand a man's sentence without having to worry about the grammar, the vocabulary, or the meanings of words. You've learnt it at some time, but by now you function automatically. It's like the way in which you come into a room: you take in everything in the room without having to take it in bit by bit. This capacity for integrating gives you understanding of both situations and characters. But it cannot be analysed into its own separate strands, which is the only thing that a proper science can do. That's what we call genius or talent for understanding how human beings behave. It is displayed in exactly the same way by a sculptor or a painter who understands the medium in which he works without being able to analyse it. That was my first point. Now what else was there?

BP-S: You told me about your typology of statesmen.

IB: One is a man who has infinite sensibility to the way that people think or feel, a natural instinct for knowing what the public will take and what the public won't take, how people will react and how they will not react, what can be done and what can't be done to them. Like, in my lifetime, Mr Roosevelt and Mr Lloyd George. The other type is represented by de Gaulle and Churchill, who were hypnotists, who had blinkers, who had very clear vision. They ignored everything which disturbed them, ignored a large part of the real world and simply bound their spell upon the people whom they tried to direct, and in this way actually changed people's own reactions. They didn't respond to reactions, they shaped them.

Conflicts of Values: Discussion of Bhikhu Parekh

BP-S: In an article by Parekh there is a long passage concerning conflicts of values. As this is a crucial point, I would like to learn what your view of Parekh's argument is. Here is the relevant excerpt:

Berlin's concept of the conflict of values is somewhat ambiguous. It is not entirely clear why and how in his view the conflicts arise. He seems to advance the following four theses.

Firstly, some conflicts of values owe their origin to the prevailing form of social organisation. They are therefore contingent and could be eliminated if the society were to be structured differently. The conflicts between liberty and equality or between spontaneity and efficiency belong to this category.

Secondly, some conflicts of values arise out of certain ineliminable features of the human condition, such as the scarcity of material resources, time and space. The conflicts between greater economic growth and a desire for greater leisure, and between the desire to be a first-rate doctor and a world-class athlete[,] would seem to arise respectively from the scarcity of material resources and time.

Thirdly, some conflicts seem to owe their origins to human nature in general or to the nature of specific human capacities. It is not necessary that a singer should lose his passion and inspiration to sing when made conscious of the unconscious motives behind his wish to sing. The conflict occurs because men are so constituted, either by nature or in a given historical epoch, that they like their activities to spring from noble motives. Again, justice and mercy conflict because they require very different attitudes to rules, human relations, and so on.

Finally, some conflicts of values are inherent in the values concerned. As Berlin's discussion of Machiavelli shows, one cannot pursue both the morality of pagan self-assertion and that of Christianity. By their very nature, they are incompatible; to pursue one is necessarily to reject the other. Such conflicts of values differ from the other three. They do not arise from factors external to the values involved, but are rooted in the very nature of the latter. As such they cannot be eliminated under any conceivable form of society, human condition and human nature. Not surprisingly, Berlin generally concentrates upon them. In doing so he establishes the reality of the conflict of values beyond a shadow of doubt. However, he also leaves the false impression that all conflicts are of this kind, and therefore ineliminable.[1]

IB: Parekh's four points really come to two points. First, there are certain conflicts of value which depend on particular circumstances. For example, if your father is drowning on your right and your mother is drowning on your left, you can't save them both. Therefore you have to choose and it's very painful. But that's due to the fact that one is on the right and the other is on the left; if they were together, you could save

---

1. Bhikhu Parekh, 'Review Article: The Political Thought of Sir Isaiah Berlin', *British Journal of Political Science* 12 (1982), 209–10.

them. The reason you can't is empirical. If you haven't got enough time to be both a dentist and a musical critic, you have to choose; but if you had plenty of time, you would first be a dentist, then a musical critic. You could do both. It simply depends upon the nature of the situation in which you find yourself. These are empirical facts, which could be otherwise. Sometimes they can be altered, sometimes they can't. But in all these cases it's a question of things that can be otherwise. Second, there is the other, conceptual, kind of conflict: mercy and justice, according to Parekh, depend on differences of attitude. But they don't: they depend on differences between the actual, core qualities of character; to do justice means to do certain things, to be merciful is to do certain other things, whatever the motive. The two things can't be combined because they're completely different, they constitute different kinds of action. So also with equality and liberty. The only example he gives is pagan self-assertion and Christianity, which clearly can't be combined. But there are others, like liberty and equality, or duty and feeling.

BP-S: So if you have only one artificial kidney and many patients who need it, this is an empirical conflict?

IB: Yes, it's an empirical fact. Of course, you might have had two. An empirical fact is something that can be otherwise. It's a historical accident that you've only one kidney. Naturally your alternatives are limited because you have only one kidney. Quite often, choice involves conflicting values. Some of these conflicts could be solved by a change in the empirical situation, which in principle could be brought about, and some couldn't. I think that is all.

The Eternally Recurring Theme: Negative versus Positive Liberty

BP-S: I have come across a challenging interpretation of the negative concept of liberty in Raymond Aron. Will you have a look at it?

Freedom, according to F. A. Hayek, is quite simply the absence of coercion. [. . .] What is the concrete freedom which serves as the model for this definition of freedom? Obviously, the freedom of the entrepreneur or the consumer: the first is free to take the initiative and to combine the means of production, the second free in the use he will make of buying power provided by his monetary income. But neither the worker in the production line, nor the employee inside a vast organisation, nor the soldier who is subject to strict discipline, nor the Jesuit who has taken a vow of obedience is free, according to this definition. Indeed, the very nature of industrial society seems inexorably to reduce the number of persons for whom this kind of freedom is accessible, at least in work.[1]

There seems to be something in it!

IB: All he is saying is that the entrepreneur is free in a way in which the worker is not. The entrepreneur is free and the consumer is free. The man who is not free is the man who hasn't got enough money to be a consumer and who hasn't got enough freedom of action to be an entrepreneur. That's what he's saying.

BP-S: As I understand him, what he wants to say is that negative liberty is not a universal value.

IB: No, I don't think he says that. What he is saying is that the entrepreneur has more negative liberty than the worker, and the consumer who has money has more negative liberty than a consumer who has none. The point I wish to make is this: the worker can't choose, because he's a worker and is under a discipline. He hasn't got the liberty of choice which the entrepreneur has. What he lacks is the means of making the choice, namely of being an entrepreneur. A worker is perfectly free to live at the Ritz; there is a difference between a situation where the worker is forbidden and where the worker hasn't got enough money. It could be said that not earning enough money is the absence of the liberty of possessing money, the absence of the means of getting money, and this is due to the fact that the capitalists have robbed him.

BP-S: But it's not only a question of means. What he says is that this model of negative liberty does not apply at work. It's not workers' inability to live at the Ritz that he has in mind, but their having the bottom status in the hierarchy of employees.

IB: So long as there are workers in a factory, they will be deprived of quite a lot of liberty. The very nature of industrial society condemns a lot of people to lack of liberty; on that he's quite right. They haven't got the means with which to be free; the means are taken away from them by somebody else. So in that sense they lack positive liberty. Positive liberty means: Who is master? Who is the boss? Am I? Or is he? In a factory, the entrepreneur is the boss. Negative liberty is a universal quality in the sense that even the worker has the negative liberty either of working or

---

1. Raymond Aron, *An Essay on Freedom* (New York and Cleveland: World Publishing, 1970), 88–9.

stopping work, either of living or dying; even that's a negative liberty. Not everything can be taken away. But the entrepreneur has a lot of positive liberty and this makes the worker lose his negative liberty. The negative liberty of workers is very limited in an industrial society.

BP-S: There's another thing. May I bore you once again? I know we've already talked about these issues . . .

IB: No, I'm not getting bored. I'm not very borable.

BP-S: If I understand you properly, the main idea which flows from your essay is that we should be clear about the ways in which we use the word *liberty*.

IB: That's right. The word *liberty* means what it means. Well, all words are ambiguous to some extent. One mustn't say that all words are clear. Of course not. All words are used in different senses and all words are general. Words aren't names. There isn't a single thing which the word *liberty* means. But the way in which people use the word *liberty* is too wide, it includes too many things which one wouldn't normally mean by liberty. Not everything good is liberty; it doesn't include everything that people want. Liberty has been too widely interpreted.

BP-S: So it's somehow dangerous to assign this wide meaning to liberty.

IB: Because liberty is a good thing, people try to get a lot of things under the blanket which they also want.

BP-S: So it's better to differentiate between goods and not to cheat about the concept in question.

IB: Well, you must be as precise as you can, but not too precise.

BP-S: What your essay, as I understand it, amounts to is a warning. But there is a crucial thing which you never say. How should one take advantage of your warning?

IB: Simply by asking yourself how you use the word. Take various types of situations, sentences, whatever you like, in which it is natural to talk about freedom. If you take fourteen contexts in which 'political freedom' is used, then you'll see that the word is ambiguous; and the question is: Is there something common to all these? If there is something common, then that's what the word *freedom* stands for. If there's nothing common, then the word *freedom* doesn't mean much, or it should be applied only to one of these things. In a way, the word *freedom* is not used in different senses. Positive and negative freedom have something in common with each other, because they ultimately refer to the possibility of choice: in one case to the removal of obstacles, in the other case to the removal of authority, which is more or less the same in some ways. Well, that's not the whole difference. In the first case, liberty means: How many doors are open? In the second case it means: Who is in charge here? Do I do what I want? Am I the source of my conduct or is it pressure from him?

BP-S: So your exhortation is that we should try to use the word . . .

IB: As we normally use it. There's no need to tighten it. Let's simply ask ourselves, 'How do we use these words? Do we use them in many different ways? If there are different ways, is there something that these ways have in common?' Maybe there isn't a common kernel. Let me give you an example which I do not use in that essay, though perhaps I should have done, and which certainly goes far beyond the two concepts. You know Wittgenstein's famous example of the family face?

BP-S: Yes, I do.[1]

IB: That could be applied to liberty, too. Liberty A resembles liberty B, liberty B resembles liberty C, liberty A is not at all like liberty C. Positive and negative liberty have some kind of family resemblance, they do.

BP-S: People read many things into you. And you leave the question of how the two freedoms should be balanced completely open.

IB: That depends on the circumstances, the concrete situation.

BP-S: But if they clashed?

IB: Well, then you've got to choose. You needn't choose the whole of A, or the whole of B; maybe a quarter A and half B, like equality and liberty. If you say, 'Why should I obey?' and 'How far should I obey?', those are two different questions. There must be a compromise. Why should I obey? Because otherwise there would be chaos. Therefore I have to have authority. I have to obey certain laws. How far do I obey? Do I have to obey if I am told to kill my mother? Then I stop obeying, because I don't want to close that door. So, as in all such cases, the question of positive versus negative liberty is: How does one blend them? How do I combine them? There's absolutely no one who can say. We do our best. The whole business about my thesis is that positive liberty has been abused in such a way that it becomes the only liberty, and the other liberty is extinguished. But the same is true of negative liberty; terrible things happen if there's too little positive liberty.

BP-S: But you once told me that if negative liberty is totally denied, there is no liberty at all.

IB: Ah, that's the other thing. That means there's no choice. That's the basic sense of liberty which means choosing between A and not-A. Unless you can choose, you are not a person. Then, after you have been given this liberty, there is then the next question: How much should be allowed to

---

1. cf. 41 above.

your power of choice and how much to the authority of others?—kings, or generals, or schoolmasters, or laws, or whatever it is. There are two senses of negative liberty. One is the basic sense without which you can't have a person at all, and the other is simply that which could come into conflict with other values, like happiness, knowledge, pleasure etc.

BP-S: Yet you write at the end of your essay that negative liberty seems to you truer and more humane.

IB: It's only for the reason that people who stress positive liberty have, on the whole, destroyed more lives than people who stress negative liberty. I shouldn't have said that.

BP-S: What made me wonder was the word *truer*.

IB: More true because the basic sense of liberty was at the back of my mind. The problem with that essay is that I did not distinguish between the basic sense and the ordinary.

BP-S: Yes, but on the whole you are more for negative liberty or not? Depends on the circumstances?

IB: Yes. I think I believe in it more. It's not that I like it more. By nature I accept authority, by nature I am very conformist. I am not *révolté* as a character, I've never risen against the society in which I live, I've never rebelled, but in theory I believe in rebellion. Temperamentally, I'm a positive libertarian. But in belief, doctrine, ideals: negative. It always happens that the weak man admires the strong, that people who are very peaceful become terribly fond of violence in theory. People on the whole live very conformist and untroubled lives. They don't find any difficulty in obeying the law or living according to the rules of ordinary bourgeois society. But I've always developed a taste for the opposite. That's clearly a not very agreeable tendency in a philosophical light.

BP-S: You are generally labelled as a terribly narrow negativist liberal, and I have always felt that something is wrong with such a characterisation.

IB: That's because people want to define human beings in terms of social relations, and I don't do that. I think that once you begin interpreting people as depending on, and being functions of, the society in which they live, it leads to suppression and miseries.

BP-S: How well I feel it, you know? The day after tomorrow I shall have to give an account of what I have done during my stay here, and I shall have to cheat.[1]

---

1. At that time I was affiliated to the Department of Humanistic Applications of Computer Science and was not expected by my superiors to occupy myself with a totally different field, i.e. political philosophy. Although, just after my graduation, I had been offered a job at the Institute of Political Science, I chose differently, because otherwise I would have had to teach Marxism and Leninism.

IB: Of course you have to cheat. Bravo!

BP-S: Each time that I write about you, giving an account of my research, I report that I have been working on your views, you see? I never mention philosophy, because officially it's not my field; I just refer to your views. Luckily enough, they never ask what the views are.

IB: Bravo! 'His well-known views.' The more you cheat, the better. Bravissimo! Don't be ashamed. You're entitled. There are two values which clash: one is telling the truth and the other is having negative liberty. When the truth is that kind of truth and negative liberty is that kind of liberty, there can't be a problem, I assure you.

BP-S: But it's distressing and sometimes I feel miserable.

IB: No, it isn't. It shouldn't be. You should certainly cheat potential torturers. Hardly anybody has denied that. If somebody wants to kill you, it's not wrong to tell them a lie.

BP-S: But I do not feel myself, you see? It's not only a question of the truth.

IB: Oh, it is, yes! What else?

BP-S: I would be so peaceful if I could say what I feel.

IB: Saying things doesn't matter. Let me give you an extreme example of the opposite. Kant, somewhere, gives the example of a man sitting in a room. Another man comes in, in order to murder a friend of his. The first man knows that the second man wants to kill his innocent friend. The murderer says, 'Where is so and so?' The first man has no right to tell a lie, he can't say the friend is out when he's in. He has to stop the second man murdering, he has to fight him, but he mustn't tell him a lie. Because if he tells him a lie, then he is using him as a means, he is deceiving him, and therefore he cannot 'determine himself in the light of the truth'. Kant's view is ridiculous if driven to such an extreme!

BP-S: Yes, of course, when you consider just one extreme case. But when your life consists of things like that all the time, you get tired . . .

IB: Because it gets you down. But provided you are quite clear that the people to whom you are lying are people who have no right to extract this information from you in accordance with any principles that you have, you're perfectly entitled to cheat. You appear to conform when you don't conform.

BP-S: But the problem is that I have not only to lie but also to steal. For instance, the paper for my PhD dissertation had to be stolen, not by myself but by a typist. Typing paper is absolutely impossible to buy. There is a special word for getting unavailable goods: to fix something. So she fixed the paper for me. You cannot have your hands clean, absolutely never.

IB: Of course you can't. Under tyranny nobody does unless they want to die.

BP-S: But, on the other hand, one has to draw a line. Once you cross it, everything is lost.

IB: Yes, but you feel all this because you're too vulnerable.

BP-S: I have a child whom I would like to bring up in the normal way.

IB: It's very difficult in that situation. There is no good way at all.

BP-S: Terribly difficult! What should I choose?

IB: You'll have to teach it how to lie and cheat, of course!

BP-S: That's the worst thing.

IB: I know it's the worst thing, but you happen to live in a terrible regime and you should lie. It's like my poor friend, a Soviet lady, who at school was asked: 'Who do you love most?' She said, 'My father.' That's wrong. Stalin was the answer. First Stalin, then father.

BP-S: That was just cruelty. It's much better now. But still, it's like wandering in the mist, all the time. The pettiest decision which you make has got this ethical dimension.

IB: You have to tell your children the truth. In the end, you want to bring them up by saying, 'Look, we're living in this kind of regime; if you tell the truth to these people, you will suffer. These people are not very nice people, but you can't help it. With these people you must be very careful; it's better not say anything at all. If you do say something, you realise it may be used to do you harm; but at home with me . . .'.

BP-S: But it's not only about saying things, it would be easier if it were. It's about cheating, lying and stealing. Like my paper. Stealing is unavoidable. Otherwise I wouldn't have my PhD.

IB: First you have to teach your children to steal, and then, at a certain point, you explain to them why it's wrong to steal and why they must go on stealing, because the situation is abnormal.

BP-S: I wish I had such good sense to use in my own conduct.

IB: It's very difficult. You have to live two lives. In other words, you have to live a family life and you have to live a public life. Everybody has to do that. Let me give you an example from Hume. Supposing you believe in property as an absolute value. You mustn't take away property from other people which they haven't given you. There is a shipwreck. Have you a right to cling to a bit of the ship, which belongs to the company, which they may want to use for some other purpose? In that situation you're fully entitled. If you are starving, you're allowed to steal food. Even on Christian principles, there is a natural law which says that if you're starving, you are entitled to steal. The law

may forbid it but Christian morality does not. That's what's called natural law in the religions.

BP-S: Yes, I know, but it corrupts one, then it's very difficult to . . .

IB: . . . divide the two.

BP-S: Yes, and that's only the beginning. It's a luxury to be able to be
honest, it's a great luxury to have this chance.

IB: I know. It's perfectly true.

BP-S: Whatever we do has an ethical dimension. That's how I feel about
living there; it's a constant ethical choice. If I am queuing and there is
only one piece of meat left, and there are ten people behind me, I am
facing an ethical choice: how much to buy? All the time, all the time.

IB: You just do what you do and you don't think very far beyond. You can't
suffer from perpetual guilt.

BP-S: Yes, I am afraid I do.

IB: I realise that. You can't suffer from perpetual remorse: 'Maybe I
shouldn't have done it, maybe it would have been better not to have
taken so much meat, maybe these people deserve more than I do.' What
you have to do is this: either you take the meat and stop thinking about
it if you can, because you can say, 'Well, next time they will take the
meat and I shall starve.' Or you don't take the meat, which is also all
right. Whichever you do is all right. In situations of extreme difficulty,
either choice is valid. There are certain situations for which ordinary
morality is not made. Life under tyranny fully justifies you in deception.
Take the war: the Germans and the Jews. The Germans come to some
town and there is a Judenrat there, the Jewish Council. And the Germans
say to the chief Jew, 'You know the names and addresses of all the Jews
who live here. We need to deport them for construction labour in
Northern Poland or in Southern Poland.' And he suspects, he already
knows, that it's not construction labour. They're going to be killed. 'If
you tell us the names and addresses, we will let you go with fifty other
people of your choice. If you don't tell us, everybody will die, because
we will find these people in the end.'

BP-S: Did such things happen?

IB: Certainly, and quite often. Now, you are the gauleiter of the Jews, and
you have to decide what to do. You have four choices. You can say, 'I am
not playing your game, I do not wish to collaborate with you, I don't
answer your question', in which case they shoot you and they shoot the
rest of them in the end, probably. Maybe some people escape but it's
unlikely. Or you say, 'All right, I'll help you', and you do it, but you tell

the Jews to escape. If you are discovered, then you of course are shot, and in the end they are, too. Or you commit suicide; that lets you out of this problem. Or you can do what they tell you, which is to give the names and addresses of everybody and save the lives of fifty people. Now, to play God, to choose people for life or death, can't be right. Nevertheless, not to do it means you've sacrificed fifty people. They'll die because you don't want to feel uncomfortable. You've allowed fifty people to die because you are not prepared to make choices, because you are not God. You have no right to choose who should live and who should die; however, you let them all die. That's what it comes to. Now, my view is that whatever you do is all right. Moral laws are not made for situations like this. Whatever you do, you can't be criticised. You do what you do. Everything is all right: to commit suicide is all right, to save the people is all right, not to save them is all right. It's beyond criticism, in a sense. Of course, if you are a pious Christian or a pious Jew, you say, 'I have no right to take any action.' You'd rather be killed yourself.

Nothing you do is wrong. In that case it's the Nazis' responsibility, not yours. But people can still criticise you afterwards. That's what Hannah Arendt used to do. It is a terrible thing to lecture these people about what they should have done. Whatever they did was beyond our criticism. When you are faced with a decision of such horror, there's no solution.

BP-S: Yes, I understand, but when one is responsible for bringing up a child, it's different.

IB: No, of course, but I have given you a very extreme case. In your case it's not quite so bad.

BP-S: Certainly. Nothing comparable. But not easy, anyway.

IB: You have to teach your children your own morality. Whatever you think right you tell them, whatever you think wrong you tell them. If you think cheating's all right, you tell them, 'Yes, in some circumstances cheating is all right, and in others it's not all right.' In the end, they will discover that what you were doing was worthwhile. But you can only teach them what you believe yourself. I'll tell you a funny story about that. Here in Oxford, there was a merchant who went to see the Master of Balliol College, who was a man called Jowett. He was a clergyman, a very famous, wise, important man. And the merchant said to him, 'Look, I wish to consult you, Sir. I don't want to cheat, but all around me every other merchant cheats. If I don't cheat, I'll be ruined. What should I do?' I don't know what you would say, but Jowett said, 'Cheat as little as you can.' For a Christian clergyman to say that is very good. Well, in a way that's right.

BP-S: But you know, if one lives in a normal, democratic country, one can, just theoretically, have this luxury of being honest. One can afford it.

IB: Certainly. But don't sacrifice your children to honesty. Don't make their lives intolerable for the sake of honesty. That's Puritanism of an extreme kind. That's also terrible. If you hang people because they've stolen a pencil, it can't be quite right.

BP-S: Yes, I know, of course I know. The problem is about finding the border in everything.

IB: As always. It's a very boring doctrine but, on the whole, it minimises suffering and is quite a decent ideal. In the end, all we want to do is to enable people to communicate with each other and to live comparatively peaceably. We just want a minimally decent society. That's all you can work for.

BP-S: You know, in some ways, if it weren't for your ideas, I would go mad, really.

IB: Thank you. You may still, but I hope not. Your moral sensitivity is so great that for you to live in even an ordinary society would be quite difficult.

BP-S: I'm hysterical. I know.

IB: No, no, I'm not saying that. But your moral sensitivity is very great. You want everyone to behave as beautifully as possible. They will never do that: 'Out of the crooked timber of humanity . . .'. I have to repeat this to you and you don't accept this right to crookedness. You assume that the crooked timber can be made straight. It can't.

1991

Two years after the collapse of Communism I visited Oxford for a short period, having been invited by John Gray to participate in a colloquium on Montesquieu. Berlin, as usual, generously spared me his time. We met three times; two conversations, those of 11 and 13 October, were recorded. The former one provided the basis for two interviews, commissioned by Polish periodicals and later published under the titles: 'Nil Desperandum' and 'I Don't Want the Universe To Be Too Tidy', both included in this volume. The themes discussed in the latter interview were inevitably related to the historic events of 1989. This topic was, of course, covered in both recorded conversations. When I return to the recordings of this time, I realise that after the collapse of Communism, liberty ceased to be the central issue that it had been during our previous meetings. We talked about three books published in 1991: the first Polish collection of Berlin's essays, a volume of articles in his honour, edited by Edna and Avishai Margalit, and John Gray's Liberalisms.[1] When we were discussing a number of points that I raised in connection with the new publications, a nagging problem, which was to dominate the later worldwide debate on ethical pluralism, cropped up—the status of freedom in a value-pluralist system. My interlocutor seemingly had no ready solution. The nagging doubt returned in 1995.

---

1. Isaiah Berlin, *Dwie koncepcje wolnosci* [*Two Concepts of Liberty*; Polish translation of selected essays by Berlin] (Warszawa: Res Publica, 1991); Edna Margalit and Avishai Margalit, eds., *Isaiah Berlin A Celebration* (London: Hogarth, 1991); John Gray, *Liberalisms: Essays in Political Philosophy* (London: Routledge, 1991).

On the Essay by Pawel Spiewak:
Liberalism, Pluralism, Relativism

BP-S: I would like to show you several excerpts from the postscript to the Polish volume of your essays, written by Pawel Spiewak. I am afraid I disagree with his interpretation of your ideas in a number of crucial respects. Here is my translation of the first passage: 'Berlin does not accept arguments of a utilitarian character. He does not connect freedom with some Utopian state of perfection and happiness. Freedom needn't lead either to progress or to regression. Freedom is, or seems to be, indispensable, for we do not know any other way to preserve pluralism.'[1]

What raises my doubts is the closing phrase: 'for we do not know any other way to preserve pluralism'. Isn't it the other way around? Do you conceive of liberty as *a means* to anything else?

IB: Liberty is itself a value without which people can't breathe, and pluralism is something which, in some sense, follows from freedom of opinion, or freedom of conviction.

BP-S: Which *follows*? But I have always thought that the pluralist view of the world is for you the point of departure. You recognise liberty as the basic value because if there is no liberty, no value can be chosen. Thus, liberty makes room for other values.

IB: Once you have choice, there is always the possibility of more than one value, of choosing this rather than that; and if that's developed, it becomes pluralism. If you believe that there is only one correct solution, you ultimately stop choice. It is correct to say that twice two is four. You can't choose whether it's four or five. You know in advance what the answer must be; you only have liberty to discover the truth. It's like the liberty to live the correct life. Once you have the correct life, there is no need for liberty.

BP-S: But am I right when I think that pluralism is, in a way, more basic?

IB: Than liberty? Liberty is not a ladder. You can't throw it away when you find something else—happiness or knowledge or the good life. Liberty is a basic value in itself, without which people can't choose. If they can't choose, they can't live, they can't think. The second sense of the word 'liberty' is absence of obstacles, which means that you must have a large selection of possible paths. That's pluralism, and that's how it connects

---

1. Pawel Spiewak, 'Isaiaha Berlina liberalny liberalizm' ['Isaiah Berlin's Liberal Liberalism'], Postscript to Berlin, *Dwie koncepcje wolnosci*, 373.

with negative liberty. The danger of positive liberty is that you're only free to do what is right, which is what Montesquieu said. But that means that you can't go to the bad. Even Kant said that it's better that people should go to the bad in their own way than that they should not be allowed to choose at all.

BP-S: Would you please have a look at the next passage? It reads as follows: 'Man is the source of values and it depends on the strength of his personality whether freedom survives and whether he is capable of making necessary compromises.'[1]

IB: No, it has nothing to do with the strength of personality. Man is the source of values, that's correct.

BP-S: In a sense.

IB: Well, he chooses them.

BP-S: But they are objective.

IB: But they're not there without him.

BP-S: Yes, sure. You have this empiricist approach.

IB: Exactly.

BP-S: But what he says here sounds relativistic.

IB: 'Source of values' really means that you commit yourself to values. It's a kind of existentialism. Man is the source of values in the sense that values are not independent entities existing apart from people. They are objective ends; but without people there are no ends. They either choose the people or people choose them. Both happen. You find yourself already possessing some ends, but you can change them. Herder is right. There is a river of culture and you are born into it; once you are grown, you already know what is good and bad, right and wrong. You know about patriotism and treachery. All these things are brought about by your parents, your nurses, your schoolmasters. And those are the values for which you live, but you can change them. So the values may not be yours, nor be created by you, but they are created by people and may be, in a way, pushed on to you; you either accept them or reject them. You can accept unconsciously, but you still accept. So Spiewak is wrong. I object to strong personalities, because they can extinguish liberty, both their own and other people's, while weak personalities can do their best to preserve it. Maybe not very much, but they can. Everybody can preserve some liberty unless they commit suicide.

BP-S: But I'm afraid he actually ascribes relativism to you. Let's look at the next excerpt: 'He doesn't care, in a sense, whether—in the privacy of

1. ibid., 380.

one's own home—one believes in magic or in science; whether one is an atheist or a model Catholic. There should be a place in this world for all attitudes—except intolerance.'[1]

IB: There's something in that. But it's not that I don't care. That's wrong. I mind very much if you believe in magic, but you must be allowed to believe in it.

BP-S: The piece is very favourable.

IB: I understand, but he's got me wrong. Well, you can tell him that it's very nice that he should be on my side, but unfortunately the good things he finds are not there.

Humean Inspiration

BP-S: Two authors whose articles have been included in this collection of essays—Stuart Hampshire and Richard Wollheim[2]—claim that there is a clearly discernible Humean inspiration in your philosophy. Do you agree? I have marked the appropriate passages:

> In all Berlin's thinking and writing one is aware of the ample, generous, humorous and seductive figure of David Hume smiling in the background [. . .] I think it is important to stress that Berlin's attitude to nationalism has both a philosophical and a historical foundation. The attitude is not just an attitude; it is part of, and follows from, a coherent moral philosophy, which in turn rests on Humean epistemology. [. . .] Always following Hume and Mill, Berlin consistently and at all times argued that there can be no place for pure a priori reasoning in ethics and politics. [. . .] He accepts from Hume the doctrine that the ultimate test of institutions and policies is to be found in human feelings as they are actually experienced and observed.[3]

You have never told me that you are influenced by Hume. You mentioned Herzen, Mill, Kant, but never Hume.

IB: I am, though what he attributes to me is not what I follow in Hume. Hume does not believe in natural necessity. He believes that there is no rational way of discovering moral truths. People have the purposes they have; reason is and always will be the slave of the passions. He also

---

1. ibid., 380–1.

2. Stuart Hampshire, 'Nationalism', in Margalit and Margalit, *Celebration*, 127–34; Richard Wollheim, 'The Idea of a Common Human Nature', in ibid., 64–79.

3. Hampshire, 'Nationalism', 129–32.

thinks most human beings are very similar, and there is tradition, and nothing wrong will happen; he's rather complacent. But he does believe, in theory, that it is not possible to discover, by rational means, what one should be or do, what is right or wrong.

BP-S: Yet he holds that there is a fixed human nature.

IB: Fairly fixed, yes. That's why most people, in the same circumstances, would probably believe the same things. But there's no way of demonstrating this. You can't show that an answer is correct, because in ethics there's nothing correct or incorrect. People believe what they believe, they want what they want, they pursue what they pursue. That I do get from Hume, certainly.

BP-S: Empiricism.

IB: Yes, that's all. But I disagree when he says that one should be calm, that one should follow nature and custom.

BP-S: Here are two passages from Richard Wollheim's article which I would like to show you. In the first one, Wollheim labels you as Humean; the second one is a quote from Hume himself:

Berlin is a particular kind of Humean. He is not the kind of Humean who utterly rejects the idea of fundamental or underlying causes as absurd; but he is the kind of Humean who rejects the idea—or, more accurately, treats it with measured diffidence—that our knowledge can actually reach to these causes. Berlin is the kind of Humean that Hume was.[1]

We are placed in this world, as in a great theatre, where the true springs and causes of every action are entirely concealed from us; nor have we either sufficient wisdom to foresee, or power to prevent those ills, with which we are continually threatened.[2]

IB: That's too strong. I don't accept that at all. Hume thinks that anything might happen, but it won't because the universe in fact pursues a certain regular path. One must assume it will, because it always has. Why shouldn't we think that it does? And if we don't believe that, we make ourselves unnecessarily unhappy. But we can't say it must. That's what I get from Hume. There is no moral must and no aesthetic must.

BP-S: So to a certain extent you are Humean.

IB: Just to that extent, I mean the empiricism and the fact that there are

1. Richard Wollheim, 'The Idea of a Common Human Nature', 78.
2. David Hume, *The Natural History of Religion*, §3, quoted by Wollheim, 'The Idea of a Common Human Nature', 79.

breaks in causality—freedom of the will, too, which Hume didn't believe in. But freedom of the will is possible, because there's no need to believe the idea that everything must follow certain paths. We behave as if this is so, because unless the future resembles the past, we don't know what to do. But it doesn't follow that it will. Our need is something different from the objective march of events. From the fact that we believe certain things, that we can't live without them, it doesn't follow that they must always be there.

Values in Marx—The Aftermath

IB: There's one essay in the collection which is critical of me. It's by Jerry Cohen, who's a Marxist. He accuses me of misinterpreting Marx. He says that I'm wrong in saying that Marx had no objective moral values.[1] I don't misinterpret Marx.

BP-S: It's much too early for me to read Marxist texts. I suppose I shall need at least twenty years to overcome the aversion.

IB: Don't read Marx. I don't recommend it. But let me tell you, he believed that values are conditioned by the productive process. When that changes, values change.

BP-S: What I mostly blame him for is his conception of man. According to Marx, man is merely raw material; he becomes something only when he enters the structure of work. Thus the true essence of man is embodied in the entirety of social relationships. So my essence is not inside me. It's somewhere beyond me.

IB: For Marx, man can be reduced to the society of which he is a member.

BP-S: He's supposed to be reduced, and that's what I experienced. You shouldn't think that you belong to yourself.

IB: You are a brick. We're building a wall, and bricks have no right to fall out of the wall.

BP-S: Yes, one cannot own anything in the world, including oneself. But this is a sin against one's dignity.

IB: Exactly. History drives you in a certain direction. Don't resist.

BP-S: It was somehow implanted in people, one could really feel it. Individuals didn't count. One experienced it even in everyday life. Nothing

---

1. 'It is unacceptably paradoxical to represent Marx as unconcerned with values. To do so is to take too seriously those macho moments when he disparaged them in the name of class militancy.' G. A. Cohen, 'Isaiah's Marx and Mine', in Margalit and Margalit, *Celebration*, 122.

really terrible happened to me. I wasn't arrested, I wasn't beaten. The only thing that happened was that I got drenched several times by a water cannon during protests.

IB: You were drenched by a water cannon. Well, that's something. Not bad, it counts.

BP-S: It's not pleasant, I should say.

IB: But in heaven you'll get good marks for that.

BP-S: I have to admit that I was scared. It makes quite a difference when you are really in danger, and I was. There were several casualties during these protests. Some people were trampled, some were beaten up, somebody lost an eye. But even in peaceful times I still felt that I was not important and nobody really was.

IB: You're quite right. Communism degrades human personality, turning it into an object.

BP-S: And then you impose this feeling on yourself. You start perceiving yourself in these terms. This was what was so painful about living under Communism.

IB: You're conditioned. You begin to believe it all and you feel that you don't exist. You feel you are merely knocked about, like a ball.

BP-S: It's very personal, but things changed when I started to read your essays. Somehow this feeling of not belonging to myself was very much connected with my life and my status at the university. After graduation, I was offered a job at the Institute of Political Science. There was a hint that I should join the Party, and I said no. And then I was offered another post; it was in a department dealing with the application of computer science to the humanities: God knows what that means. It had nothing to do with the things I love. And then, just before the Solidarity period, I came across your writings, and during the period of martial law I read them and I just recovered!

IB: Well, at least I have saved one soul.

BP-S: And now that the spell has been broken and things are becoming normal, it feels like saying hello to yourself. All of a sudden, you come back to yourself and you start feeling responsible.

IB: You become yourself, yes. You are restored to yourself. It's a rehabilitation. You are reintegrated.

BP-S: Not feeling quite myself was the most difficult thing for me. I could stand everything, constant scarcity, queues, ration coupons, but not this. I was on the edge of a breakdown . . .

IB: That's because you're too honest. Because you don't want to pretend.

You don't want to play a part. You're no good at acting. The way to save oneself is by acting, telling lies. There's a great case for telling lies. You shouldn't say that all lying is bad. Lies can be very good things if, for instance, they save someone's feelings. Suppose somebody says to you, 'How did so and so die?' As a matter of fact, he died while trying to kill some innocent person, but you don't tell the truth because it hurts too much. That's why I say that knowledge and happiness can be disunited, can be incompatible. There is a case for telling lies to save people misery, or to save oneself under a despotic regime.

BP-S: But it's degrading.

IB: You're much too tender; you have a very delicate moral conscience. And I congratulate you on that. But one survives a bad time by learning to act. I've never had to do it. But in your position it was nearly impossible to avoid. And the fact that you didn't act has left your nature completely unscarred, unharmed. You may have no moral wounds. Nothing to regret.

BP-S: I owe it to my father. He set the moral pattern for me. He was quite severely persecuted for his convictions just after the war. He was labelled in his secret police record as 'an enemy of the Soviet Union'. He worked for local government and, despite constant pressure, never joined the Party. That's why, though he was very clever, he didn't have a career.

IB: He remained uncompromised? That's wonderful. That's what Poles are for. The great thing about Poland, for all its many faults, is the courage of Poles. They stand up. That's why the first crack against the regime was in Poland and nowhere else.

BP-S: But this courage used to be somewhat crazy, totally ignoring the cost.

IB: I know, but it's better to have crazy courage than to be cowardly. I don't blame cowards. At least cowardice doesn't lead to bloodshed. It's terrible to be too brave, because that means that you kill or are killed. Nevertheless, in times of crisis there is something dignified and noble about standing up.

BP-S: To me, these things are deeply embedded in our history. You know, we had this period of crazy liberty, which must have somehow survived in our genes. Though, of course, as Plato says, too much liberty is paradoxical.

IB: When?

BP-S: The seventeenth, eighteenth century. In the West there were absolute regimes, and we had this institution of *liberum veto*.[1] This amounted to

---

1. The institution of *liberum veto* operated in Poland in the years 1652–1791.

a requirement that votes should be unanimous, which was completely impractical and absurd. For over two centuries we also had the institution of 'free election'.[1] One vote was enough to reject everything.

IB: Bravo! It was mad and it was wonderful.

BP-S: It was absolutely mad and it led to anarchy.

IB: There is something grand about resistance. You have resisted and your friends are resisting now. The gate has opened. I'm glad you lived to see it.

BP-S: I couldn't believe it, really.

IB: You have a long life before you: happy, democratic and free. A life of choices and resistances. Don't believe that what is now will be for ever. That is never true. Things may become worse, but they can also become better. Nothing stands in the world. It's a platitude to say so, but that's why you can plan and behave as if tomorrow will be better.

BP-S: I hope so.

The Impact of Theories

BP-S: May I bore you a little bit once again? I have one last question. John Gray in his latest book writes something about which I am sceptical. I wonder what you think about it? Here is the appropriate passage: '[I]t is distinctive of a post-liberal form of theorising, I suggest, that in abandoning the search for universal principles of justice or rights, and returning thought to the vicissitudes of practice, it also relinquishes the liberal illusion that theory can ever govern, or even substantially illuminate, practice.'[2]

IB: Not true.

BP-S: I have experienced the power of theories.

IB: Exactly, but theory can and should affect practice; there's nothing wrong with that. If you have the correct theory, there's no reason why it shouldn't influence practice. To reject theory as such, because all theory is a prison, all theory is an ideology, all theory is chains, is a mistake.

BP-S: I asked him about this and he said that the only thing theories can do is destroy.

IB: No, they can build.

BP-S: Can you think of an example?

IB: John Stuart Mill had a theory. Even Locke in his day built something.

---

1. Election *viritim*, that is the principle that the king was elected by the whole gentry, was in effect in Poland over the span of years 1573–1791.

2. Gray, *Liberalisms*, 236.

American democracy had theory behind it. Jefferson and Madison and all these people were brought up on classical theory. America is a country built entirely upon theory. It has no religion. It has a national theory. It is the first State created by metaphysics and sheer theorising. America is not perfect, but nevertheless the theory by which Americans live, the famous American way of life, the democracy in which they believe, is a force for good and not for evil. There are other examples. The Russian government of 1917, the provisional government between February and October, was absolutely built on theory. It didn't last, but it was the only time Russia was free. In that period between February and October there was a real liberal theory in existence and people felt liberated. It was a happy moment for a great many people. Or take the French Revolution. The doctrine of 'liberty, equality, fraternity' meant something; the destruction of feudal rights and the destruction of the oppressive Church were good. It was done in the name of theory and it did nothing but good. Then it went too far; it resulted in terror and terrible tyranny. To say that theory as such is destructive and enslaving is false. There's a great deal to be said for theory provided it's not an embracing, monistic ideology. Pluralism is a theory.

BP-S: John Gray's outlook constitutes a theory. The theory that theories are bad is a theory itself.

IB: Gray sees abstract theory as a kind of weight that oppresses you. You have to learn everything from practice. There's a lot of truth in that, but it goes too far.

BP-S: It's an exaggeration.

IB: Principles are part of a theory. When people follow principles, it's not disgraceful. When someone says, 'Why don't you cheat if you're on a bus and you know that you'll escape notice because you are very skilful? You'll give your fare to the poor.' You say, 'But I can't.' Why not? Principle. It's quite all right. There's nothing wrong with having principles. Bad principles are bad and good principles are good. It's as simple as that. What is bad and good? That can't be explained. Everybody knows that inside. That's what you knew when you explained why you didn't like the regime. You knew that destruction is bad, that slavery is bad, that being dehumanised is bad. How did you know that?

BP-S: I just knew.

IB: Precisely, that's all I mean.

1995

My last two meetings with Berlin (17 and 24 May 1995) were dominated by the crucial questions posed by John Gray in his newly published monograph, especially the thorny problem of the relationship between pluralism and liberalism. The issue had already been tackled at our previous meetings. In 1988 Isaiah Berlin, when I asked him about the connection between the two main themes in his political philosophy, answered as follows:

> My pluralism probably springs from my liberalism and my liberalism from my pluralism, but both from the incompatibility of values. That's a psychological statement about me. I was a liberal before I ever thought about being a pluralist. Why was I a liberal then? Because I saw no reason for forcing people, for frustrating people's goals, even if I disagree.

Yet three years later he remarked that 'pluralism in some sense follows from freedom of opinion'. I felt confused about this knotty point, especially after having found in Ramin Jahanbegloo's Conversations with Isaiah Berlin two statements concerning the issue in question, in successive sentences, that are difficult to reconcile.[1] Armed with John Gray's monograph I took the offensive, determined to arrive at a final solution. I witnessed Berlin considering the problem. He looked for the answer to my nagging questions; first at our two meetings and then in correspondence. His views kept changing as he approached the solution which he eventually offered me.

---

1. 'I believe in both pluralism and liberalism but they are not logically connected. Pluralism entails [. . .] a minimum degree of toleration.' Jahanbegloo, *Conversations*, 44; cf. 82 above, 225, 287, 290 below.

Since Berlin's death, the pluralism–liberalism nexus has proved to be one of the most vividly discussed issues within the pluralist movement. I am aware that some of Berlin's intellectual heirs, especially those who are in favour of neat solutions, may be disappointed at his somewhat disordered observations and their vague outcome. They may be dissatisfied, exactly as I once was, with Berlin's evasiveness and inconsistency. Yet I hated the thought of censoring his views; I think they should be presented and faced as they were. There are two factors to be taken into account by potentially discontented readers. First, these were completely unprepared, spontaneous conversations. Thus it would be unreasonable to expect the views expressed in them to be well thought out, clear and precise. Second, it would be equally unreasonable to assume that a philosopher who had refrained through all his long life from building a rigid system, and who often used to offer 'yes-and-no', half-way solutions, would have decisively cracked a tangled and controversial problem. His role as a thinker was, as I perceive it, to put a stick into a hornets' nest rather than to offer resolutions for thorny dilemmas. Perhaps the clue that he gave me over a decade ago will inspire further discussion. If so, it will perform a role like that of other ideas which, though not fully spelled out by Berlin, are implicit in his intellectual legacy, and can be teased out by careful and sympathetic imaginative reconstruction of his vision.

17 May 1995

The Relationship Between Liberalism and Pluralism

BP-S: There was one issue raised by John Gray in his recent book which most of all captured my attention: his controversial view on the relationship between liberalism and pluralism. I remember that we have already tackled this problem before. Yet could you possibly come back to it again?

IB: From liberalism you can't get to pluralism, because you might have a very despotic and completely dogmatic liberalism which says, 'This is the truth; what I, a liberal, say is true, and everything else is false. I don't allow any disagreement. I have discovered the answer, how to live, and the answer is liberal.' So you can be a liberal without being a pluralist.[1] Every movement is capable of being despotic, coercive: people are not allowed to— whatever it is—be conservatives; people are not allowed to be Roman Catholic. Secular liberalism can become a dogmatic movement.

BP-S: But you'll have to allow some measure of liberty.

IB: Oh yes, but not pluralism. Liberty, of course—that's what 'liberal' means. Certainly. In a liberal regime you are not prevented from doing a thousand things. But it doesn't mean that from that you can deduce the

---

1. Berlin also dealt with this theme in a conversation in April 1988: 'You are an objective monist, you know twice two is four, you know that tomorrow is Monday and you know that democracy is good and tyranny is bad. But you are tolerant. It's a perfectly possible position. Absolutist liberals all knew that certain values were eternal, objective, true for all men. But they did not believe in coercion. They would rather that people were mistaken than that they should go to jail. That's a case of non-pluralistic liberalism.'

possibility of a multiplicity of values. Maybe yes, maybe not. You might be very monistic as a liberal. I don't think liberals are monistic, but in theory you can imagine a monistic liberalism which simply says, 'This is the answer.' This might be so for John Stuart Mill, for instance.

BP-S: Or Friedrich Hayek.

IB: Hayek, yes. All right.

BP-S: The free market is the answer to everything.

IB: But that's dogmatic. In other words, most liberals, obviously, are likely to be pluralists, but there's no logical nexus. The other way, yes. From pluralism to liberalism there is a connection—a direct, not a loose, connection. Because if you're a pluralist, then of course you must allow for the possibility of wide differences. That's what pluralism is: I understand the ways of the other culture; I understand how people can have values different from mine. I can understand how people can live lives which are founded on different principles from mine. I don't accept them, but I see how one could be a human being, a virtuous and perfectly decent human being, and yet do that. I can see what it's like to have been a Roman. I don't like the idea that Romans executed criminals or slaves on the stage—they actually killed them—but I see there is a culture which would permit that kind of thing; it is not inhuman, and that kind of life is possible. Once you allow that, you can't not be liberal. Illiberal pluralism doesn't exist. So there is a connection. Because once you allow the possibility of equally valid systems of belief which are different from yours, which you may hate, but which you don't want to suppress, which you allow to be ways of life, you can understand why people live like that. You really can understand what their values are.

Let me go back a little: I don't accept the a priori view of universal values. On the other hand, quasi-universal values do exist—values which a great many people in a great many countries at a great many times have believed are in effect what unites us. Everybody is for truth and against falsehood; everyone is in favour of courage; everyone is in favour of some degree of justice, and people who deny that are outside the range. Within that, differences can occur—that's what pluralism is—of a kind which makes it possible to communicate with people in these other cultures, even if you reject them. Given that, you are a liberal. You must allow freedom of belief, freedom of culture, freedom of constellations of values.

BP-S: Does this answer the examples that Gray gives? Because he says that pluralism undermines universalistic claims; that there could be particularistic authoritarian regimes—he gives the examples of Shinto, of

Orthodox Jews;[1] he gives the example of a nun who enters a convent, and once she has taken this decision, the range of her choices is strictly limited, but still it's a worthwhile sort of life.

IB: She accepts it as a way of life. What follows from that?

BP-S: We can imagine a regime which is very authoritarian, like Shinto. In a way it doesn't deny pluralism because it may accept different particularistic regimes which have completely different sets of values.

IB: 'Accept?' I'm not sure. If you have a very authoritarian regime it is unlikely to accept different regimes. It may be on terms with them, may have to deal with them, but it won't accept their validity.

BP-S: But if it's not universalistic? How about Orthodox Jews?

IB: They are probably universalistic too. People should, all of them, be Jews. Everything else is false. No. They are not pluralists. If you belong to a religion, for instance, particularly to a dogmatic religion which says, 'The truth is what we believe, and everything everyone else believes is false', then you are certainly against other beliefs. You may be unable to fight against them for material reasons; but if you could, you would. Islam would like the whole world to be Muslim. Quite a good example: all these ayatollahs in Iran believe that the world will never be a proper world until everybody is a Muslim. Everything else is an obstacle to the right world. There is a perfect world—the world of Islam. They are not pluralists. They can't be. Nor are they liberal.

BP-S: Yet it's definitely not the example of Islam that Gray has in mind. Would you please have a look at this passage:

Let us consider first the last of the three arguments which aim to link value-pluralism with liberalism—the argument that authoritarian or illiberal societies or regimes are bound to deny the truth of value-pluralism. This is true only of those illiberal orders which ground themselves on the Western universalist premises that the truth of value-pluralism demolishes. It is true that value-pluralism undermines the universalist claims made by illiberal societies that are Marxist, utilitarian or positivist, Platonist, Christian or Muslim, at their foundations; but human history to date, and the human prospect for the likely future, abounds with illiberal cultures that are particularistic, not universalistic, in the values they claim to embody. Authoritarian regimes sustained by Hindu, Shinto or Orthodox Jewish doctrine, or which seek simply to preserve a local way of life, make none of the universal claims that value-pluralism subverts. All that needs to be claimed on behalf of such illiberal societies is that they harbour worthwhile forms of

---

1. Gray, *Isaiah Berlin*, 151, quoted below on this page and the next.

life which will be compromised, or destroyed, by the exercise of freedom of choice. If this once be admitted, why should the value of unimpeded choice always trump that of the forms of life that are undone by such choice? How *could* it, if value-pluralism is true?[1]

IB: Yes, I understand this. He makes the distinction between universal monism—that's what I would call it—which says this is the only way, you can't go against it, no choice is possible, and Shinto, Orthodox Judaism etc., which simply want to preserve certain ways of life but take no interest in anything outside themselves, in other words, don't stop other people from behaving as they do. I don't think it's a very real distinction. Jews or Shintoists or Hindus do that because, presumably, either they are not interested in other people, and therefore other people don't exist for them in that sense, or because they have no possibility of making the world totally Hindu or totally Jewish or totally Shinto, but if they could they would. It's obviously true that there are local communities which don't stop other people from behaving as they like. That's all we'd say. Marxism is universalistic, Christianity's universalistic, whereas these are sects or limited religions, which say: Within our particular world, we don't allow choice of a certain kind; but what you do outside is none of our business.

BP-S: But they could be pluralist in that sense?

IB: Well, they're saying: We don't mind what happens—you're not a Shintoist—do as you like. It's like your nun. Inside the convent, you are not free. In the street, anybody may do as they like.

BP-S: So Gray is right?

IB: Value pluralism subverts universal claims. But these bodies don't make universal claims, he says. Therefore pluralism does not subvert them.

BP-S: And the other way round. They might be pluralist.

IB: Well, what does that mean? That means they don't mind you behaving as you like?

BP-S: What he says is that you cannot make a case for liberalism from the truth of pluralism.

IB: No, what he's saying is that universalism cannot be reconciled with pluralism. There are universal claims—only one way of life is right. Where things are not universal, where they are local, then they are compatible with pluralism, and pluralism is compatible with them.

BP-S: Surely his point is that, if you are a pluralist, it doesn't mean that you

---

1. See previous note.

must accept liberalism. You might be a pluralist Shinto and not accept liberalism.

IB: His point is this: If you ever make universal claims for certain values, you have knocked out the possibility of choice between these values and others; but if you don't make that universalist claim, and you say: 'We Shintoists live that way; how you live doesn't matter, live as you like, we will not interfere—we don't forbid you to be non-Shinto', that is pluralism.

BP-S: So pluralism does not entail liberalism. That's what he wants to prove, using this.

IB: That pluralism can entail Shinto, in other words?

BP-S: Yes.

IB: No, pluralism does entail liberalism. The Shintoists are liberal with respect to the rest of the world. If you are a pluralist, there must be somewhere where a choice different from your own is permitted.

BP-S: But Gray says that being a pluralist does not entail liberalism.

IB: Well, I think it does.

BP-S: Because the Shintoist would be a liberal with regard to the rest of the world.

IB: Yes. Otherwise he wouldn't be a pluralist. That's why pluralism must entail liberalism, in that sense.

Choice as a Part of Human Nature— Basic Liberty—Liberty and Interference

BP-S: You wrote that an inescapable necessity of the human condition is choice-making.[1] So let us think about this nun. This is my own doubt about this example. She has made this choice and so she has a narrower range for choosing.

IB: She has given up her liberties.

BP-S: And many of her choices. Is she therefore less human?

IB: No. Nor less free. She has deliberately done it. She closed the door. She made her choice. She could easily stop it. She could open the door again. She could leave the convent, she could suddenly turn atheist.

BP-S: How about concentration-camp prisoners? Are they less human?

IB: No, because they can choose. They are prevented by other people from

---

1. '[L]iberty—without some modicum of which there is no choice and therefore no possibility of remaining human as we understand the word.' Berlin, 'The Pursuit of the Ideal', in *The Proper Study of Mankind*, 10.

realising their choices, but they know what they would do if they could. Choice doesn't entail the possibility of realising a choice once made. Choice means the possibility of conceiving how things could be different from what they are. If I am tied to a tree, I am not free, but I don't become inhuman. I become inhuman only if my desire for more choice has evaporated—if I no longer want to choose, if I no longer know what choosing is.

BP-S: If I understand you properly you are now referring to basic liberty. We have talked about it before, but I can't remember any explanation of the notion of basic liberty in your writings.

IB: I'd better explain it. I ought to have made it clear in my book and I didn't. This really needs supplement. There are two senses of 'liberty'. One is ordinary political liberty—negative liberty and positive liberty— values which I pursue. I pursue a society in which people are free to do everything which the law allows; but of course there are other values that may collide with liberty, like security, like equality, which are not wholly compatible with it—liberty has to be to some extent limited. I can't allow people to be free to murder, to lock other people up, to have people beaten in the street. I restrain liberty in order to allow room for certain other values like security, happiness, justice—all kinds of other things. Liberty is squeezed back by the need to realise certain other values, and you do your best to achieve a compromise. That's the normal sense: political liberty. That's the sense in which Fascism denies it.

Then there is a basic sense, which is choosing. Choosing is simply the capacity for choice; that cannot be eliminated by anything. You can't say it's a great bore to have to choose, it's rather difficult to have to choose, choosing is often very painful. Let me give you a pill after which you will never choose again. You will do everything more or less mechanically. You will do various things because you want to. No alternatives will ever appear to you. Would you like to take this pill? That would dehumanise you. That's the basic sense—not political liberty at all. That's the sense of liberty in which choosing is part of the evidence for being a human being. The ability to realise your choice has nothing to do with it. You may not be able to realise it. You choose not to be tied to the tree. You can't help it if you're tied. But you enjoy being tied? No: you choose freedom. I'm sorry I can't give it to you. But you choose it.

BP-S: So while negative liberty assumes a social context, basic liberty concerns only the individual?

IB: Yes. And it is essential to being a human being, for me. Anyone who can't choose, who is psychologically unable to choose, is to that extent not quite human. For example, people can be hypnotised. A brainwashed person is to some extent dehumanised. He doesn't choose. Successful brainwashing means you just follow a line. Someone says, 'What about other possibilities?' 'What do you mean, other possibilities? They don't occur. I can't think about them. I don't know what you mean. The only right thing to do is this, and I do it.' 'But don't you think you might perhaps do something else? You don't want to, but you could do something else? You can imagine yourself as doing something different from what you're doing.' 'No, I can't do that.' Then you are, to a certain extent, less human.

BP-S: When we discussed brainwashing your answer was that it's an obstacle to one's positive liberty; you didn't talk about basic liberty.

IB: I know. That's why I have to make this difference between basic liberty and these political liberties. It's certainly an obstacle to positive liberty—I'm not now master—but it's even more of an obstacle to the basic liberty which underlies it, which I ought to have made clear.

BP-S: Underlies both sorts of liberties, negative and positive?

IB: Yes. Both depend on it.

BP-S: So it concerns the abilities of a person.

IB: Of course. If you brainwash people in such a way that they can't choose, then they are like people under hypnosis. If you brainwash them enough they behave like zombies, like dolls; then I think you have robbed them of some degree of their humanity.

You are different from a dog. It doesn't choose. A dog follows instincts, an animal doesn't seem to do that much choosing; if I offer a piece of meat it can't not go towards it. Even brainwashing allows people some basic liberties. You can either get up from the chair or sit down. You can either light a cigarette or not light it. Some basic liberty is preserved, but a lot has gone. Choices have become limited. When they have become zero, then you cease to be a human being.

BP-S: You never wrote about this?

IB: No. I should have done. It was quite wrong to have left it out; I regret it. I've spoken about it, I've lectured on it, I've told people, but I've never written it up, no.

BP-S: When John Gray writes about your conception of negative liberty, he says that 'negative unfreedom need not presuppose the deliberate interference by others which occurs when force or coercion is deployed'.[1]

IB: It can be limited by human behaviour which in fact shuts a door which would otherwise be open. Sometimes I deliberately tie you to a tree and

1. Gray, *Isaiah Berlin*, 27.

put you in gaol. I pass a law which forbids you to go to a hotel which excludes Jews or excludes blacks. That's a deliberate limitation of negative liberty; but I can also create a situation in which you simply can't do it, because you are in no position to do it—it's not intended particularly to shut you out, but does in fact.

BP-S: This implies that a socio-economic system considered unjust and exploitative constitutes an obstacle to negative freedom. I am afraid that this sounds truly Marxist to me. So there is no difference between the liberal and the Marxist understanding of liberty? That's what it sounds like!

IB: Yes there is, because Marxism says that the only kind of liberty is economic liberty; but there are thousands of other kinds.

I'm just trying to think what human beings can do without positively wanting to stop you, but which in fact stops you. For example, the fact that shops are shut on Sundays—that's not Marxist. You can't buy anything on Sunday. The intention is to allow people who have shops to have a free day, to give liberty to shopkeepers to have a day on which they needn't serve. You have to give holidays to certain workers, which means that on those days you can't get this and you can't get that. It's not intended to stop you, but it has that effect.

There is a notice saying 'Don't walk across the grass.' That is a real prevention of negative liberty. Now let's think of something that doesn't do that: parliamentary elections in which you have to have the majority of the votes. That stops you, if you are in the minority, from putting in the person whom you want to put into Parliament. That's a curtailment of negative liberty, not so intended. You have majority rule. Majority rule means that certain things can't be done. You may accept it, or you may not. If you're an anarchist you don't accept it. If you're not an anarchist, you do. But it's certainly a human act which in fact shuts a certain door; rightly in this case. What Gray says is that deliberate curtailment of liberty is not the only curtailment there can be. It can be the consequence of some law, or some arrangement, which doesn't mean to stop liberty, but has that effect.

What Are Values?—Goods and Evils

BP-S: Gray writes here: 'It is not obvious what "values" designate—goods, options, virtues, whole conceptions of the good or entire cultural traditions or forms of life, or merely wants and preferences.'[1]

---

1. ibid., 49.

IB: I'll tell you what values are. Values are goods, not virtues, not whole conceptions of the good or cultural traditions. Values are the things in the light of which I live my life. Values are that which in the end I appeal to.

BP-S: Do they have to be good? I mean I may choose something which is bad.

IB: Yes, but if you choose it for its own sake, it's a value for you. There is no need to be good. Values are values. Values are those ends—not just by themselves, but concatenations, horizons—they are like networks of those things that I do because they are what they are, not a means to something else; ends for the sake of which I do what I do. By values I mean what I regard as purposes in terms of which I live my life, interwoven with other purposes, creating a kind of network of purposes. Fanatics have one purpose, you and I have seventeen. That's all I mean by values.

BP-S: You often use the term 'ultimate values'.

IB: Ultimate values are those purposes which are themselves not means to other things; that for the sake of which you do what you do.

BP-S: Is it your own term?

IB: I can't tell you where I got it from. I think it's quite normal: final values, ultimate values, final ends. Things which are done for their own sake. Things you do because they are what they are and not because they're a means to something else, or even related to something else.

BP-S: Gray also writes that your pluralism concerns conflicts both between goods and between evils. Is that so? There might be conflict between evils?

IB: Of course there can be. You could have a conflict between Fascism and Communism. But the main thing I'm interested in is, of course, conflict of good with good.

BP-S: What, according to you, is good and what is evil? I don't know what your standard is.

IB: Ah, that's a separate question, a central question in moral philosophy. I think that some goods, the great goods, are what a lot of people in a lot of countries at a lot of times take to be good. That's the central core. Apart from that, good is simply, as Hume says, that in the light of which people live their lives. But 'Evil be thou my good', which is what Satan says in Milton's poem—that I've never understood. That means evil is what I pursue. Iago in Verdi's opera *Otello* sings, 'Praise to the god of evil.' His aim is to do harm. I understand that. I don't believe in objective good or objective evil as a priori. I'd be delighted to believe that, but I don't.

BP-S: But good is objective in the sense that it's not a question of belief only, it's knowable in the empirical way?

IB: Yes. Mill, for example, says 'Happiness is the only good.' I don't think it's the only good. Why does he say it? Because, he says, that's what people think, that's what people accept. I don't know why he says that. His defence of utilitarianism is that whatever you think you're doing, in the end you'll find that all you want to do really is what is useful. Not true. I can disprove it to you by an example—quite an amusing example of good and evil. But I can't answer your question. All I can say about good and evil is that they are what we accept or reject in the end. Not we individually, we as a culture, we as a group. Otherwise communication is impossible.

BP-S: But in this sense these values are objective.

IB: Only in the sense that they belong to my *Kulturkreis*, to my culture, my way of life, which I live with other people. What the Chinese think doesn't affect me. That's their view of life.

   Let me give you an example where utilitarianism fails. Supposing there's an island on which there are two cities which don't communicate with each other: complete insulation. Each city is very sadistic; the only thing they enjoy is the thought of other people's sufferings. Each city believes, falsely, that the other is going through the pains of hell. They are not: but each thinks that way about the other. And it makes them happy. Each city is happily contemplating the false proposition that the others are being tortured. What is wrong with such an island? Something is not quite right. There's a great deal of happiness in both cities, so what is wrong? Something is wrong, because we think that gloating when people are tortured is bad. Not only because that leads people to inflict harm, but in itself, intrinsically; the idea of enjoying people's tortures we rule out as evil. What do I mean by evil? Heaven knows. That which I, my culture, my group, people I live among, people I know, people I can talk to, all accept as evil. I can't go beyond that. And millions of other people have thought the same. It's entirely empirical.

BP-S: Yes, but on the other hand you call good and evil categories. How do you reconcile the two views? I remember that I asked you this question: If all the values are entirely empirical, why don't you just call them sociological generalisations?

IB: They embody rules, they embody ideals.

BP-S: But they are entirely empirical at the same time?

IB: Only because everything is. For me, in the end, everything is empirical.

Experience is all we have. Where else can you turn, if you are not a Christian, if you don't believe in God's word, if you don't have an intuition of certain things as absolute (which I don't)? That's what it means to be an empiricist. That's why people attack me, people who really believe in an a priori conception of certain things.

A book which made a difference to me was G. E. Moore's *Principia Ethica*. He says that goodness is a simple, unanalysable quality, and you see it as you see yellow, by direct perception. You see it with your own eyes. I think that if a negative instance occurs, the hypothesis that telephones can't change into geese has to be abandoned. I don't think it will, but in principle it could happen. Whereas people who really believe in absolutes, like Moore, who thinks goodness is a simple quality which you perceive, like yellow—yellow can't stop being yellow; it can't change to something else—people like that really believe in objective unchanging values, seen by a special magic eye. It would be very nice if that were true, it would make life much simpler, but I don't believe it.

BP-S: So values are stable, but on the other hand they are not.

IB: Also not, I agree. They are not as fixed as all that.

BP-S: So the answer is yes and no.

IB: The answer is always yes and no. To all empirical questions, to all questions of life. Are you in love with so and so? Yes and no.

BP-S: Like my ex-President [Lech Walesa]: 'I am for and even against,' he said once.

IB: Marvellous.

24 May 1995

The Knotty Problem Reconsidered:
Does Pluralism Entail Liberalism?

BP-S: John Gray's main thesis, which we discussed last time, is that liberalism is merely one item on the pluralist's menu of options. You answered that pluralism must entail liberalism. But in your conversations with Ramin Jahanbegloo you say, 'Pluralism and liberalism are not the same or even overlapping concepts. There are liberal theories which are not pluralistic. I believe in both liberalism and pluralism, but they are not logically connected.'[1] You say that they are not connected?

IB: No. I meant only that there is no logical entailment. Pluralism might be held completely fanatically. That's to say you have your belief, you think all the other beliefs are completely false, and you proscribe them. You could be pluralist but not tolerant at all. You could be a pluralist and say, I fully understand what this other view is, I am deep inside what the Romans said, I fully understand what nationalism is, I also understand what anti-nationalism is. I understand all these things: but they must be kept out, otherwise they're a danger to the State. Therefore I impose some kind of very rigid orthodoxy. I explain the other movements all right, I understand them, I see that one could belong to them, and yet I don't let them in. There aren't such people—this is purely theoretical—but there could be somebody who was like that.

---

1. Jahanbegloo, *Conversations*, 44; cf. 82, 211 above, 287, 290 below.

BP-S: What you are saying now is very different from what you said at our last meeting.

IB: No, it's exactly the same. This is merely an imaginary case of an extreme kind, and not likely to happen. What I said last time was that pluralism does entail liberalism; that's right, and I do think that. If you're a pluralist you must, since you have an understanding of views other than your own, allow a world in which all these things are pursued by people, even if they are incompatible, and even if you are against some of them. But you could have an isolated case of a man who says: I understand perfectly what these movements are, I understand very well why people believe them; I think they're honest, the people who believe them, I think that some of them may be profound. But I want one doctrine to prevail.

BP-S: So in a way you don't object to Gray's main thesis? Authoritarian regimes like Shinto and Orthodox Judaism, according to him, don't mind about anybody who's outside, but they do restrict the people who are inside.

IB: That could happen, but it's not what I would call pluralism. It is an extreme case of a very eccentric pluralism which believes in the necessity of having a single doctrine in the State. It is quite intolerant. They say: I understand all these other things, I have been through them myself. I was a Communist once, I was a Tolstoyan once, I was this, I was that, I fully understand how one can be. But I'm not going to allow it, because it endangers the State, because we're in a position where we can't allow free speech. I don't think there are cases of this, but in theory this could be a position.

BP-S: So there is no universal case for liberalism?

IB: There's no logical connection, that's all I'm saying. There is a psychological connection, there's a political connection, but not a logical connection. I'm just being rather pedantic.

Perfection

BP-S: There is a passage in John Gray's 'Constancy and Difference' that I'd like to ask you about:

> The idea of incommensurability in ethics is an offence to all the standard positions in moral theory, but it is more than that. It is a criticism of the conception of perfection by which Western thought has been animated at least since Plato and the doctrine of the Form of the Good. More, it is a criticism of the idea of deity which permeates Western theology, in both its Augus-

tinian and its Thomistic traditions, in which it is an attribute of the deity's perfection that it comprehends in its nature all goods. If the idea of incommensurability in fundamental values is sound, then the very idea of perfection, as that has been understood in these central Western traditions, is incoherent. This has the most radical and subversive implications for traditional ways of thinking. It implies that the notion—which is integral to all universalist religions—that there is one best way of life, at least in principle, that is binding on all human beings, is misconceived. And it has the consequence that the project of a theodicy, in which the conflicts of values which distinguish our actual experience are revealed to be merely apparent, is also misconceived. In these traditional understandings, apparent conflicts among ultimate values express imperfections in our understanding, or perhaps in human nature. On Berlin's view, as I understand it, such conflicts betray no imperfection in our perceptions or our nature; they reflect the way things are ultimately in the world. The reality and depth of these conflicts attests to a defect in the very idea of perfection rather than to any imperfection in our understanding.[1]

IB: I fully accept that.

BP-S: Isn't it too strong?

IB: No. It is very strong, but it's right. Perhaps one should add that there is an idea of perfection, but it's not something we understand. Maybe there is another world in which all justice and mercy are one, in which everything is one, knowledge and happiness can be combined, and so on. But it's beyond our understanding. Augustine believed in negative theology; that means that anything we say about God is false because we are human, we are finite, his qualities are not our qualities, and anything you like to say about him by analogy with what goes on in the world cannot be true because he is beyond all this. We have to say that we don't know what he's like: we believe but we don't understand. That's the only way out.

Categories Revisited

BP-S: Another important thing. Gray writes:

So far we have found Berlin treating [categories] as anthropological generalisations, which are presumably known empirically. At the same time, when he discusses the question of our knowledge of these 'categories'

---

1. English original of Dutch translation of John Gray, 'Constancy and Difference: Isaiah Berlin's Contribution to the Life of the Mind', *Nexus* 12 (1995), 5–15.

explicitly, we find him denying that they, or our knowledge of them, are straightforwardly empirical, even though he insists that they cannot be insulated from the growth of scientific knowledge.[1]

IB: That I can explain. The point is there are certain presuppositions of our daily experience which we accept and which we don't question.

BP-S: That sounds very Kantian, doesn't it?

IB: Well, it is Kantian . . .

BP-S: But everything is empirical.

IB: . . . but it could change. Kant is wrong. Kant believes that causality is something in terms of which we interpret the world. But it could change. If all material objects turned to clouds, causality would be very difficult to apply. This telephone cannot turn into a goose, but suppose it could; then our physics, our biology would be completely upset. In other words there are categories—let's say there are frameworks in terms of which we can't help thinking—but they could change.

BP-S: But is our knowledge of them straightforwardly empirical?

IB: Everything is. We understand them because that's how we think.

BP-S: But this is what he writes about your essay 'Does Political Theory Still Exist?':

> Here Berlin's argument follows those of philosophers such as Hampshire and Strawson [. . .] in setting as a task of philosophical enquiry the specification—via a sort of quasi-Kantian transcendental deduction—of the necessary 'categories' of human agency. It is these categories, and not any substantive claims about human motivations or interests, that give most of the content to the idea of human nature in Berlin's account of it.[2]

IB: That's correct. The point about these necessary categories is that they are things which we don't question, which we take for granted—all men do—that there are lumps in the universe which are not clouds, that there is a past and present, that time passes; the ideas of time, space, material objects, as in Kant. But there are things that are not quite so firm, like good and bad, wrong and right. Here there is a certain degree of flexibility. Some categories are rigid and some are a little bit more elastic.

BP-S: But you would call our getting to know them quasi-Kantian?

IB: If you like to call it that, yes, because Kant also believed that we know nothing beyond empirical experience: we don't know the noumenal

---

1. Gray, *Isaiah Berlin*, 67.
2. ibid., 14.

world. Or rather, he does think we know some things—God, freedom and immortality. Apart from that (which I don't accept), and apart from his special kind of moral knowledge, yes, I would say it's Kantian, in the sense that these are the categories by which we think. But they could change, in which case we'd be thrown into chaos, we wouldn't know what to do. Certain things are given; we accept them because we can't help it. But the 'can't help it' is an empirical proposition. I can't help not growing twenty feet tall; I can't help not being able to fly to Sirius with wings: but these are empirical propositions. You can call them necessary if you like, but they are not logically necessary. I go back to Hume: the world is as it is, and there are certain firm categories in terms of which we think. We think in terms of good and bad, we think in terms of true and false. You could imagine a world in which people did not think in terms of good and bad, but it's not our world. You wouldn't know what they meant, you wouldn't be able to understand them—but you could try to conceive of such a world.

Articles
1989–2005

BP-S: *Wouldn't it be too bold of me to write at the end of each paper that I thank you for looking through them? Are they good enough to warrant a mention of your name?*

IB: *I don't mind that. But you needn't. Let them be yours—entirely. Don't say I looked through them. It weakens the originality of your work. And it might look as if I had coerced you into being my creature, my tool. You should defend your independence in terms of negative and positive liberty. Both.*

All Souls College, Oxford, 13 July 1986

These articles were written between the years 1986 and 2005. The first three were discussed with Berlin. The other two amount to the continuation of my work on his ideas. While writing them I made heavy use of our correspondence and conversations. This was a way of sharing the, at that time, unpublished material that I had at my disposal. As these sources are now being made public, there is perhaps a case for not extracting so many passages from them. However, almost all these papers have already been either published or presented elsewhere, so that they have acquired an independent status. This is why I decided to include them in essentially their original form, despite many redundancies and overlaps.

One More Voice on Berlin's Doctrine of Liberty

I

Isaiah Berlin's famous essay on political freedom, 'Two Concepts of Liberty',[1] was described by Marshall Cohen as 'academic, inflated and obscure'.[2] It is perhaps an indication of the value of the essay that it should produce such a violent reaction. However, this characterisation of the essay has relevance to the problem of political liberty itself, for there is no doubt that the concept is of its nature obscure. Nevertheless, though philosophically so vague, the burning issue of liberty cannot be treated as merely academic in the contemporary world. Let this serve as justification for my adding one more voice to a long and complex discussion.

II

Participants in the debate have recognised different threads of Berlin's essay as the most significant ones. Many have concentrated on his conception of negative freedom, some criticising its narrowness and tracing its links with

---

1. Berlin, 'Two Concepts of Liberty', in *Liberty*, 166–217.
2. Marshall Cohen, 'Berlin and the Liberal Tradition', *Philosophical Quarterly* 10 (1980), 216.

classical liberalism.[1] It seems to me, however, that the main value and originality of Berlin's approach lies not so much in his discussion of negative liberty but in his perceptive critique of the positive concept. The proportions of the essay devoted to the two aspects in a way confirm this impression. Berlin devotes nine pages to his exposition of the negative concept, whereas his critique of the positive concept occupies twenty-four pages. Some commentators have discussed both threads of the essay. Nevertheless, what most of them have concentrated upon has been the distinction between the two concepts, not the critique of the positive one.[2] Several authors claim to have solved the problem by arguing away the distinction.[3] A significant exception is Charles Taylor, who questioned Berlin's whole approach to the relationship between the negative and positive concepts.[4] But in my opinion the only author to have taken up and elaborated upon the most original part of Berlin's doctrine, namely the critique of the positive concept, is C. B. Macpherson. This is the only discussion that does not evade in one way or another Berlin's central thesis that positive doctrines of liberty are particularly susceptible to distortion.[5] C. B. Macpherson attempts to refute Berlin's main argument in the following way. He quotes Berlin's statement of the four central assumptions of the positive view of liberty:

> first, that all men have one true purpose, and one only, that of rational self-direction; second, that the ends of all rational beings must of necessity fit into a single universal, harmonious pattern, which some men may be able to discern more clearly than others; third, that all conflict, and consequently

1. See Arnold S. Kaufman, 'Professor Berlin on Negative Freedom', *Mind* 71 (1962), 241–3; Cohen, 'Berlin and the Liberal Tradition', 216–27; Hillel Steiner, 'Individual Liberty', *Proceedings of the Aristotelian Society* 75 (1974–5), 33–6; John Gray, 'On Negative and Positive Liberty', in *Liberalisms*, 62–4. For discussion on the disadvantages of the rigid negative approach, see also Alan Ryan, 'Freedom', *Philosophy* 40 (1965), 108–11.

2. See Gray, 'On Negative and Positive Liberty', 48–51; John Gray, introduction to *Conceptions of Liberty in Political Philosophy*, ed. Zbigniew Pelczynski and John Gray (London: Athlone, 1984), 4–6; Henry J. McCloskey, 'A Critique of the Ideals of Liberty', *Mind* 74 (1965), 483–6; Leslie J. Macfarlane, 'On Two Concepts of Liberty', *Political Studies* 14 (1966), 77–81; David Nicholls, 'Positive Liberty', *American Political Science Review* 56 (1962), 114–15, note 8. For an objection on the ground of the incompleteness of the two concepts of liberty see also Stanley I. Benn, 'Freedom and Persuasion', *Australasian Journal of Philosophy* 45 (1967), 260–2.

3. See Gerald MacCallum Jr., 'Negative and Positive Freedom', *Philosophical Review* 76 (1967), 312–34; Joel Feinberg, *Social Philosophy* (Englewood Cliffs, NJ: Prentice-Hall, 1973), 9–14; William A. Parent, 'Some Recent Work on the Concept of Liberty', *American Philosophical Quarterly* 11 (July 1974), 149–67 (see especially 152 and 166).

4. Taylor, 'What's Wrong with Negative Liberty', 175–93.

5. Macpherson, *Democratic Theory*, 95–119. Though Cohen does actually engage in a discussion of Berlin's critique of conceptions of positive freedom, he conducts it from a position of fundamental disagreement: see Cohen, 'Berlin and the Liberal Tradition', 218, 221–7.

all tragedy, is due solely to the clash of reason with the irrational or the insufficiently rational—the immature and undeveloped elements in life whether individual or communal—and that such clashes are, in principle, avoidable, and for wholly rational beings impossible; finally, that when all men have been made rational, they will obey the rational laws of their own natures, which are one and the same in them all, and so to be at once wholly law-abiding and wholly free.[1]

Macpherson maintains that only the first assumption is inherent in all doctrines of positive freedom. In other words, he questions Berlin's thesis of the necessary logical bond between the notion of 'freedom to' and rationalist monism. According to Macpherson the first assumption is even inconsistent with the last three. For what flows from the acceptance of the 'positive' idea of freedom is not 'a preordained harmonious pattern'[2] but a 'proliferation of many ways and styles of life'.[3]

A hint of the same view, that there is no logical connection between rational self-direction and rationalist metaphysics, has been expressed by John Gray: 'I suggest that some useful variant of the idea of a real or rational will may survive the demise of the rationalist metaphysics and philosophical psychology in which it has traditionally been embedded.'[4] Robert Kocis's conception of rational self-direction is also similar to that of Macpherson: '"self-actualisation" is not a single goal, but a series of (probably conflicting) goals';[5] 'there are many forms of self-realisation'.[6]

Berlin maintains his view and simultaneously rejects Macpherson's objection. According to him, the first assumption implies that to every problem there is in principle only one objective solution. If there is no answer, in principle, to a question, or if there are two answers, it cannot be a real question. Thus, 'my realisation of myself as a rational being must rest on the perception of what the problem is. To this question there is in principle only one true answer. What is true of me is also true of you in similar circumstances, because we are both human beings.'[7]

At this point the door is open to rationalist metaphysics. Thus the idea of rational self-realisation logically entails the conviction expressed in the last three assumptions, if it is taken strictly.

---

1. Berlin, 'Two Concepts of Liberty', in *Liberty*, 200: cf. 142 (note 1) above.
2. Macpherson, *Democratic Theory*, 112
3. ibid., 111.
4. Gray, 'On Negative and Positive Liberty', 59.
5. Kocis, 'Toward a Coherent Theory of Human Moral Development', 375.
6. ibid, 386.
7. Isaiah Berlin in conversation with Beata Polanowska-Sygulska, 5 July 1986.

III

This question has yet another dimension. The problem of human liberty is an object of concern in many intellectual fields other than general political theory —philosophy, social psychology, or literature, for example. It is the role of the last to reflect the mood of contemporary culture. My impression is that one does not often nowadays come across the metaphor of freedom as an experience of space in an upward flight. Naive as this remark may be, the ancient myth of Icarus can be taken as the incarnation of the idea of 'freedom from'. This very notion, though limited to the social context, seems to form the basis of the classical liberal image of freedom. The vision one encounters today has much more affinity with Kierkegaard's choice of the existential stage of development or Heidegger's postulate of authentic existence than with Icarus's flight. It is no longer space devoid of obstacles but the horizon of choice that stands for human liberty. Let me back this digression up with some quotations which, though chosen at random, speak for themselves. This is how two modern writers, Thomas Merton and Alberto Moravia, see human liberty:

> I cannot make the universe obey me. I cannot make other people conform to my whims and fancies. I cannot make even my body obey me. When I give it pleasure, it deceives my expectation and makes me suffer pain. When I give myself what I conceive to be freedom, I deceive myself and find that I am the prisoner of my own blindness and selfishness and insufficiency . . . we too easily assume that we are our real selves, and that our choices are really the ones we want to make, when, in fact, our acts of free choice are (though morally imputable, no doubt) largely dictated by psychological compulsions, flowing from our inordinate ideas of our own importance. Our choices are too often dictated by our false selves.[1]

> [A] man has a beautiful life when he is free, when he lives according to his own principles, directing himself by his own internal inspiration, and not humbly sticking to universally valid norms. To live beautifully means to choose one's own way and follow it despite the price one has to pay. To me that man has lived his life beautifully who has had an opportunity to reveal the whole fullness of his personality, not the one who has lived 'respectably'. A man does not live to be 'respectable', but to express himself as a personality. To me an opportunity of human fulfilment is a synonym for freedom.[2]

---

1. Thomas Merton, *No Man Is an Island* (London: Hollis & Carter, 1955), 20–1.
2. From an interview with Alberto Moravia published in a Polish periodical: 'Podroz po wyboistej drodze z Alberto Moravia' ['A Journey along a Bumpy Road with Alberto Moravia'], *Forum* 48 (1977), 18.

It was the contemporary reality that generated existentialism and induced this very notion of human freedom.

IV

Let us now return to the social context. Reading Fromm's *Fear of Freedom*, one cannot help noticing certain parallels: 'positive freedom consists in the spontaneous activity of the total, integrated personality'.[1] While Merton and Moravia drew their visions of liberty from the standpoint of the isolated individual, Fromm's conception undoubtedly involves a social context. And this is where the political theorist should apply all his imagination. The following excerpt strikes a reader of Fromm as especially significant: 'Positive freedom also implies the principle that there is no higher power than this unique individual self, that man is the centre and purpose of his life: that the growth and realisation of man's individuality is an end that can never be subordinated to purposes which are supposed to have greater dignity.'[2] It is worth mentioning that a similar idea was put forward by one of Berlin's critics, namely by Charles Taylor:

> [E]ach person has his/her own original form of realisation. Some others, who know us intimately, and who surpass us in wisdom, are undoubtedly in a position to advise us, but no official body can possess a doctrine or a technique whereby they could know how to put us on the rails, because such a doctrine or technique cannot in principle exist if human beings really differ in their self-realisation.[3]

Does this mean that both authors somehow want to protect their doctrines against potential distortions? Why did they take such precautions? Were they aware that their conceptions were vulnerable to perversion? Let us now examine the origin of such an apprehension.

An explanation of this problem is provided by 'Two Concepts of Liberty'. The adherents of the positive view of freedom, however, would challenge Berlin's critique and probably his line of defence. It seems valid to follow their argument and to examine the theoretical consequences that may be drawn from their vision of liberty. Let us concentrate upon one concrete doctrine, namely that of C. B. Macpherson. What follows from his simulta-

---

1. Fromm, *Fear of Freedom*, 222.
2. ibid., 228.
3. Taylor, 'What's Wrong with Negative Liberty', 180.

neous acceptance of the first assumption (that is, that all men have one true purpose, and one only, that of rational self-direction) and rejection of the rationalist monism which he claims is inherent in the last three assumptions? If there is no universal pattern and liberty is understood in the positive way, a countless number of collisions is bound to emerge. This is because any social doctrine aiming at regulating relationships among men must provide some universal principle. Classical liberalism structured society by granting every individual an independent sphere. There is no way in which liberty identified with self-realisation and abstracted from any universal pattern of development could perform the same role. What is it then that can make the positive doctrine of freedom a social one, not merely an individualist, possibly existentialist, conception of personal self-fulfilment?

It is my thesis that every defence of positive liberty presupposes some *tacit, universal value* that fulfils the task of structuring society. This value is seen as indispensable and fundamental. At the same time, given the great persuasive appeal of the term 'liberty', it is hard for a theorist to abandon the concept. Thus he expands or even changes its meaning in order to protect the preferred value. Is this the case in Macpherson's discussion? Let us come back once again to his paper. The following excerpt seems to support my contention. '[I]f the chief impediments to men's developmental powers were removed, if, that is to say, they were allowed *equal freedom*, there would emerge not a pattern but a proliferation of many ways and styles of life which could not be prescribed and which would not necessarily conflict.'[1]

However, the removal of the 'chief impediments', which is essential to achieving 'equal freedom', implies the emergence of an authority which would perform the task. By providing equal conditions for self-realisation, the authority must simultaneously define them. Thus it will not be merely the scope of an individual's independent sphere that will be decided upon by some external authority, but also *the very content of his freedom*. This model is bound to produce a limited range of patterns (if not one), rather than a proliferation of many ways and styles of life.

In conclusion, it seems to me that Berlin's main thesis that positive conceptions of liberty are particularly susceptible to distortions remains valid. For if a doctrine of 'freedom to' is to fulfil a social function, it must provide some principle, whether explicit or implicit, by which to structure society. In both cases the term 'liberty' loses its original connotation as a sphere of independence and will mean whatever a theorist wishes.

---

1. Macpherson, *Democratic Theory*, 111–12.

Two Visions of Liberty

Berlin and Hayek

I

Isaiah Berlin and Friedrich August Hayek—the two most powerful contributors to modern liberal philosophy—have marked their participation in contemporary discussion in very different ways. Berlin's single essay, having produced vast and passionate argument, though published over a quarter of a century ago, is still passionately discussed and widely referred to by the continuators of the new movement in ethical thought that he initiated. Hayek's great system of ideas, expressed in many volumes and papers, has attracted comparatively less comment since its peak of popularity at the time of Ronald Reagan and Margaret Thatcher. The different intellectual backgrounds of the two theorists have shaped the character of their achievements. Berlin, being a philosopher, has concentrated upon the purely philosophical aspect of liberty. Hayek, as an economist with a deep knowledge of legal and political issues, has mainly developed the economic dimension of freedom. Dissimilarities between the two contributions makes it particularly tempting to search for common ground.

II

One may ask whether it is at all possible to compare such different achievements. The task is more complex than might appear at first sight. For it is not only the disparity of the preoccupations of the two authors that makes their approaches so distinct. It is my interpretation that the main difference lies in their levels of theorising. While Hayek remains mostly on the theoretical level, building up his own body of doctrine, Berlin formulates a meta-theory of liberty, i.e. a theory of theories. Let me now elaborate on the latter remark. Ascription to Berlin by his critics of an assumed liberal doctrine of freedom has long been a source of serious misinterpretations. Berlin's analysis of the two concepts of liberty, and his thesis that the negative one gives better safeguards for individual freedom, is essentially a discussion, rather than a body of doctrine.[1]

However, some part of Hayek's reflections, pertaining to the philosophical dimension of freedom, also belongs to the meta-theoretical level. The following provisions would make a comparison between Berlin's and Hayek's approaches possible. First, what can be considered is the philosophical aspect of liberty, which has been developed by both authors. The basic sources of their views, then, would include Berlin's 'Two Concepts of Liberty', with the introduction to the later edition, and Hayek's *The Constitution of Liberty*, which contains the fullest presentation of this topic. Only occasionally will I rely on other writings. Second, the legal and the economic dimensions of liberty, so fully developed in Hayek's doctrine, will receive only brief comment. Though Berlin does not, in principle, take up these problems, his standpoint can be derived, to a certain extent, from his writings. I shall draw a comparison between the legal and economic views of the authors within the limits set by Berlin's preoccupations.

III

Despite his strong grounding in economics, Hayek appreciates the great importance of political philosophy:

> [T]hough I still regard myself as mainly an economist, I have come to feel more and more that the answers to many of the pressing social questions of our time are to be found ultimately in the recognition of principles that lie outside the scope of technical economics or of any other single discipline. Though it was from an original concern with problems of economic policy that I started, I have been slowly led to the ambitious and perhaps presumptuous task of approaching them through a comprehensive restatement of the basic principles of a philosophy of freedom.[2]

---

1. Berlin confirmed this intuition of mine in a conversation in July 1986: 154–5 above.
2. Friedrich A. Hayek, *The Constitution of Liberty* (London: Routledge & Kegan Paul, 1960), 3.

Hayek ends where Berlin starts, with his warning against the undervaluing of political thought: 'when ideas are neglected by those who ought to attend to them—that is to say, those who have been trained to think critically about ideas—they sometimes acquire an unchecked momentum and an irresistible power over multitudes of men that may grow too violent to be affected by rational criticism'.[1]

Both authors ascribe special status to liberty within their systems of ideas. They justify their positions, however, in different ways. For Berlin, the value of liberty flows from his recognition of the plurality of human aims and the indispensability of making choices: 'The world we encounter in ordinary experience is one in which we are faced with choices between ends equally ultimate, and claims equally absolute, the realisation of some of which must inevitably involve the sacrifice of others.'[2] 'If, as I believe, the ends of men are many, and not all of them in principle compatible with each other, then the possibility of conflict—and of tragedy—can never wholly be eliminated from human life, either personal or social.'[3] It is Berlin's thesis that men put such high value on liberty just because of this 'inescapable characteristic of the human condition'.[4]

Hayek puts forward a quite different justification for the special position of liberty. His contention flows straight from the idea of spontaneous order in society that forms the central core of his political philosophy: 'the case for individual freedom rests chiefly on the recognition of the inevitable ignorance of all of us concerning a great many of the factors on which the achievement of our ends and welfare depends'.[5]

According to Hayek the level of our ignorance increases with scientific advance, for '[t]he more men know, the smaller the share of all that knowledge becomes that any one mind can absorb. The more civilised we become, the more relatively ignorant must each individual be of the facts on which the working of his civilisation depends.'[6]

On John Gray's interpretation, most of the knowledge on which social life depends is of a primordially practical character. Thus, it cannot be concentrated in a single brain, natural or mechanical, not because it is very complicated, but rather because it is embodied in habits and dispositions, and it governs our conduct via rules which are often inarticulate.[7] Our inevitable ignorance creates

---

1. Berlin, 'Two Concepts of Liberty', in *Liberty*, 167.
2. ibid., 213–14.
3. ibid., 214.
4. ibid.
5. Hayek, *The Constitution of Liberty*, 29.
6. ibid., 26.
7. John Gray, *Hayek on Liberty* (Oxford: Basil Blackwell, 1986), 25.

the need for providing conditions in which the greatest variety of experiences and opportunities will be generated: 'Liberty is essential in order to leave room for the unforeseeable and unpredictable.'[1] In Hayek's view the value of liberty stems from its indispensability to the further advance and preservation of civilisation. Both authors point to hypothetical situations in which liberty would lose its value. Thus, for Berlin, this would be the moment of realisation of the perfect State, abolishing all the conflicts between human aims, while for Hayek it would be the achievement of omniscience, embracing all future wants and desires. The counterfactuality of these two visions confers value on liberty. The status of freedom in Berlin's and Hayek's views, though similar, is not identical. Berlin, in the introduction to his essay, rejects the objection that he makes liberty an absolute value: 'Nothing that I assert [. . .] about the frontiers of individual liberty (and this applies to the liberty of groups and associations too) should be taken to mean that freedom in any of its meanings is either inviolable, or sufficient, in some absolute sense. It is not inviolable, because abnormal conditions may occur.'[2]

Nevertheless, just because of the fact that freedom is 'an inalienable ingredient in what makes human beings human',[3] it should be curtailed only under exceptional circumstances. Thus, though not an absolute value, it undoubtedly possesses a special status 'precisely because we regard such situations as being wholly abnormal, and such measures as abhorrent, to be condoned only in emergencies so critical that the choice is between great evils, we recognise that under normal conditions, for the great majority of men, at most times, in most places, these frontiers are sacred, that is to say, that to overstep them leads to inhumanity'.[4]

Unlike Berlin, Hayek seems to ascribe an absolute character to liberty: 'Like all moral principles, it demands that it be accepted as a value in itself, as a principle that must be respected without asking whether the consequences in the particular instance will be beneficial.'[5] Only such an understanding of liberty, in Hayek's opinion, creates safeguards for its respectability: 'freedom can be preserved only if it is treated as a supreme principle which must not be sacrificed for particular advantages'.[6] For liberty is not merely one particular value, but the source and condition of most moral values.[7]

---

1. Hayek, *The Constitution of Liberty*, 29.
2. Berlin, Introduction, in *Liberty*, 52.
3. ibid.; cf. 262, 286 below.
4. ibid., 52–3.
5. Hayek, *The Constitution of Liberty*, 68.
6. Friedrich A. Hayek, *Law, Legislation and Liberty*, 3 vols. (London: Routledge & Kegan Paul, 1982), 1: 57.
7. Hayek, *The Constitution of Liberty*, 6.

IV

In spite of some differences, Berlin's and Hayek's philosophical conceptions of liberty show general similarity. Both authors accept the negative approach and associate liberty with a respected sphere of independence. They ascribe other interpretations to efforts aimed at the protection of values distinct from liberty. But here the kinship between the two standpoints ends, and we encounter a serious difference. Berlin approves of the two equally valid understandings of the concept of liberty, namely the negative and the positive ones. He identifies the first interpretation with the lack of obstacles to potential choices, and the second with the wish on the part of the individual to be his own master. The two concepts may, to a certain extent, overlap, but they are not the same. While 'freedom from' is a political ideal, 'freedom to' constitutes a moral demand. However, the positive concept, when connected with the idea of two selves and extended to certain supra-individual entities, may threaten political liberty. Thus it is 'freedom from' that, according to Berlin, provides a 'truer and more humane ideal'.[1] Unlike Berlin, Hayek accepts only one understanding of liberty. He admits that the term may also be used in several other long-established senses, though not without care. Nevertheless, 'in our sense *freedom* is one, varying in degree but not in kind'.[2]

Hayek's approach can be represented by the following formula—'liberty means a state in which a man is not subject to coercion by the arbitrary will of another or others'.[3] This definition comprises several elements that demand further elaboration. In principle, only an individual can be a subject of liberty. Hayek's terminology reflects this conviction through his frequent use of the phrase 'individual liberty'. He indicates that the term 'personal freedom' would also be legitimate. Berlin, too, relates the 'safer' and, thus, preferred understanding of liberty to the individual. Nevertheless, he is not as precise as Hayek in terminological questions. Usually he employs the phrases: 'negative liberty' or 'freedom from'. Sometimes, however, he uses the terms 'individual', 'social' or 'political liberty' as implicit synonyms. Incidentally, it is significant that Hayek understands 'political liberty' quite differently. In his interpretation the term is much closer to Berlin's 'positive freedom'. This point is elaborated later in this paper.

Both authors place negative, individual liberty in a social context. This

---

1. Berlin, 'Two Concepts of Liberty', in *Liberty*, 216; cf. 89 above, 225, 286 below.
2. Hayek, *The Constitution of Liberty*, 12.
3. ibid., 11.

point is underlined in this remark of Hayek's: '"freedom" refers solely to a relation of men to other men, and the only infringement of it is coercion by men'.[1] Berlin's viewpoint on this question seems to be similar, though less narrow—he relates violations of liberty solely to the 'interference of other human beings', both direct or indirect, intentional or unintentional.[2] Let us now concentrate on the actual wording of the two approaches. While Hayek defines freedom as the lack of coercion, Berlin employs for the same purpose the following phrase: the lack of obstacles to potential choices. Despite the difference in the definitions, freedom, in both cases, is identified with a certain sphere of independence. This understanding is strictly 'negative', for it includes neither 'inner' nor 'outer' conditions of realising the liberty of the individual. Here we encounter another distinction between the two approaches. Berlin defines the sphere of non-interference very loosely, not tackling the question of its borders. He remarks only that 'the minimum area that men require if [. . .] dehumanisation is to be averted, a minimum which other men, or institutions created by them, are liable to invade, is no more than a minimum; its frontiers are not to be extended against sufficiently stringent claims on the part of other values, including those of positive liberty itself'.[3] He insists, however, that this minimum area must be respected if we are not to 'degrade or deny our nature'.[4]

Hayek justifies the postulate of preserving an independent sphere in a different way: 'The rationale of securing to each individual a known range within which he can decide on his actions is to enable him to make the fullest use of his knowledge, especially of his concrete and often unique knowledge of the particular circumstances of time and place.'[5] This argument is closely connected with his idea of spontaneous order in society. Unlike Berlin, Hayek provides a criterion for the delimitation of an independent private sphere. He contends that such borders should not be treated as fixed once for all. Moreover, they cannot be marked by the will of any man or group of men. The solution to the problem 'rests on the recognition of general rules, governing the conditions under which objects and circumstances become part of the protected sphere of a person or persons. The acceptance of such rules enables each member of a society to shape the content of his protected sphere and all members to recognise what belongs to their sphere and what does not.'[6] It is

1. ibid., 12.
2. Berlin, 'Two Concepts of Liberty', in *Liberty*, 169–70.
3. Berlin, Introduction, in *Liberty*, 53.
4. Berlin, 'Two Concepts of Liberty', in *Liberty*, 173, quoting Constant: see 37 above, note 6.
5. Hayek, *The Constitution of Liberty*, 156.
6. ibid., 140.

not possible, then, to enumerate all the rights and protected interests that should be recognised as belonging to the respected area. Nevertheless, Hayek comments upon several of the most typical elements which, according to him, are inherent in this sphere: private property, a right to privacy and secrecy, and the conception of a man's house as his castle.

Finally, let me discuss the significant changes that have taken place in the views of both authors. What strikes the reader of Berlin and Hayek, the latter in particular, are the modifications introduced by them with reference to the character of individual liberty (namely its 'subjectivity' or 'objectivity'). In the first edition of his essay Berlin defined freedom subjectively, as the lack of obstacles to realisation of man's desires. Thus, the scope of liberty depended on an individual's own estimation. In his introduction to the later edition, he changed the wording of his standpoint, putting forward a new understanding of freedom as the lack of obstacles to the potential human choices. In this way the notion acquired an objective character. Hayek's formulations have evolved in the opposite direction. When compared with his older definition, the later one, put forward in *Studies in Philosophy, Politics and Economics* and enriched by the following modification, has become openly subjective: 'To constitute coercion it is [. . .] necessary that the action of the coercer should put the coerced in a position which he regards as worse than that in which he would have been without that action.'[1] These shifts in the positions of both authors have been caused by the critical discussions of their ideas.

My own view is, however, that the 'objective' understanding of freedom provides a 'safer' definition, in so far as it secures better safeguards for protecting liberty. When an individual is conceived of as having a decisive voice on the scope of his liberty, the term becomes relative and thus opens the door to techniques of manipulation.

V

Let us now briefly consider Hayek's catalogue of other interpretations of the concept of liberty. It may be instructive to look for their counterparts in Berlin's work and to compare the attitudes of both authors. Hayek starts his analysis from the concept of 'political freedom', understood as 'the participation of men in the choice of their government'.[2] In his opinion such an inter-

---

1. Friedrich A. Hayek, *Studies in Philosophy, Politics and Economics* (London: Routledge & Kegan Paul, 1967), 349.

2. Hayek, *The Constitution of Liberty*, 13.

pretation should not be confused with the notion of individual liberty, for 'a free people in this sense is not necessarily a people of free men'.[1] What Hayek calls 'political freedom' is, for Berlin, one of the forms of positive freedom (i.e. that of collective self-direction). Though Berlin also employs this term, he understands it quite differently, namely as individual liberty. Despite this ambiguity, Berlin's attitude towards the aforementioned form of collective freedom seems to be very close to that of Hayek: 'The desire to be governed by myself, or at any rate to participate in the process by which my life is to be controlled, may be as deep a wish as that for a free area for action, and perhaps historically older. But it is not a desire for the same thing. So different is it, indeed, as to have led in the end to the great clash of ideologies that dominates our world.'[2] Another form of collective freedom is striving for national independence. Once again, Berlin and Hayek insist that this interpretation should be differentiated from the notion of individual liberty. Berlin expands this understanding to cover other social groups, such as classes, races, communities, or professions. Thus both authors draw a distinction between individual and collective freedom, and warn against confusing them.

The next meaning discussed by Hayek is that of 'inner', 'metaphysical' or 'subjective' freedom. In his interpretation, such an understanding implies that a man should be guided in his actions by his own considered will, by his reason or lasting conviction, rather than by momentary impulse or circumstance. Besides, while choosing between alternatives, a person should not be subject to ignorance or superstition. According to Hayek, the 'opposite of "inner freedom" is not coercion by others but the influence of temporary emotions, or moral or intellectual weakness'.[3] It follows then, that this meaning is different from that of 'individual liberty', and should not be confused with it. While Hayek confines himself to drawing the above distinction, Berlin devotes the major part of his essay to its discussion. His rough counterpart to Hayek's 'inner freedom' is 'positive freedom' or 'freedom to'. But the two understandings are not identical. For 'inner freedom', according to Hayek, can be obstructed by emotions or moral or intellectual weakness, while 'positive freedom', in Berlin's interpretation, can also be curtailed by other people:

> I wish my life and decisions to depend on myself, not on external forces of whatever kind. I wish to be the instrument of my own, not of other men's, acts of will. I wish to be a subject, not an object; to be moved by reasons,

---

1. ibid.
2. Berlin, *Two Concepts of Liberty*, 178.
3. Hayek, *The Constitution of Liberty*, 15.

by conscious purposes, which are my own, not by causes which affect me, as it were, from outside. I wish to be somebody, not nobody; a doer— deciding, not being decided for, self-directed and not acted upon by external nature or by other men as if I were a thing, or an animal, or a slave incapable of playing a human role, that is, of conceiving goals and policies of my own and realising them.[1]

Berlin differentiates between the two historical forms of the idea of 'freedom to', namely that of ascetic self-denial and the positive doctrine of liberation by reason. Incidentally, he uses the very term 'inner freedom' for the first, historically older, form. He warns against dangerous perversions of the concept of 'freedom to', which are likely to occur when the notion becomes connected with the idea of the two selves. The most original and valuable part of the essay is devoted to tracing the intellectual sources of these distortions.

While Berlin identifies the greatest danger to liberty as the concept of 'freedom to', expanded over supra-individual entities, Hayek sees the menace elsewhere. To him it is the identification of freedom with 'the physical ability to do what I want'[2] that provides the most serious threat to liberty. For it leads to the assimilatioin of liberty and collective power. Thus both authors oppose the collective interpretation of the notion of freedom, though they describe the process of expanding the concept differently. They also warn against confusing liberty with other values and thus extending its original meaning. According to Berlin: 'Everything is what it is: liberty is liberty, not equality or fairness or justice or culture, or human happiness or a quiet conscience.'[3] This thought is also present in Hayek's work: 'Liberty does not mean all good things or the absence of all evils.'[4]

At this point let me convey some general impressions that I have gained from the writings of the two authors on the philosophical dimension of freedom. As a theorist, Hayek seems to place a high value on consistency and clarity of formulation. However, it is possible that because of this he occasionally falls into formalism, while trying to 'bridle' a subject-matter that by its very nature eludes theoretical rigour. Berlin's investigations, on the other hand, cannot be described as precise. This is not merely a question of style: he appears to build his doctrine upon the assumption that there are no final solutions to the problem of liberty. The following excerpt supports this intuition: 'the vagueness of the concepts, and the multiplicity of the criteria

---

1. Berlin, 'Two Concepts of Liberty', in *Liberty*, 178.
2. Hayek, *The Constitution of Liberty*, 16.
3. Berlin, 'Two Concepts of Liberty', in *Liberty*, 172.
4. Hayek, *The Constitution of Liberty*, 18.

involved, are attributes of the subject-matter itself, not of our imperfect methods [. . .] or of incapacity for precise thought'.[1]

VI

Berlin does not, in principle, develop the legal aspect of freedom. One may try, however, to derive his position, to a certain extent, from the remarks and hints scattered in the essay. Also the selection of quoted authors itself in some way reveals his standpoint. Thus, while reflecting upon negative liberty Berlin approvingly quotes Hobbes: 'A free man', said Hobbes, 'is he that [. . .] is not hindered to do what he has a will to.'[2] Hobbes's thought is then elaborated upon: 'Law is always a fetter, even if it protects you from being bound in chains that are heavier than those of the law, say some more repressive law and custom, or arbitrary despotism or chaos. Bentham says much the same.'[3] Later on, in the context of a discussion of Mill's approach, Berlin reconstructs the negative conception of liberty in its classical form in the following way: 'all coercion is, in so far as it frustrates human desires, bad as such, although it may have to be applied to prevent other, greater evils; while non-interference, which is the opposite of coercion, is good as such, although it is not the only good'.[4] It is very significant that Berlin quotes Locke in the second part of the essay, which is devoted to positive freedom. He connects Locke's thesis, 'Where there is no law there is no freedom',[5] with 'the forms of liberalism founded on a rationalist metaphysics'.[6] All of them are versions of the following creed: 'A law which forbids me to do what I could not, as a sane being, conceivably wish to do is not a restraint of my freedom.'[7] To sum up, Berlin's standpoint seems to be close to that of Bentham: 'Every law is contrary to liberty.'[8]

The heredity of classical liberal thought suggests quite different things to Hayek. In his interpretation of thinkers like Adam Smith or John Stuart Mill, 'Freedom of economic activity had meant freedom under the law. [. . .] The "interference" or "intervention" of government which those writers opposed

---

1. Berlin, 'Two Concepts of Liberty', in *Liberty*, 177, note 1.
2. ibid., 170, note 3, citing *Leviathan*, chap. 21: ed. Richard Tuck (Cambridge: Cambridge University Press, 1991), 146.
3. ibid.
4. ibid., 175.
5. ibid., 193.
6. ibid., 195.
7. ibid.
8. ibid.

as a matter of principle therefore meant only the infringement of that private sphere which the general rules of law were intended to protect.'[1] Seeing in these rules the basic safeguard of individual liberty, Hayek contends that 'We owe our freedom to restraints of freedom.'[2] For man's development did not take place in conditions of liberty. 'Freedom was made possible by the gradual evolution *of the discipline of civilisation, which is at the same time the discipline of freedom.*'[3] It is significant that Hayek finds support for his thesis in Locke: 'who could be free, when every other man's humour might domineer over him?'[4] Hayek's strong belief in the unbreakable link between the philosophical and legal aspects of freedom resulted in the emergence of his theory of 'the rule of law'. He develops this in the second part of *The Constitution of Liberty*. However, because of the lack of any counterpart in Berlin's conception I shall confine myself to indicating this striking difference between the two doctrines.

The last problem to be discussed is the 'economics of freedom'—within the bounds of the two conceptions. While Berlin expresses his views on the topic merely in the form of several incidental suggestions, Hayek devotes the principal part of his doctrine to it. Because of this difference in proportion I shall comment upon the question only briefly. In his essay, Berlin hardly takes up the economic dimension of freedom at all. Thus, from his acceptance of the negative understanding, some critics derived an extreme negativist attitude towards all forms of interventionism. Such an interpretation led Berlin to express his view in the introduction to the later edition of the essay: 'Legal liberties are compatible with extremes of exploitation, brutality and injustice. The case for intervention, by the State or other effective agencies, to secure conditions for both positive, and at least a minimum degree of negative, liberty for individuals is overwhelmingly strong.'[5] Nevertheless, Berlin confined himself to rejecting the laissez-faire approach that had been, quite mistakenly, ascribed to him, and did not develop the issue. In another essay entitled 'Political Ideas in the Twentieth Century' we encounter a revealing passage: 'It is neither realistic nor morally conceivable that we should give up our social gains and meditate for an instant the possibility of a return to ancient injustice and inequality and hopeless misery. The progress of technological skill makes it rational and indeed imperative to plan.'[6] Thus

---

1. Hayek, *The Constitution of Liberty*, 220.
2. Hayek, *Law, Legislation and Liberty*, 3: 163.
3. ibid.
4. ibid., quoting John Locke, *Second Treatise on Government*, chap. 6, sect. 57.
5. Berlin, Introduction, in *Liberty*, 38.
6. Berlin, 'Political Ideas in the Twentieth Century', in *Liberty*, 91.

it is simply not true that Berlin holds an extreme negativist view. His plea for negative liberty should be interpreted on the meta-doctrinal level—as an advocacy of the concept that is more resistant to dangerous distortions. But this discussion should not be mistaken for a body of doctrine, which Berlin simply did not develop. His pluralistic vision of reality, on the other hand, implies that liberty is one of many values, and thus may be curtailed for the sake of some of them. Yet there is a sense defended by him in which the negation of liberty is the negation of choice; and choice is involved in choosing any value, whether inimical to a given liberty or not.

As far as Hayek's approach is concerned, this image changes rapidly. The largest part of *The Constitution of Liberty* is devoted to the incarnation of the principle of liberty in economic life. Hayek's economic conception provides an application of the idea of spontaneous order. Thus the only successful regulator of this sphere of social life is the free market since planning is impossible because of man's unavoidable ignorance of dispersed knowledge. Hayek argues against the coercive measures taken by the Welfare State, which, in his view, encourage inflation. His critique constitutes a strong plea against a State monopoly in particular spheres of economic life. According to Hayek, such a monopoly in fact provides a hidden form of egalitarian redistribution, based on some non-existent principle of social justice.

Once again, because of the lack of a counterpart within Berlin's conception I shall not elaborate on this topic but confine myself to the following conclusion: While Berlin, believing in the plurality of values, seeks the solution in 'some logically untidy, flexible and even ambiguous compromise',[1] Hayek demands the reinstatement of the free market, which is treated by him as a sort of panacea.

To sum up, Berlin's and Hayek's visions of freedom show affinity in the philosophical dimension. The two approaches are strikingly different as far as the legal aspect of liberty is concerned. The economic views of both authors, to the extent to which they may be compared, also seem distinct. Berlin, when I asked him to express his opinion of Hayek's doctrine, answered: 'I think he is too narrow, too rigid. Such an approach can lead to a fiercely competitive society, which can produce a terrible perversion of what I call both negative and positive liberty. But I do not wish to attribute to him the wish for any such result; only the provision of insufficient protection against it.'[2]

---

1. ibid., 92.
2. Isaiah Berlin in conversation with Beata Polanowska-Sygulska, 13 July 1986.

The Twilight of 'Liberty' as an Abstract Ideal?

I

This article analyses two different approaches to social freedom, viz., tackling the issue in the traditional, general way, and giving up the abstract ideal either for the sake of 'minimising unfreedom' or for the sake of particular liberties.

The respective positions of Berlin and Hayek on the one hand, and Popper, Aron and Dworkin on the other, are presented as an illustration of the two approaches. The standpoints of Berlin and Popper are given special consideration, as they are most richly underpinned by these authors' methodological views. The consequences of adopting each of the two approaches, and especially their bearing on individual liberty, are analysed.

It is suggested that the old abstract ideal of liberty provides better safeguards for individual freedom.

II

Aron, Berlin, Dworkin, Hayek and Popper on Liberty

Reading contemporary liberal philosophers, one encounters surprisingly divergent approaches to the central concept of liberty. Raymond Aron concludes in his *An Essay on Freedom* that 'there is no totality which can be called *the* freedom of individuals or *the* freedom of nations'.[1] Ronald Dworkin seems to represent a similar position: 'there is no such thing as any general right to liberty'.[2] Aron's and Dworkin's demand that general reflection on liberty should be abandoned brings to mind Karl Popper's postulate that one should deal with liberation rather than with the ideal of social liberty. On the other hand Friedrich Hayek firmly insists that 'while the uses of liberty are many, liberty is one'.[3] Berlin, criticising the contemporary 'tendency to circumscribe and confine and limit',[4] and 'to reduce all issues to technical problems',[5] recognises social liberty as a traditional philosophical subject and deals with it in a general way.

It will be interesting to learn the intellectual sources of these two kinds of approach. What are the arguments for and against each of them? And which of them seems to create better safeguards for individual liberty? I shall attempt in this article to search for answers to these questions. I shall mainly concentrate upon Popper's and Berlin's approaches, since they seem to rest on a more developed methodology.

III

Popper and Berlin: Liberation or Choosing the 'Safer' Concept of Liberty

When, at the beginning of his celebrated essay, Berlin proposes to analyse two central senses of the protean word 'freedom',[6] the reader cannot help juxtaposing this intention with Popper's thesis that it is *unimportant* to discuss words and meanings.[7] This statement stems from his methodological anti-essentialism. Is, then, Berlin's account of liberty essentialist? It does not seem so, for the following reasons. First, Berlin's conception is not an insight into the nature of freedom, but a critical examination of the two main meanings that have been historically ascribed to it. Second, his thesis of the par-

---

1. Aron, *An Essay on Freedom*, 145.
2. Ronald Dworkin, *Taking Rights Seriously* (London: Duckworth, 1978), 277.
3. Hayek, *The Constitution of Liberty*, 19.
4. Berlin, 'Political Ideas in the Twentieth Century', in *Liberty,* 89–90.
5. ibid., 82.
6. ibid., 168.
7. Karl R. Popper, 'Winch on Institutions and the Open Society', in *The Philosophy of Karl Popper,* ed. Paul Schilpp (La Salle, IL: Library of Living Philosophers, 1974), book 2, 1166.

ticular susceptibility to distortions of the positive doctrines of liberty seems to be testable, as far as the practical consequences of adopting each of the two concepts are concerned. Third, his definitions of both positive and negative liberty should be labelled as nominalist, for they must be read, as Popper demands,[1] from the right to the left: 'The first of these political senses of freedom or liberty [. . .] *I shall call* the "negative" sense. [. . .] The second [. . .] *I shall call* the "positive" sense.'[2]

Fourth, Berlin's essay aims primarily neither at clarification of the concept of liberty nor at making it more precise. What Berlin examines are the theoretical consequences resulting from the acceptance of each of the two understandings of liberty. Thus, his considerations appear to be directed outwards and not towards the concept, which seems to be a distinctive feature of the essentialist method. Therefore, it looks as if Berlin's analysis of liberty cannot be characterised as typically essentialist.[3]

Popper claims to have introduced the term *essentialist* (and *essentialism*) in *The Poverty of Historicism* and in *The Open Society and Its Enemies*.[4] His account of the essentialist method as consisting in penetration to the essence of things in order to explain them[5] has been widely adopted. It must be borne in mind, however, that the term has a broader connotation in the whole of Popper's philosophical system. It is crucial to elaborate on this point, even though this is contrary to Popper's recommendation that we should avoid discussing words and meanings. There are contexts in *The Open Society* in which the essentialist position is understood in the way defined above ('the essential nature of the State',[6] 'the true nature of the State'[7]). Elsewhere in the book, however, the reader may learn that the essentialist method consists not only in looking into the real nature of things, but also embraces the sort of semantic analysis found in Wittgenstein's *Tractatus*.[8] The broadest interpretation of the term can be deduced from Popper's *anti-essentialist exhortation*: '*Never let yourself be goaded into taking seriously problems about words and their meanings. What must be taken seriously are questions of fact, and assertions*

---

1. Popper, *The Open Society*, 2:14; cf. 61–2 above.
2. Berlin, 'Two Concepts of Liberty', in *Liberty*, 169 (my emphasis); cf. 52 above.
3. There is, however, a touch of essentialism in the following remark:
'Pluralism, with the measure of "negative" liberty it entails, seems to me a *truer* and more humane ideal.' ibid., 216 (my emphasis); cf. 89, 245 above, 286 below.
4. Popper, *Conjectures and Refutations*, 169, note 5.
5. Popper, *The Poverty of Historicism*, 28.
6. Popper, *The Open Society*, 1: 112.
7. ibid., 115.
8. See the criticism of Wittgenstein in *The Open Society*, 2: 9, 20; *The Philosophy of Karl Popper*, book 2, 1171; and Popper, *Unended Quest*, 116.

about facts: theories and hypotheses; the problems they solve; and the problems they raise.[1] It is very striking that according to this formulation even radical nominalism would have to be labelled as essentialist.

Leaving aside the controversial problem of essentialism, it is worth stressing that Popper's and Berlin's approaches to social liberty are conspicuously different. Berlin's abstract question, 'Which of the two historically significant concepts of liberty, "negative" or "positive", is theoretically safer with regard to respecting individual freedom?' cannot be fruitfully discussed on Popper's grounds. We should give up thinking about social liberty in a general way. If I interpret him correctly, Popper himself would ask a different question: 'What should we do under given circumstances to minimise violations of liberty?' Thus, it is not different *conceptions of liberty* and their theoretical consequences that should be critically examined, but *liberation* understood as a proposal for political action. Only such a demand can be sensibly discussed and put into practice. It is through the application of the method of trial and error that the 'piecemeal social engineer' could minimise infringements of individual liberty and thus proceed towards liberation. Popper's approach stems from his conviction of 'a really fundamental similarity between the natural and social sciences'. In consequence, traditional political theory with its elucidation of concepts would have to be given up: 'All those theories must be translated, as it were, into the language of demands or proposals for political actions before they can be seriously discussed.'[2]

It is very significant indeed that the quoted statement comes from *The Open Society*. On the one hand Popper, in his great book, outlines an idea of 'piecemeal social engineering' which is supposed to conform to his thesis of the affinity between the social sciences and the experimental natural sciences. On the other hand, he *seriously discusses* the political theories of Plato, Hegel and Marx without having previously translated them 'into the language of demands and proposals for political actions'. Does not the mere fact of Popper's formulation of his famous critique confirm the validity of discussing essentialist theories? And yet, according to his own recommendation, such theories are philosophically unimportant. One could defend Popper's position by claiming that he mounted his attack just because of the great perils inherent in essentialist political theories, and that his anti-essentialist exhortation will prevent the formulation of dangerous theories in the future. But the author of *The Open Society*, in the fervour of polemics, happens to have betrayed his own, rigorously postulated, anti-essentialism.

---

1. Popper, *The Open Society*, 2: 19; cf. 61, 176 (note 1) above.
2. ibid., 1: 112.

For his widely discussed condemnation of Plato's politics hinges on Popper's claim that a distorted concept of justice is applied in the *Republic*. As this is a crucial point, I shall take the liberty of quoting the relevant passages from *The Open Society*. The reader is introduced into the central core of the author's argument by being asked: 'What do we *really* mean when we speak of *Justice*?'[1] The question strikes us as, true to type, essentialist. For what is being asked about here is the meaning of 'justice'. Popper is aware of this awkwardness, for he then tries to belittle it: 'I do not think that verbal questions of this kind are particularly important, or that it is possible to make a definite answer to them, since such terms are always used in various senses. However, I think that most of us, especially those whose general outlook is humanitarian, mean something like this',[2] and then follows a characterisation of the humanitarian understanding of 'justice'. The next most revealing passage makes it clear that Popper fights Plato's essentialist philosophy precisely with essentialist means:

> If Plato had meant by 'justice' anything of this kind, then my claim that his programme is purely totalitarian would certainly be wrong and all those would be right who believe that Plato's politics rested upon an acceptable humanitarian basis. But the fact is that he meant by 'justice' something entirely different. What did Plato mean by 'justice'? I assert that in the *Republic* he used the term 'just' as a synonym for 'that which is in the interest of the best State'.[3]

Thus, although elsewhere Popper says that 'nothing depends on words, or on "conceptions"',[4] this proves to be untrue in the case of his own substantive argument.

There is another puzzle in Popper's approach. The questions he would regard as genuinely important, that is 'What should we do in these circumstances?', 'What are your proposals?',[5] presuppose previous convictions about aims and values. Translation of political theory into the language of proposals and demands would result in stopping the debate over priorities as such. But they would be assumed in the proposed aims to be realised through 'piecemeal social engineering'. Thus reduction of the discussion only to technological means would imply only superficial silencing of the eternal controversies. It is very striking that Popper on the one hand claims to be a pluralist and stresses

---

1. ibid., 89 (my emphasis).
2. ibid.
3. ibid.
4. *The Philosophy of Karl Popper*, book 2, 1166.
5. I owe this interpretation to Magee, *Popper*, 106.

that clashes of values and principles are fundamental for the open society,[1] and on the other recommends giving up the disputes over them.[2]

Both motifs—the dangerous distortions of concepts and the plurality of values—bring to one's mind Berlin's political theory. They are approached here, however, in a different way because of Berlin's distinct methodological convictions. For Berlin does not denounce enquiry into words and meanings as philosophically unimportant; on the contrary, he maintains that 'the only way in which we can interpret the world is by examination of the words and concepts in terms of which we think of this world; we learn from juxtaposing dissimilar concepts, categories etc., and we discover what at least we ourselves believe, seek, and believe others to believe, seek, and suspect them, if they disagree, of confusion or self-deception (sometimes justly, sometimes not)'.[3]

Recognising that research on crucial words in influential doctrines is highly significant, Berlin examines two central concepts of liberty—'negative' and 'positive'—understood respectively as the lack of obstacles to potential human choices and as self-realisation. He enquires into their metaphysical presuppositions and their implications. He arrives at the conclusion that distortions of both concepts have led to socially intolerable practices, but the perversions of positive freedom have more frequently

---

1. '[T]here always exist irresolvable clashes of values: there are many moral problems which are insoluble because moral principles may conflict. [. . .] clashes of values and principles may be valuable, and indeed essential for an open society.' Popper, *Unended Quest*, 116.

2. '[S]o much of the talk about values is just hot air. So many of us fear that we too would only produce hot air or, if not that, something not easily distinguished from it. To me these fears seem to be well founded.' ibid., 193. The anomaly in Popper's approach has already been commented upon by Rush Rhees: 'free criticism has not the function in social affairs that it has in science. And experimenting and learning by mistakes are not the same here either. These points are both connected with the fact that controversies in social affairs are not about the solution of problems, as they are in science. If we speak of "social problems", that is something different. [. . .] Criticism may lead men to alter policies. And reasons may lead men to adopt them. But often they do not. When they do it is not like science. Arguing for a policy is not like establishing a theory, and raising objections to a policy is not like criticising a theory. In any case, if "public control through free criticism" means control by all citizens, this is unlike science because there are not common standards and methods of criticising social policies.' Rush Rhees, *Without Answers* (London: Routledge & Kegan Paul, 1969), 62–3. A similar point has been made by Peter Winch: 'discussion and criticism are possible only if there is agreement amongst the participants about what hypotheses or policies are to be discussed. But the hypotheses formulated by the social engineer as worthy of discussion will be those which have a bearing on the achievement of the ends which he has. So, unless his ends are shared by a large number of other people, he is unlikely to arrive at hypotheses which others will be willing to discuss with him and he will thus not have the benefit of criticism[,] which is essential if his activities are to be carried out in a rational way. Hence there is a premium—deriving from the nature of rationality—on having social aims which are likely to be widely shared.' Peter Winch, 'Popper and Scientific Method in the Social Sciences', in *The Philosophy of Karl Popper*, book 2, 898.

3. Letter of 22 April 1987, 58 above.

been used to defend oppression and injustice than those of negative liberty. Berlin's liberalism is embedded in his radical pluralism of aims and values. Such a vision of reality implies a traditional conception of political theory as 'an enquiry concerned not solely with elucidation of concepts, but with the critical examination of presuppositions and assumptions, and the questioning of the order of priorities and ultimate ends'.[1] Since the core of political theory is the dispute over its central value-concepts, 'the prospects of establishing a science in this field [. . .] seem remote'.[2] For the subject-matter of political theory differs from 'any other empirical enquiry in being concerned with somewhat different fields; namely with such questions as what is specifically human and what is not and why; whether specific categories [. . .] are indispensable to understanding what men are; and so, inevitably, with the source, scope and validity of certain human goals'.[3] For Berlin, political theory could be transformed into an applied science only conditionally on a universal acceptance of a single dominant model.[4]

The difference between Popper's and Berlin's methodological views touches on fundamentals. The fragmentary analysis set out above does not provide an adequate basis for drawing categorical conclusions. But we can definitely say that Berlin's approach can detect dangerous perversions of political concepts, while Popper's nominalistic method leaves them out of account. It is only when Popper adopts 'essentialist' means that he becomes able to fight such distortions. Moreover, the belief, common to both thinkers, in the inevitability of clashes of values seems to cohere better with Berlin's traditional political theory than with Popper's social technology.

IV

Aron and Dworkin: Liberties Instead of Liberty

Another recommendation to abandon a general idea of liberty comes from Raymond Aron. His approach, however, stems more from his political than (as in Popper's case) his methodological commitments. Criticising Hayek's understanding of liberty as the absence of coercion, Aron claims that it is only the freedom of the entrepreneur, or of the consumer, which has served as the model

---

1. Berlin, 'Does Political Theory Still Exist?', in *The Proper Study of Mankind*, 66.
2. ibid., 65.
3. ibid., 74.
4. See ibid., 66–71.

for this definition. In Aron's view such an approach confuses one aspect of freedom with the whole of freedom and underestimates the power of egalitarian demands.[1] The way out is to assume the existence of *individual freedoms* rather than one *fundamental freedom*.[2] This is tantamount to abandoning philosophical reflection for the sake of sociological analysis. In Aron's opinion, dealing with individual freedoms calls for the adoption of a neutral and analytic sense of liberty. He employs Felix Oppenheim's definition, which meets the required demands: 'I am free to do something provided nobody prevents me from doing it or makes it punishable for me to do it, or provided nobody makes it either necessary or mandatory for me to do so.'[3] Thus social freedom is at the same time freedom *to* and freedom *from*. According to Aron this implies that every member of a society is unfree with regard to innumerable acts and free to do numerous acts because of the law which forbids other people to prevent me from doing them.[4] Thus every law takes certain freedoms away from some, but at the same time confers freedoms on others or on all.[5] This argument leads Aron to the significant thesis of the non-existence of a totality which can be called the freedom of individuals or nations.

A somewhat similar conclusion has been reached, though in a different way, by Ronald Dworkin. For the author of *Taking Rights Seriously*, the foundation of the liberal society is not liberty in the neutral sense, as has traditionally been claimed, but equality of concern and respect. Dworkin is strongly opposed to the idea of liberty as license, which he defines as 'the degree to which a person is free from social or legal constraint to do what he might wish to do'.[6] He condemns it as being neutral with respect to forms of behaviour. He chooses Berlin's concept of 'freedom from' as an illustration of this approach.[7] Dworkin claims that the idea of liberty as license is untenable, and tries to argue it away. The consensus in favour of some *right to liberty* seems to him absurd. The conclusion is firm: there exists no general right to liberty. We have only 'distinct rights to certain liberties like the liberty of free expression and of free choice in personal and sexual relations'.[8] As there is no right to liberty, the conflict between liberty and equality vanishes and the argument for any given specific liberty may be entirely independent of the argument for any other.[9]

---

1. Aron, *An Essay on Freedom*, 88–9.
2. ibid., 142.
3. Oppenheim, *Dimensions of Freedom*, 118.
4. Aron, *An Essay on Freedom*, 144.
5. ibid., 145.
6. Dworkin, *Taking Rights Seriously*, 262.
7. ibid., 267.
8. ibid., 277.
9. See ibid., 274, 277–8.

V

Berlin and Hayek: Restoration of the Old Ideal

It is justified that Dworkin and Aron should have chosen just Berlin's and Hayek's views of liberty as a target for their criticisms. For the latter authors consistently stick to the general idea of social freedom. It would be interesting to look for, and enquire into, their counter-arguments to criticism of their approach. Berlin, asked by me to express his opinion on the topic, answered:

> [I]t's is not an accident that all these liberties are called liberties. It is not just a coincidence that economic liberty, liberty of worship, liberty of association, liberty of speech are all called *liberties*. There is something in common, there is a kernel [. . .] When people say [. . .], 'I've lost my liberty', it's not meaningless. You don't say, 'Please be precise. You've not lost your liberty to breathe, you've not lost your liberty to frown, you've not lost your liberty to bend your finger. What do you mean?' What they mean is freedom to perform the kind of acts which I need to perform if I am to be fully myself.[1]

One of the crucial notions underlying Berlin's reflections on liberty is the conviction that the idea of choice is intrinsic to the concept of man. If a man were denied *any choice* he would cease to be fully human. Thus it is not only the freedom of the entrepreneur or of the consumer that provides the model for the negative (and the general) understanding of liberty. Neither is it true, according to Berlin, that social freedom is at once freedom *to* and freedom *from*. That is because a man struggling against his chains or a people against enslavement need not consciously aim at any definite further state. A man need not know how he will use his freedom; he just wants to remove the yoke.[2] The point of Berlin's argument seems clear enough—he aims at protection of individual freedom as 'an inalienable ingredient in what makes human beings human'.[3] This preoccupation is even more explicit in Hayek:

---

1. Conversation of 13 July 1986, 159 above.
2. See Berlin's reply to Gerald McCallum Jr., who represents a similar position to that of Oppenheim: Introduction, in *Liberty*, 36, note 1. For an excellent critique of what he calls the 'restrictivist' approach to social liberty see also John Gray, 'On Liberty, Liberalism and Essential Contestability', *British Journal of Political Science* 8 (1978), 386–7, and 'On Negative and Positive Liberty', *Liberalisms*, 45–6.
3. Berlin, Introduction, in *Liberty*, 52; cf. 244 above, 286 below.

Liberties appear only when liberty is lacking: they are the special privileges and exemptions that groups and individuals may acquire while the rest are more or less unfree. Historically, the path to liberty has led through achievement of particular liberties. But that one should be allowed to do specific things is not liberty, though it may be called 'a liberty'; and while liberty is compatible with not being allowed to do specific things, it does not exist if one needs permission for most of what one can do. The difference between liberty and liberties is that which exists between a condition in which all is permitted that is not prohibited by general rules and one in which all is prohibited that is not explicitly permitted.[1]

Hayek also points out that it is impossible to compile a complete catalogue of rights: 'Today we must be particularly aware that, as a result of technological change, which constantly creates new potential threats to liberty, no list of protected rights can be regarded as exhaustive. [. . .] The greatest threats to human freedom probably still lie in the future.'[2] Thus both Berlin and Hayek put new life into the traditional, general idea of social freedom which in their opinion provides better safeguards for individual liberty.

VI

Final Remarks

Having analysed the two approaches to social liberty in the light of the positions of their supporters, we have reached the point where some conclusion is supposed to be drawn. Yet as I believe in an ineradicably disputable character of the idea of social liberty, I contend that no ultimate solution can be found. Was there any point, then, in the whole discussion? I think that at least one thing can be learnt from it. The proposal to abandon the traditional idea of liberty always seems to involve an intention to further some other aim. In Popper's case it is his *unity of scientific method*, in Aron's the *meeting of egalitarian demands*, and in Dworkin's *abolishing of the conflict between liberty and equality*. In consequence, alas, it is individual liberty that is the loser. It is conspicuous that Aron himself should

---

1. Hayek, *The Constitution of Liberty*, 19.
2. ibid., 216.

admit this: 'Against totalitarian regimes it is both easy and necessary to involve the old wisdom: absolute power corrupts absolutely; freedom implies a sphere in which the individual is his own master and answerable only to himself.'[1]

1. Aron, *An Essay on Freedom*, 160.

Pluralism and Tragedy

Isaiah Berlin, generally recognised as the author of the conception of ethical pluralism,[1] reflected upon his contribution to this idea (in an interview given to me in 1991) in the following way: 'I cannot believe I am the first person to have said that some ultimate values are incompatible. Maybe I am; but it's rather like the first man who said "Two plus two equals four." [. . .] It seems so obvious to me.'[2]

Pluralism is an intermediate standpoint in ethics, situated between monism and relativism, and offering a unique description of ethical life. According to monism there is only one reasonable system of values, the same for all human beings. Different kinds of ethical relativism assume that all values are merely expressions of personal preferences or social conventions, varying from place to place. From a pluralist standpoint human values are objective and knowable, but they are irreducibly plural. They can be neither ranked in a comprehensive hierarchy nor reduced to a common measure that

---

1. This claim, though, has recently been questioned by the discovery of much earlier publications referring to ethical pluralism. See Sterling P. Lamprecht, 'The Need for a Pluralistic Emphasis in Ethics', *Journal of Philosophy, Psychology and Scientific Methods* 17 No. 21 (1920), 561–72; and A. P. Brogan, 'Objective Pluralism in the Theory of Value', *International Journal of Ethics* 41 No. 3 (1931), 287–95. Berlin never mentioned these articles (or their authors), and may never have read them; it seems unlikely that he would have forgotten them if he had, and the striking similarities of wording may be coincidental.

2. See 124 above.

has universal binding force. What is more, some human aims and values may be incompatible and incommensurable. There exists no ultimate standard that would allow for rational resolution of collisions among them. As the conflict among values is inevitable, the idea of perfection (which assumes completeness) is logically incoherent, and total ethical harmony is beyond human reach. Charles Taylor commented upon Berlin's contribution to this standpoint in the following way:

> Isaiah's plurality thesis was not only a blow to various totalitarian theories of positive liberty, it was also deeply unsettling to the moral theories dominant in his own milieu. It is one of the paradoxes of our intellectual world, which will be increasingly discussed in the future, why this latter point was not realised. The bomb was planted in the academy, but somehow failed to go off.[1]

The odds are that it was a bomb with delayed ignition. The pluralist standpoint, only loosely sketched in Berlin's writings, has been made more precise in more recent publications.[2] According to William A. Galston this view can be characterised by the following basic tenets:

1. Value pluralism is not relativism. The distinction between good and bad, and between good and evil, is objective and rationally defensible.
2. Objective goods cannot be fully rank-ordered. This means that there is no common measure for all goods, which are qualitatively heterogeneous. It means that there is no *summum bonum* that is the chief good for all individuals. [. . .]
3. Some goods are basic in the sense that they form part of any choiceworthy conception of a human life. [. . .]
4. Beyond this parsimonious list of basic goods, there is a wide range of legitimate diversity—of individual conceptions of good lives, and also of public cultures and public purposes. [. . .]
5. Value pluralism is distinguished from various forms of [. . .] 'monism'. A theory of value is monistic [. . .] if it either (*a*) reduces goods to a common measure or (*b*) creates a comprehensive hierarchy or ordering among goods.[3]

---

1. Charles Taylor, 'Plurality of Goods', in *The Legacy of Isaiah Berlin*, ed. Ronald Dworkin, Mark Lilla and Robert B. Silvers (New York: New York Review Books, 2001), 117.
2. See, among others, Maria Baghramian and Attracta Ingram, eds., *Pluralism: The Philosophy and Politics of Diversity* (London: Routledge, 2000); George Crowder, *Liberalism and Value Pluralism* (London and New York: Continuum, 2002); William A. Galston, *Liberal Pluralism: The Implications of Value Pluralism for Political Theory and Practice* (Cambridge: Cambridge University Press, 2002).
3. Galston, *Liberal Pluralism*, 5–6.

George Crowder articulates a different version of pluralism that stresses the tension inherent in the incommensurability thesis. In his view there are four basic components inherent in this theory:

First, pluralists claim that there are certain fundamental universal values, the enjoyment of which contributes to human flourishing. [. . .] Second, the things that are valuable for human beings—including both universal and local values—are plural or several. [. . .] The third component of pluralism is the most distinctive. This is that values are not only plural but may be radically so: they may be incommensurable with one another. [. . .] For the value pluralist, no basic value is inherently more important or authoritative or weightier than any other, and none embraces or summarises all other values. [. . .] Fourth, these plural and incommensurable values may in particular cases come into conflict with one another. That is, they may be incompatible or mutually exclusive, such that one is realisable only at the cost of sacrificing or curtailing another.[1]

Berlin found it difficult to assume sole credit for initiating the new pluralist direction in ethics: 'I cannot believe that I am the first person to think of something so obvious as to say that some ultimate values conflict with others.'[2] Nevertheless, it was his work that 'has helped spark what may now be regarded as a full-fledged, value-pluralist movement in contemporary moral philosophy'.[3] Moreover, pluralism is a movement within which 'contrary standpoints and schools have already emerged'.[4]

II

On Crowder's interpretation, the central implication of the pluralist outlook is that problematic choice is the necessary consequence of conflict among incommensurables.[5] Both he and John Gray have investigated the subject of value conflicts. Gray singles out three levels at which we can experience clashes of aims and values: (1) within any morality or code of conduct—among ultimate values (e.g., between liberty and equality), (2) within com-

---

1. Crowder, *Liberalism and Value Pluralism*, 2–3.

2. Conversation of October 1991, 123 above.

3. Galston, *Liberal Pluralism*, 5.

4. The following standpoints are recognised in the literature: 'liberal' and 'anti-liberal' pluralism (see Crowder, *Liberalism and Value Pluralism*, chaps. 3 and 4); 'tragic' and 'benign' pluralism (see Jonathan Riley, 'Crooked Timber and Liberal Culture', in Baghramian and Ingram, 120–55).

5. Crowder, *Liberalism and Value Pluralism*, 3.

plex values themselves (e.g., between freedom 'from' and freedom 'to'), and (3) among whole ways and styles of life (e.g., represented by different cultural forms).[1] Crowder points to two principal sources of value conflict. First, the ability of human beings to realise different values is limited by empirical circumstances. Given the laws of physics it is impossible to be at the library and at the beach simultaneously. Second, some clashes arise from the very nature of the values concerned. A life of independent, unencumbered self-reliance necessarily excludes a life dedicated to a large family and marital intimacy.[2]

A crucial question arises—is it possible to make rational choices in situations of value-conflict? This issue has given rise to two opposing standpoints within the pluralist movement. The first one, sometimes (rather misleadingly) labelled 'tragic pluralism', questions the rational solubility of all conflicts. According to this outlook situations occur in which reason encounters an impassable barrier—incommensurability of the ultimate values which people pursue for their own sake. The only way out of such a stalemate would be to make a radical, arbitrary choice, which implies some necessary loss. Versions of this standpoint are represented not only by Berlin, but also by Stuart Hampshire, Joseph Raz and John Gray.[3]

Other adherents of pluralism, labelled 'benign', express greater optimism about the possibility of integrating rival values, even though they recognise the inevitability of tragic loss. Thomas Nagel adopts this point of view when he advocates 'the search for higher-order values, or for methods that permit the conflicts to be resolved'.[4] Taylor entertains similar hopes: 'It always makes sense to work toward a condition in which two cherished goods can be combined, or at least traded off at a higher level. [. . .] Such adjudication and balance are possible if we approach value pluralism in an Aristotelian framework.'[5] It seems that such optimistic expectations, which were expressed at a conference convened by the New York Institute for the Humanities in the autumn of 1998 to mark the first anniversary of Berlin's death, were fulfilled four years later. Crowder, in his *Liberalism and Value Pluralism*, put forward the thesis that it is possible to choose rationally among conflicting values. In Crowder's view pluralism implies two kinds of guidelines—particularist and universalist—capable of guiding rational choice among plural values. The former makes rational choice possible by

1. Gray, *Isaiah Berlin*, 42–3.
2. Crowder, *Liberalism and Value Pluralism*, 55–6.
3. I share Crowder's interpretation on this point: see *Liberalism and Value Pluralism*, 6 note 3.
4. Thomas Nagel, 'Pluralism and Coherence', in *The Legacy of Isaiah Berlin*, 110.
5. Taylor, 'Plurality of Goods', 118.

attention to the context in which it is taken. The latter advocates the application of a set of universal principles which, according to Crowder, are implicit in pluralism itself.[1]

Despite these differences, both approaches within value pluralism share an important feature—'they take value conflict seriously'.[2] Both recognise the phenomenon of the incommensurability of values, as well as the fact that the unavoidable loss inherent in making a 'radical' or a 'hard' choice can never be fully compensated for. Thus, conflicts of values and the choices made among them sometimes have a tragic dimension. Of the whole spectrum of problems tackled by the contributors to the pluralist standpoint in ethics, let us now concentrate on what is considered the tragic element of value pluralism. In particular, let us analyse the opposing positions represented by Berlin and a Polish philosopher, Ryszard Legutko. According to Berlin the phenomenon of the tragic is best understood from the pluralist standpoint in ethics, while in Legutko's view pluralism is actually an anti-tragic conception, and it is only the monistic perspective that allows us to recognise the losses inherent in value conflicts as human tragedies.

III

In an article published in *Critical Review* in 1994,[3] Ryszard Legutko fiercely criticises the commonly accepted thesis that value-pluralism best reveals the tragic dimension of the human condition.[4] The polemic he initiated has continued.

As Legutko's arguments seemed to be crucially important, I reported them to Berlin, who criticised them in a letter to me dated 28 June 1997.[5] Legutko answered a year later in two texts published in Polish.[6] This did not mark the end of the disagreement, however. In 2002 George Crowder joined

---

1. Crowder, *Liberalism and Value Pluralism*, chaps. 3, 5, 6, 7, 8, 10.

2. This 'Dworkinian paraphrase' comes from Steven Lukes; see his *Moral Conflict and Politics* (Oxford: Clarendon Press, 1991), chaps. 1, 2.

3. See 94 above, note 1.

4. ibid.

5. See 101–2 above.

6. Ryszard Legutko, 'O postmodernistycznym liberalnym konserwatyzmie' ['On Postmodern Liberal Conservatism'; not the same as the article published with this title in English], in *O czasach chytrych i prawdach pozornych* [*On Sly Times and Sham Truths*] (Krakow: Stalky i Spolka, 1999), 75–101, and 'O obiektywnym pluralizmie wartosci' ['On Objective Pluralism of Values'], in *Liberalizm u schylku XX wieku* [*Liberalism at the Close of the 20th Century*], ed. Justyna Miklaszewska (Krakow: Meritum, 1999), 25–37.

the discussion. Since it is likely that the polemic will remain lively, it is worth reconstructing its course hitherto.

Legutko puts forward the thesis that pluralism is entirely devoid of tragic features. First, it ignores the religious dimension of the ultimate. Second, it lacks two ingredients essential for recognising tragedy: the notion of necessity and the notion of unity. When there is no impersonal necessity—fate or a higher moral imperative—there is no tragedy.[1] There is also no tragedy when there is no sense of the unity of morality:

> If it were possible to speak about the phenomenon of the tragic, one would have to assume not only that values have an objective character, but that they are also united so strongly—moreover, objectively, or even, as in the tragedians, metaphysically, i.e. in the form of some general Justice—that we must feel obliged to pursue the most important of them, even if they happen to be contradictory. Thus the tragic assumes the conception of the objective unity of values and the necessity of an uncompromising pursuit of them, quite apart from our own preferences, even at the cost of suffering and ultimate sacrifice.[2]

In Legutko's view, moral pluralism is inherently anti-tragic.[3] For example, in the light of value-pluralism Antigone and Creon 'are at best impractical doctrinaires, and at worst stubborn blockheads, unable to see that the only sensible solution for them was a compromise which, unaccountably, they refused to make'.[4] Contrary to Berlin's thesis that the idea of incommensurability, which lends a tragic dimension to human choices, comes from the thinkers of the counter-Enlightenment, and that the Greeks were unable to identify it, Legutko firmly emphasises that it was precisely the ancients who discovered and interpreted the notion of the tragic. He contends that on the basis of pluralism human choices—particularly those made among lower goods—are in fact trivial, not tragic; pluralism gives tragedy a frivolous interpretation. What is tragic—asks Legutko—in choosing between two clearly incommensurable values—becoming a priest or a soldier? The answer is that such a dilemma is no more tragic than staying at home in the summer or going on a vacation.

Berlin's epistolary reply is a record of his spontaneous reflections; thus it does not fully satisfy the demands of precision and coherence. Its most important counter-arguments are expressed in the following passages:

---

1. 'On Postmodern Liberal Conservatism', 6.
2. 'O postmodernistycznym liberalnym konserwatyzmie', 81.
3. 'On Postmodern Liberal Conservatism', 6.
4. ibid.

It is very well for him [Legutko] to say that a man can choose to be a priest or a soldier, and if he chooses one then he doesn't regret the other—of course, there is no agony here—as he says, I go for a walk or not. The agony comes in, and with it the tragedy (for this is what tragedy is about), when both values pull strongly at you; you are deeply committed to both, you want to realise them both, they are both values under which your life is lived; and when they clash you have to sacrifice one to the other, unless you can find a compromise which is not a complete satisfaction of your desires, but prevents acute pain, in short, prevents tragedy. That is the value of compromise.[1]

It is significant that Legutko ignored the above crucial passage in his analyses. Berlin elaborated on the nature of the tragic in the following way: 'The tragedy is for the Athenian audience, who presumably believe in both sets of values, both the unwritten laws, the eternal code which Antigone obeys, and Creon's belief that the State is the ultimate source of authority. [. . .] Whichever side wins, the loss of the other side is a source of pain to the audience, which believes in both these irreconcilables. This is tragic.'[2] Legutko's retort is bald and flat: 'I find it difficult to argue this point, because this is exactly the stance which I myself took.'[3]

Crowder offers a different interpretation of the Creon–Antigone conflict. In his view, the tragic quality of certain human choices flows from the sense of loss that is an inescapable consequence of sacrificing one of the conflicting values. Such loss is in a sense absolute: it is not compensated by the gains in the rival value. It is in these—typically pluralist—terms that Crowder perceives the tragic dimension of the dilemma faced by Creon. He 'must decide between upholding the laws of the State in his political role, which oblige him to execute Antigone, and honouring the claims of family relationship in his role as Antigone's uncle and prospective father-in-law. His decision in favour of the State's law does not blind him, at least at the end, to the absolute nature of the price for that decision.'[4]

IV

It is impossible to give a simple answer to Legutko's penetrating and multi-faceted critique, but I would just observe that, paradoxically enough, he is at

---

1. Letter of 28 June 1997, 101 above.
2. ibid.
3. 'O postmodernistycznym liberalnym konserwatyzmie', 100.
4. Crowder, *Liberalism and Value Pluralism*, 71–2.

the same time right and wrong. He correctly points out that in the phenomenon of the tragic—as it was understood and interpreted by Sophocles—the idea of the unity of values was inherent. Unfortunately, this is not an original argument. A dozen or so years before Legutko raised his objection, nearly the same thought was expressed by Alasdair MacIntyre, also in the context of a criticism of Berlin's ethical standpoint. According to MacIntyre, Sophoclean tragedy is powerful precisely because it assumes that there is one objective moral order, but because of flawed human understanding men are unable to harmonise rival moral truths.[1] MacIntyre stressed that Sophocles' viewpoint was unique in Greek thought, and contrasted it with Plato's and Aristotle's conception of virtues. A similar observation was made earlier by Berlin: 'Some sceptical thinkers in the ancient world—Carneades, for example [. . .] uttered the disquieting thought that some ultimate values might be incompatible with one another, so that no solution could logically incorporate them all. [. . .] Something of this, too, seemed to lie at the heart of the tragedies of Sophocles, Euripides.'[2]

Nevertheless, the above passages do not completely put Legutko's thesis to rest. A crucial question arises—does the absence of the category of unity, an absence embedded in the pluralist outlook, imply the elimination of tragedy altogether? And is the perspective of Sophocles the only one from which phenomenon of the tragic can be perceived? The answer to both questions is—no.

Modern philosophy has given rise to a variety of interpretations of tragedy. This theme is present in the reflections of Pascal, Hume, Hegel, Schopenhauer, Heidegger and Sartre. Hegel's contribution marked a crucial breakthrough by initiating a new paradigm of tragic action in terms of a conflict of duties, rather than in terms of suffering, pity and purgation. Let us concentrate on the theory of tragedy put forward by Max Scheler in his *Zum Phänomen des Tragischen*, 1915. Apart from the deep chasm separating Scheler's emotional apriorism from the empiricist perspective characteristic of pluralists, and, moreover, Scheler's hierarchical system from the pluralist vision of ethics—it seems, paradoxically enough, that the interpretation of the tragic he presents largely corresponds with the pluralist viewpoint. Scheler perceives the tragic not just as an aesthetic, but as an ethical, category, and concentrates on its objective properties: '"Tragic" [. . .] this heavy cool breath, given by things themselves, this dark glimmer surrounding them, from which a particular property of the world—and not of our "I", its feelings,

---

1. Alasdair MacIntyre, *After Virtue* (London: Duckworth, 1985), 143.

2. Isaiah Berlin, 'Herder and the Enlightenment', in *Three Critics of the Enlightenment*, ed. Henry Hardy (Princeton, NJ: Princeton University Press, 2000), 233.

experiences of sympathy and fear—dawns upon us.'[1] Thus tragic complications are inherent in objective reality, and not in subjective human reactions to
it. They may occur only 'in the sphere of *values and relationships between
them*'.[2] In a world devoid of values—a purely physical world—there is no
tragedy. Scheler distinguishes three notions—tragic 'curse', tragic 'knot', and
tragic fault. The phenomenon of the tragic includes the destruction of some
value; it occurs in the clearest and sharpest form when holders of *equally* high
values seem to be doomed to demolish and erase one another.[3] Such a curse
is ingrained in reality, which is constructed in just this way: the curse is
involved in the constitution of the world. This constitution seems to be on the
look-out for such events, to which it itself gives birth.[4] Another important trait
of the tragic event is its inevitability. The 'inner' necessity of the destruction
of values results not from outer factors, but from the permanent nature of
things and from people's experience of a tragic fate.[5] Reality, 'lying in wait'
for conflict, permanently 'ties itself' in tragic 'knots', because the causal
course of events does not care for values. The culminating point of the tragic
is guilt, into which the hero falls; it is the guilt, which, as it were, comes to the
hero, and not he to the guilt. The position in which he finds himself precludes
right resolution. 'The moral or the "culpable guilt" is grounded in *the act of
choice*; the tragic or the "non-culpable guilt" in *the sphere of choice*.'[6]

Of the two ingredients which according to Legutko are indispensable to
the tragic, Scheler includes only one—the category of necessity. However, he
understands it differently from Legutko—not as a destiny or a moral imperative, but as the inevitability of the destruction of a value. Such an understanding fully conforms to the viewpoint of pluralism, which strongly
stresses the unavoidability of the loss inherent in the collision of values.

One might say that, over the span of ages, the theory of tragedy has undergone an evolution which results in a shift in the weight assigned to different
aspects of tragedy. In consequence, some of them are now perceived as more
significant, while others have been de-emphasised. The former undoubtedly
include axiological conflict and the loss it entails, the latter, unity of values
and human struggle with unpredictable, irrational forces. Both value conflict

---

1. Max Scheler, *Vom Umsturz der Werte: Abhandlungen und Aufsätze* [*Gesammelte Werke*, vol.
3] [*On the Revolution in Values: Treatises and Articles* [*Collected Works*, vol. 3]] (Bern: Francke
Verlag, 1955), 151. All translations from Scheler are my own.
    2. ibid., 153.
    3. ibid., 155.
    4. ibid., 157.
    5. ibid., 161.
    6. ibid., 168.

and loss are greatly emphasised by pluralists. Nevertheless, none of them identifies a tragic element in every act of choosing. John Gray, accused by Legutko of a 'frivolous' interpretation of the tragic, by no means holds such a view: 'The fact that good harbours conflicts of value does not mean that the human condition must always be tragic. To be sure, tragic choices cannot be eliminated from ethical life. Where universal values make conflicting demands, the right action may contain wrong. Then there is surely tragedy.'[1]

Does Legutko rightly ascribe an anti-tragic character to pluralism? In other words, does the pluralist viewpoint make it impossible to find oneself in a position in which there is no good way out, and which inevitably leads to 'falling'—if not into guilt—then into responsibility for unavoidable loss? Gray declares that life is much more complex than traditional ethics. In his view, it is great literature, and life itself, that throw most light on existential complications.[2]

In his autobiography, the Polish film director Krzysztof Kieslowski recalls a difficult choice he once made:

> Martial law—it was all so terrible. It seemed to me that it was something the nation would never forgive the regime, and that people would revolt. I instantly began signing some letters of protest, some petitions. At first it was very hard for my wife. She felt I was responsible for her and for the child. She was right. At the same time I knew that I was responsible for more than that. And this was exactly an example of the inability of making a good choice. If the choice was right from the social point of view, it would be wrong from the family point of view. One should always seek a lesser evil. This lesser evil boiled down to my going to bed and simply falling asleep, like a bear.[3]

Did not the situation in which this man—a modern incarnation of Antigone—found himself necessitate the destruction of some good, whether he believed in the 'objective unity of values' or not? And if he did not, would we have the right to call him a 'stubborn blockhead' because of the moral discomfort which he felt? Finally, is it the thesis of the objective unity of values that throws more light on his position, or is it Berlin's explication of the agony experienced by the man who is drawn in different directions by colliding

1. John Gray, *Two Faces of Liberalism* (New York: New Press, 2000), 10.
2. 'Zycie jest bardziej zlozone niz tradycyjna etyka' ['Life is more complex than traditional ethics'], Bronislaw Wildstein in conversation with John Gray, in Bronislaw Wildstein, *Profile wieku* [*Profiles of the Century*] (Warsaw: Politeja, 2000), 176.
3. Krzysztof Kieslowski, *Autobiografia: O sobie* [*Autobiography: About Myself*], ed. Danuta Stok (Krakow: Znak, 1997), 93.

values? One may discuss whether the good relinquished by Kieslowski was great enough to call his choice a tragic one. But in any case, one of the two colliding values was irrevocably sacrificed for the sake of the other one.

However, there are existential complications which do not raise such doubts. In a conversation with Bryan Magee, Berlin considered the possibility of making a rational choice in a hypothetical situation where there are not enough dialysis machines, and it is necessary to make a decision about which of two patients—a great scientist or an innocent child—is to be rescued.[1] The answer was to him self-evident—in the situation of a conflict between two incommensurable ultimate values a rational choice is out of the question. There is no way to justify such decisions rationally, taken as they are in the face of profound dilemmas.

Life has brought about a realisation of this theoretical vision. Consider what an eminent Polish nephrologist Franciszek Kokot once recalled:

> I often felt like a hangman. A patient needed dialysis and I didn't have enough apparatuses. I ordered him to wait and [. . .] it was as if I had performed the death penalty. The patient usually died before his turn came. I always left everything to chance. When I had several patients, I connected to the apparatus the one who turned up first. I treated them all the same, whether it was a worker, a cleaner, a priest or a teacher. Then I was not psychologically burdened with a choice. This I couldn't stand. If I had decided myself that I would, for instance, connect this one to a dialysis machine, and the other one not, it would mean that I would consciously sentence one of them to death. Once I had a call from a local committee of the Communist Party:—'Please include in the programme of dialyses comrade X,' demanded some Party secretary. I replied: 'Comrade, you are welcome. Tomorrow I'm sending you a list of twenty dialysed patients. Please cross out one name and enter your candidate.' He didn't dare.[2]

A conscious adherent of ethical pluralism would interpret his position in just this way. Life made him face a choice among distinct, ultimate, and incommensurable values; such a conflict excluded—to his mind—making a rational decision. The aforementioned comrade interpreted the situation exactly in the same way, though he was probably experienced in making hard choices. Let us characterise the situation in Scheler's terms. There is no doubt that an inevitable, necessary loss was inherent in any decision that

---

1. Bryan Magee, 'Dialogue with Isaiah Berlin', in *Men of Ideas: Some Creators of Contemporary Philosophy* (London: BBC, 1978), 31.

2. 'Czesto czulem sie jak kat' ['I Often Felt Like a Hangman'], J. Watola and D. Kortko in conversation with F. Kokot, *Magazyn Gazety Wyborczej*, 10 January 2002, 26.

could be made by the agent. Reality tied itself into a tragic knot—in the face of a clash of equally high values the agent had no chance of finding a good way out. He did his best to avoid responsibility, but the non-culpable tragic guilt came to him by itself. Just because of it he sometimes 'felt like a hangman'. There is no doubt that the position in which he found himself bears all the hallmarks of the tragic in Schelerian terms.

The status of moral conflict has been the subject of pluralists' analyses, including those of Steven Lukes and George Crowder.[1] According to them, monistic theories seek to avoid recognition of moral conflict in two ways— either by interpreting it as a result of an error, of ignorance, or of individual or social pathology (Plato, Aristotle, Aquinas, and their successors), or by proposing an overarching principle that provides us with a practical decision-making procedure for all possible moral contexts (modern Kantianism and utilitarianism). Relativism deprives moral conflict of any meaning by explaining it away, that is by proposing a structure in which all allegedly colliding demands—each in its own place—deserve acceptance. Subjectivist theories remove the sting from moral conflict in another way—by erasing the notion of conflicting claims based on reasons. For instance, emotivism sees morality as just a way of expressing or inducing states of mind and feeling.[2] It is only pluralism, which recognises the plurality of values, their incompatibility and incommensurability, that fully accounts for moral conflict. It is only the pluralist perspective that allows for an adequate explication and depiction. It is only pluralism that, to use a Dworkinian phrase, 'takes moral conflict seriously', makes sense of it and assigns a meaning to this basic ethical experience.[3] Pluralists do not cling dogmatically to their standpoint and are aware that their adversaries are not devoid of counter-arguments. As Crowder openly admits: 'The case for incommensurability, and for value pluralism more generally, is not logically watertight, but few if any interesting claims about the nature of morality are wholly impregnable in that sense.'[4] Is it possible, then, that pluralism, which takes moral conflict seriously and thus most fully reveals it, constitutes, as Legutko maintains, an 'inherently anti-tragic' conception? Moreover, was it actually conceived as such? While a negative answer to the first of these questions may be subject to discussion, such an answer to the second seems irrefutable, for things are exactly the other way round. Stressing the impossibility of achieving an ultimate har-

---

    1. See Lukes, *Moral Conflict and Politics*, chap. 1; and Crowder, *Liberalism and Value Pluralism*, 64–73.

    2. Lukes, *Moral Conflict and Politics*, 3–4.

    3. ibid., 20.

    4. Crowder, *Liberalism and Value Pluralism*, 72.

mony (because of the incommensurability of the values pursued by human beings), pluralists strongly emphasise that the possibility of insoluble conflicts irrevocably wrecks the hope of eliminating the suffering and tragedy of human life.

Finally, does the phenomenon of the tragic constitute, according to pluralists, 'an anachronism and a generally dangerous thing?'[1] On the contrary, moral agony and painful dilemmas, sometimes entailing the necessity of making a tragic choice, are present in the very centre of human experience. Compromise is not conceived as merely the 'pasting up' of a crack—by its nature irremovable—but as the only available pragmatic way out of the dilemma, and also as the source of relief from suffering.[2] Legutko's thesis becomes intelligible and valid, however, when one takes it as directed at relativism. He remarks: 'In a fragmented world, where there is no moral centre, but only peripheries, each periphery becomes its own disconnected centre: so many options are regarded as equally good that few may feel degraded by alternative ways of life or alternative moral outlooks.'[3] But this vision does not conform to the pluralist viewpoint. Pluralism assumes not only universal values, but also a kind of ethical knowledge.[4]

V

At the same time, it seems that Legutko's polemic is to a certain extent correct—because, from a psychological perspective, the monist vision, in its ancient embodiment, is the one in which the phenomenon of the tragic acquires most condensation and depth. Belief in the objective unity of values promises peace and harmony; that is why the agony and the feeling of being torn apart which are experienced by the tragic hero become intensified by his discovery of an insoluble conflict and the recognition of its nature. Such an experience makes him aware that, to speak in Schelerian terms, he happens to live in a world in which 'something like this is possible'. This is the hour when the veil which protects him is torn apart; the moment when he loses the feeling of safety and the sense of orientation in the world. The ethical system

---

1. Legutko, 'O postmodernistycznym liberalnym konserwatyzmie', 101.
2. I develop this point in my *Filozofia wolnosci Isaiaha Berlina*, 152.
3. Legutko, 'On Postmodern Liberal Conservatism', 6.
4. This idea is well elucidated by John Gray: 'Value-pluralism is closer to ethical theories which affirm the possibility of moral knowledge than it is to familiar kinds of ethical scepticism, subjectivism or relativism. It enables us to reject some judgements about the good as being in error.' Gray, *Two Faces of Liberalism*, 6; see also 54–5.

to which he adheres proves to be unable to interpret the situation in which he has found himself. As Taylor says, in order to fit everything together, monism has to forget nine-tenths of human motivations and values.[1] From the psychological point of view, the position of the 'ancient hero' is much more difficult than the situation of a person who is aware of the tragic trait in reality, and knows that life sometimes brings about insoluble dilemmas. Subjectively, monism proves to be more densely permeated with tragedy. On the other hand, pluralism—thanks to its 'taking moral conflict seriously'—openly admits that difficult, often insoluble dilemmas are deeply embedded in the human condition. In this way it reveals the objective, tragic dimension of man's position in the world. It stresses the necessity of choice and the inevitability of loss. And in this respect pluralism proves to be more tragic than monism.

---

1. Taylor, 'Plurality of Goods', 67.

Value-Pluralism and Liberalism

Connection or Exclusion?

I

Isaiah Berlin's 'master idea' of pluralism was labelled as 'a death-blow to the central classical Western tradition'[1] and 'the bomb [...] planted in the academy [which] somehow failed to go off'.[2] Yet, as I have stated elsewhere, it proved to be a bomb with a delayed fuse.[3] Because it *did* go off. During the last decade value-pluralism has been one of the most hotly debated positions, both in ethics and in political philosophy. Moreover, it is already a movement within which opposing standpoints and schools have emerged, these being 'liberal' and 'anti-liberal' pluralism; 'benign' and 'tragic' pluralism.[4] In the field of political philosophy, the most keenly disputed issue, which dominates the debate from the pluralist standpoint, seems to be the pluralism–liberalism nexus, i.e. the controversy concerning whether pluralism provides liberalism with some positive support or actually subverts it. The question had already been raised in the 1980s. Robert Kocis, while criticising the two, in his opinion, contradictory strains in Berlin's thought—Kant's moral universalism and Herder's pluralism—questions underpinning the idea of liberty, as a value endowed with a special status, with the pluralist vision.[5]

---

1. John Gray, 'The Unavoidable Conflict', *Times Literary Supplement*, 5 July 1991, 3.
2. Taylor, 'Plurality of Goods', 117; cf. 266 above.
3. Beata Polanowska-Sygulska, 'Pluralism and Tragedy', included in this book.
4. See 267 above, note 4.
5. Kocis, 'Toward a Coherent Theory of Human Moral Development', 374–5.

Michael Sandel refers to the following thought of Schumpeter's, quoted with marked approval by Berlin in his 'Two Concepts of Liberty': 'To realise the relative validity of one's convictions and yet stand for them unflinchingly is what distinguishes a civilised man from a barbarian'[1]—and asks these most significant questions:

> If one's convictions are only relatively valid, why stand for them unflinch-ingly? In a tragically configured moral universe [. . .] is the ideal of freedom any *less* subject than competing ideals to the ultimate incommensurability of values? If so, in what can its privileged status consist? And if freedom has no morally privileged status, if it is just one value among many, then what can be said for liberalism?[2]

Sandel's objection tackles the crucial problem of how ethical pluralism provides a basis for privileging liberty. The dispute about this dilemma developed rapidly in the 1990s. The early George Crowder, assuming value-pluralism to be true, examines its implications for liberalism. These investigations lead him to the following conclusion:

> [V]alue puralism has, of itself, no tendency to support the case for liberalism. The attempt to move from pluralism to liberalism encounters various difficulties but one persistent problem is outstanding. The mere fact that values are 'plural' [. . .] tells us nothing about which of the vast range of values known to us from human experience are the values we ought to choose for ourselves and our social institutions. Pluralism tells us that we must choose but not what to choose. It gives us no reason not to embrace values that have, by themselves or in combination with others, illiberal implications.[3]

Among a number of contributions which were made in the early 1990s,[4] there were two substantial ones which marked a breakthrough in the discussion on the pluralism–liberalism nexus. Both were initiated in 1993 and developed in subsequent publications. According to both, there is no logical connection between pluralism and liberalism; pluralism in fact undermines

---

1. Joseph A. Schumpeter, *Capitalism, Socialism, and Democracy* (London, 1943), 243, cited by Berlin in 'Two Concepts of Liberty', in *Liberty*, 217.

2. Michael Sandel, introduction to *Liberalism and Its Critics* (Oxford: Basil Blackwell, 1984), 8.

3. George Crowder, 'Pluralism and Liberalism', *Political Studies* 42 (1994), 303.

4. See, e.g., George Kateb, 'Notes on Pluralism', *Social Research* 61 (1994), 511–37; Ira Katznelson, 'A Properly Defended Liberalism: On John Gray and the Filling of Political Life', *Social Research* 61 (1994), 611–30; Charles E. Larmore, 'Pluralism and Reasonable Disagreement', *Social Philosophy and Policy* 11 No. 1 (1994), 44–60.

liberalism. Thus, liberalism should either be entirely rejected by pluralists, or, at best, recognised as a contingent local tradition. Those contributions were made by John Kekes and John Gray. The cases made by both these anti-liberal pluralists triggered a lively debate. Their critical stance initiated research into Berlin's argument for liberalism from a pluralist perspective. Berlin himself joined the discussion, though he expressed himself mostly in private conversations and correspondence[1] and did not communicate his views in public. Anti-liberal polemic prompted liberal-minded pluralists to react; hence a stream of publications written from this position. The most persuasive liberal contributions were made by William Galston and the later George Crowder, who had radically changed his views.

Tackling such an extensive issue as the relationship between pluralism and liberalism requires restricting the field of research. So I shall confine myself to a number of the most important themes. Having adopted a historical approach to the debate on the subject-matter in question, I shall, in the first place, roughly present the anti-liberal polemic, paying most attention to John Gray's standpoint. Secondly, I shall briefly reproduce my own analysis, undertaken in the 1990s, and inspired by personal contact and correspondence with Berlin. Thirdly, I shall give an account of Berlin's reaction to Gray's critique. Fourthly, I shall outline the liberal response to the anti-liberal polemic. At this stage I shall concentrate on George Crowder's investigations, which constitute the most powerful case for liberal pluralism. In conclusion, I shall aim at finding out whether Crowder's argument is tenable.

II

Arguing against the compatibility of pluralism and liberalism in his *The Morality of Pluralism* (1993), Kekes maintains that contemporary liberals attribute the status of an overriding procedural value to the following values: Rawls—to justice, Berlin—to human rights, Dworkin—to equality, and Raz—to freedom. Their commitment to the overridingness of the fundamental procedural liberal value is in fact tantamount to their rejection of pluralism, if it is to be taken seriously. 'Liberalism and pluralism thus cannot be held together,'[2] concludes Kekes. The political system that, according to him, is most hospitable to pluralism is conservatism, with its respect for local tradition, which provides a suitable ethical context for resolving conflicts of

---

1. Included in this book: conversations of May 1995 and correspondence of 1997.
2. John Kekes, *The Morality of Pluralism* (Princeton, NJ: Princeton University Press, 1993), 207.

values. He develops his argument for conservatism from the pluralist stand-point in his subsequent works: *Against Liberalism* (1997) and *A Case for Conservatism* (1998). Kekes's critique of liberal pluralism was well countered by George Crowder (2002). A brief account of his argument will be given in due course. At this stage it is worth mentioning that if there is any value with a special status in Berlin's liberalism, it is liberty. Yet it by no means has the status of an overriding value. This vague and ambiguous point will be elaborated upon later in the text.

John Gray questioned Berlin's thesis of the necessary connection between pluralism and liberalism in exactly the same year as Kekes (1993), in a collection of essays entitled *Enlightenment's Wake*. Yet his broadest and most penetrating analysis of the topic in question was carried out in his influential book *Isaiah Berlin*, published in 1995.[1] This is the work which is most responsible for having spawned a broad stream of writings on ethical pluralism over the last decade. From 1995 onwards a wide range of authors have joined the discussion, and have also concentrated on the pluralism–liberalism nexus.[2] It is worth giving an account of Gray's critique, all the more so because Berlin's last observations on this topic were prompted by Gray's polemic.

Gray first characterises Berlin's liberalism as 'a liberalism of a distinctive and highly original kind', 'the most profoundly deliberated and most powerfully defended' and 'by far the most formidable and plausible so far advanced, inasmuch as it acknowledges the limits of rational choice and affirms the reality of a radical choice'.[3] He stresses the fact that this original

---

1. See 80 above, note 3.

2. See, among others, Steven Lukes, 'Pluralism Is not Enough', *Times Literary Supplement*, 10 February 1995, 4–5; Pratap B. Mehta, review of John Gray, *Isaiah Berlin*, *American Political Science Review* 91 No. 3 (September 1997), 722–4; Michael Walzer, 'Are There Limits to Liberalism?', *New York Review of Books*, 19 October 1995, 28–31; Jeffrey Friedman, 'Pluralism or Relativism?', *Critical Review* 11 No. 4 (1997), 469–80; Daniel Weinstock, 'The Graying of Berlin', *Critical Review* 11 No. 4 (1997), 481–501; Albert Dzur, 'Value Pluralism versus Political Liberalism?', *Social Theory and Practice* 24 No. 3 (1998), 375–92; Hans Blokland, 'Berlin on Pluralism and Liberalism: A Defence?', *European Legacy* 4 No. 4 (1999), 1–23; William A. Galston, 'Value Pluralism and Liberal Political Theory', *American Political Science Review* 93 No. 4 (December 1999), 769–78; Hans Joas, 'Combining Value Pluralism and Moral Universalism: Isaiah Berlin and Beyond', *Responsive Community* 9 No. 4 (Fall 1999), 17–29; Michael H. Lessnoff, 'Isaiah Berlin Monism and Pluralism', chap. 8 in *Political Philosophers of the Twentieth Century* (Oxford: Blackwell, 1999); essays collected in Arien Mack, ed., *Liberty and Pluralism* [*Social Research* 66 No. 4 (Winter 1999)]; essays collected in Baghramian and Ingram, eds., *Pluralism: The Philosophy and Politics of Diversity*; Jonathan Riley, 'Interpreting Isaiah Berlin's Liberalism', *American Political Science Review* 95 No. 2 (2001), 283–95; Jonathan Riley, 'Defending Cultural Pluralism within Liberal Limits', *Political Theory* 30 No. 1 (2002), 68–97; Galston, *Liberal Pluralism*; Gerald F. Gaus, 'Pluralistic Liberalism: Making Do Without Public Reason?', chap. 2 in *Contemporary Theories of Liberalism* (London: Sage, 2003), 25–55; Steven Lukes, *Liberals and Cannibals: The Implications of Diversity* (London: Verso, 2003).

3. Gray, *Isaiah Berlin*, 145.

liberal doctrine is supported in Berlin by the 'master' thesis of pluralism. Having put such a high value on Berlin's achievement, Gray then tackles the problem of the relationship between pluralism and liberalism. He analyses three strands of reasoning whereby value-pluralism might support liberal values and practices:

1. The argument 'that it is by the choices protected by negative freedom that we negotiate our way among incommensurable values': to which he answers that 'Choice-making [. . .] goes on, even in the absence of negative freedom', as it is 'an inescapable necessity of the human condition'.[1]
2. The argument that, 'if the radical value-pluralist thesis of the rational incompatibility of goods and evils is true, then the State can never have sufficient rational justification for imposing any particular ranking of values on people'.[2] In Gray's opinion this argument also fails:

For a particularistic illiberal regime need not claim, when it imposes a particular ranking of incommensurable values on its subjects, that this ranking is uniquely rational, or even that it is a better ranking than others that are presently found in the world. It need only claim that it is a ranking embedded in, and necessary for the survival of, a particular way of life that is itself worthwhile, and that this ranking, and the way of life it supports, would be imperilled by the unimpeded exercise of choice.[3]

3. '[T]he argument that authoritarian or illiberal societies or regimes are bound to deny the truth of value-pluralism': Gray agrees 'that value-pluralism indeed undermines the universalist claims made by illiberal societies that are Marxist, utilitarian, positivist, Platonist, Christian or Muslim, at their foundations', but he insists that 'human history to date, and the human prospect for the likely future, abounds with illiberal cultures that are particularistic, not universalistic, in the values they claim to embody'. He then gives examples of authoritarian regimes 'sustained by Hindu, Shinto or Orthodox Jewish doctrine' which, in his view, 'seek simply to preserve a local way of life' and 'are not committed to asserting the unique or universal authority of the ways of life which they protect, nor [. . .] to denying the value of other ways of life'. In Gray's view, just because such 'particularistic cultures' avoid universalistic reasoning, they would 'appear particularly

1. ibid., 143, 159.
2. ibid., 144.
3. ibid., 153.

well-placed to perceive and accept the truth of value-pluralism and its corollary, the worth and validity of radically different forms of life'.[1]

Gray's analyses lead him to a conclusion which forms the main thesis of the whole book: liberalism is not supported by value-pluralism; pluralism is a deeper truth and 'a truth that undermines liberalism as a political ideal with a universal claim on reason'. '[T]here can be, and need be, no universal justification for liberalism. [. . .] It is instead best understood as a particular form of life, practised by people who have a certain self-conception, in which the activity of unfettered choice is central.'[2] In his later work Gray sustains and develops his radical critique of liberal pluralism: 'if a strong version of pluralism is true, liberalism is indefensible'[3]—'Pluralism and liberalism are rival doctrines.'[4] Thus, value-pluralism as a theory of ethics does not point to liberalism. A political ideal that fits best with the pluralist outlook is *modus vivendi* which 'expresses the belief that there are many forms of life in which humans can thrive'.[5] The ideal of *modus vivendi*, as advocated by Gray, has pertinently been described as 'a form of loose political "pragmatism"',[6] searching for peaceful coexistence by way of reaching compromise in situations of conflict. The problem is that such a political ideal rests on recognition of peace as both an overriding and a universal value. Gray is aware of this difficulty; this is why he makes the following reservation: 'The pursuit of *modus vivendi* is not a quest for some kind of super-value. It is a commitment to common institutions in which the claims of rival values can be reconciled. The end of *modus vivendi* is not any supreme good—even peace. It is reconciling conflicting goods.'[7]

Yet if the ideal of *modus vivendi* is meant to be taken seriously, it must assume universal commitment to the overridingness of 'reconciling conflicting goods'. I raised this objection in an essay published in the Polish periodical *Przeglad Polityczny* in 2002,[8] and then in a letter to John Gray. This is how he responded to my criticism:

1. ibid., 151–2.
2. ibid., 146. 161.
3. John Gray, 'Where Pluralists and Liberals Part Company', in Baghramian and Ingram, 86.
4. ibid., 101.
5. John Gray, *Two Faces of Liberalism* (New York: New Press, 2000), 5.
6. I owe the phrase to Crowder, *Liberalism and Value Pluralism*, 119.
7. Gray, *Two Faces of Liberalism*, 25.
8. Beata Polanowska-Sygulska, 'Dwie twarze liberalizmu' [review of John Gray, *Two Faces of Liberalism*], *Przeglad Polityczny* 56 (2002), 150.

The question about the universality of *modus vivendi* that you raise in your covering [letter] is a fundamental one. My view is that though some values (human goods and bads) are universal, that's to say species-wide, there can't be a universally authoritative morality. Different individuals and cultures resolve conflicts amongst universal human values differently, and not unreasonably so. So if *modus vivendi* means peace, there's nothing universal about it; but if it means all human beings are inescapably faced with conflicting values, then it is universal. The key point is that most liberals inherit from Christianity the idea of somehow saving the human species from itself—an idea I find rather absurd. *Modus vivendi* aims to avoid this idea.[1]

Unfortunately, this argument does not seem to resolve the lingering doubt about *modus vivendi*. Even if the ways of resolving conflicts among universal human values are different in different cultures, the value of 'reconciling conflicting goods' as such is being advocated universally. Therefore such an ideal fits in poorly with the pluralist outlook in ethics. The world in which there would be serious commitment to the ideal of *modus vivendi* would be a world of peacefully co-existing individuals and cultures. Yet according to Gray's own formulation, 'the goods of human life are many'.[2] Why then should peaceful coexistence be so desirable? Moreover, sometimes short-term peace and compromise need to be rejected for the sake of a lasting peace and a satisfactory compromise. Thus, the value of peace proves to be, like other goods, 'internally complex' and 'inherently pluralistic'.[3] The highly abstract and strictly formal principle of *modus vivendi* apparently assumes that peaceful coexistence is a harmonious whole and gives no suggestions how to resolve conflicts *within* the value itself, e.g., how to deal with the 'paradox' of peace just specified.

III

John Gray's discussion not only led to the emergence of two schools—liberal and anti-liberal—within the pluralist movement; Berlin himself entered the dispute. As it transpired, I was privileged to meet and then correspond with him in 1995, shortly after the publication of Gray's groundbreaking monograph. I reported on Gray's most recent work, asked many questions concerning his contribution to pluralism, and expressed my doubts. Berlin,

---

1. Email to Beata Polanowska-Sygulska, 23 January 2003.
2. Gray, 'Where Pluralists and Liberals Part Company', 25.
3. Gray, *Isaiah Berlin*, 43.

inspired by Gray's critique, discussed with me the problems posed by his opponent. Unfortunately, he did not publish a response to Gray. The main sources for his views are the transcripts of our conversations and his letters to me. None the less, before I get down to his last thoughts on the pluralism–liberalism nexus, I shall give an account of my reconstruction of the view he expressed in his written work.

In Berlin's texts the crucial problem of the relationship between pluralism and liberalism is not focused on. His main essays seem to suggest that the special status of freedom follows from the fact that it is involved in each act of choice, and that protection of at least a minimal sphere of negative liberty provides a safeguard for preservation of humanity: 'liberty—without some modicum of which there is no choice and therefore no possibility of remaining human as we understand the word';[1] 'to be free to choose, and not to be chosen for, is an inalienable ingredient in what makes human beings human';[2] 'to contract the areas of human choice is to do harm to men in an intrinsic, Kantian, not merely utilitarian, sense'.[3] The vein of the 'pluralist foundation' for the liberal institutions is taken up twice in 'Two Concepts of Liberty': 'If [. . .] the ends of men are many, and not all of them are in principle compatible with each other, then the possibility of conflict—and of tragedy—can never wholly be eliminated from human life, either personal or social. The necessity of choosing between absolute claims is then an inescapable characteristic of the human condition. This gives its value to freedom as Acton had conceived of it—as an end in itself.'[4] At the end of the essay Berlin puts forward the thesis of the necessary connection between pluralism and liberalism: 'Pluralism, with the measure of "negative" liberty that it entails, seems to me a truer and more humane ideal than the goals of those who seek [. . .] the ideal of "positive" self-mastery.'[5]

The above quotations seem to suggest that Berlin's standpoint with regard to the point at issue is definite: pluralism *implies* liberalism. Berlin's replies to the objections raised by Kocis and Crowder may be recognised as a confirmation of this reading. In the article 'Reply to Robert Kocis' Berlin resolutely rejects his adversary's critique, maintaining that Kocis's interpretations are inadequate.[6] In a rejoinder to Crowder written with Bernard Williams, Berlin also rejects Crowder's argument, charging him with a dis-

1. Berlin, 'The Pursuit of the Ideal', in *The Proper Study of Mankind*, 10.
2. Berlin, Introduction, in *Liberty*, 52; cf. 244, 262 above.
3. ibid., 44.
4. Berlin, 'Two Concepts of Liberty', in *Liberty*, 214.
5. ibid., 216; cf. 89, 245, 255 above.
6. Berlin, 'Reply to Robert Kocis', *Political Studies* 31 (1983), 388–93.

torted reconstruction of the idea of pluralism and of an immensely abstract level of argument.[1] The image of Berlin's position, which had seemed up to now coherent, and not to allow for doubt, is entirely ruined by his statement made in a conversation with Ramin Jahanbegloo. He answers Jahanbegloo's question of whether the concept of pluralism is supposed to defend 'the old liberal political theory' in the following way: 'Pluralism and liberalism are not the same or even overlapping concepts. There are liberal theories which are not pluralistic. I believe in both liberalism and pluralism, but they are not logically connected.'[2] Yet in just the next sentence he maintains that: 'Pluralism entails [. . .] a minimum degree of toleration',[3] and in another context, referring to the turning-point brought about by the Counter-Enlightenment thinkers, he adds, 'If you allowed that there can be more than one valid answer to a problem, that in itself is a great discovery. It leads to liberalism and toleration.'[4]

One must agree with John Gray when he claims that Berlin's own statements on the cardinal question of the relations of pluralism with liberalism 'are not entirely of one voice'.[5] The same ambiguity occurs in relation to a closely connected issue, relevant to justification of the value of liberty on the basis of ethical pluralism, namely Berlin's differentiation between 'basic liberty of choice' and 'negative liberty'.

Analysis of the few contexts in which Berlin takes up the subject of basic human liberty leads one to suppose that it is precisely to the basic freedom of choice that social liberty owes its special status among other values. Berlin firmly emphasises the fact that basic freedom is necessarily assumed in any moral doctrine. In his published writings the differentiation in question is hardly referred to. But he offers a more detailed characterisation in correspondence. It is worth quoting the relevant passage:

> there are two sorts of choice which I did not develop in the books of essays or dialogues. [. . .] One is basic choice, that a human being is not fully human, not human at all, unless he can choose between A and B: I may be tied to a tree, or subject to torture, or whatever, but I can choose either to accept this or try to fight against it, to bend my little finger or not bend it, or whatever; I must have some basic powers of choice in some region—if I am deprived of choice, then I become a robot, hypnotised, to that extent not

---

1. Berlin and Williams, 'Pluralism and Liberalism: A Reply', 306–9.
2. Jahanbegloo, *Conversations*, 44; cf. 82, 211, 225 above, 290 below.
3. ibid.
4. ibid., 73.
5. Gray, *Isaiah Berlin*, 150.

free, therefore not human. That kind of freedom, the power of basic choice, however limited, is part of what it is to be a human being, not an animal driven entirely by instinct. Then there is political choice, which is what my essay on the two freedoms was founded on: that means something different—that there are as many doors open for me to walk through as can be opened—freedom from interference, negative freedom. It is not the only value; if it conflicts with positive freedom, or with security or with other social values, needs of other members of the population, then it may have to yield to these other values—and so uncomfortable compromises have to be achieved. But this kind of liberty is political, and must not be confused with basic human liberty, which is a biological/psychological entity. There is no human culture at all, among the plural cultures, which does not entail basic liberty—suppression of that is dehumanisation of the human being who is being oppressed or tortured.[1]

Thus special status is attached to basic freedom of choice, while negative liberty constitutes just one among other social values. Claude Galipeau once asked Berlin about the source of negative freedom's privilege: '[W]hy should one hold to negative liberty as being a value which is *absolutely* crucial for society, or *all* societies?'[2] The answer he received seems to be related to the quoted passage: '*Because*, unless there is choice, there's no morality at all. [. . .] If there is no choice, I don't see that you are fully human. If you are a robot, why talk about morality?'[3] This again points to basic freedom as the value endowed with a special status. It is basic freedom that is involved in each act of choice; it is basic freedom that constitutes an indispensable attribute of humanity and, as Kant taught, the basis of any morality.

This clear vision is again distorted by another statement of Berlin's: 'negative liberty is also such that in its absence other values collapse also, because there is no opportunity to practise them, there are no opportunities, no constellations of diverse values—in the end, no life'.[4] Does negative liberty then also have special status? However, if this were so, what would this special status consist in? After all, negative liberty is a value like others and may have to be limited for their sake. Is it perhaps that its distinctive position springs from the fact that it constitutes an embodiment of basic liberty of choice, which is a con-

1. Letter of 18 February 1997, 87 above.
2. Claude Galipeau, unpublished conversation with Berlin, 23 May 1988, 35.
3. ibid., 35–6.
4. Jahanbegloo, *Conversations*, 151. Bernard Williams expresses a similar thought: 'if there are many and competing genuine values, then the greater the extent to which a society tends to be single-valued, the more genuine values it neglects or suppresses. More, to this extent, must mean better.' Introduction to Berlin, *Concepts and Categories*, xvii.

dition of morality? This connection makes negative liberty neither a supreme value, nor an absolute one—and yet distinguishes it from all the others as the value which demands a special protection. Such an interpretation seems to be acceptable. Yet it is most difficult to reconcile it with Berlin's categorical statement, expressed in his reply to Robert Kocis's critique:

> [A] basic liberty of choice, by individuals or societies, of some ends as being preferable to others [. . .] is presupposed in the pluralism which I defend, or [. . .] by any doctrine that deserves to be described as ethical. But this is [. . .] something altogether different from, nor even connected with, the concept of "negative liberty", which in my lecture applied in any case to political life only.[1]

The foregoing quotations do not provide an unambiguous answer to the question of the mutual relation between pluralism and liberalism, in particular of the source of negative liberty's privilege on the basis of ethical pluralism. Neither did John Gray find a solution to these key questions in Berlin's writings. Therefore it will be worth coming back to his analyses, the more so because Berlin found them extremely thought-provoking. Gray's thesis that it is possible to create oneself through choice-making even in the absence of political freedom is no doubt justified because the lack of negative liberty is not tantamount to annihilation of basic liberty of choice. It is the latter that is inherent in one's being fully human. Berlin's statement, characterising the situation of slaves, brings an open confirmation of Gray's interpretation. According to Berlin it is not true that slaves are deprived of basic freedom. Slaves can choose. For instance, they can choose whether to lift a little finger or to bend it.[2] Gray's observations, which in his opinion undermine the two subsequent arguments for a necessary connection between pluralism and liberalism, were extensively discussed by Berlin and myself.[3]

Gray's example of illiberal cultures that are not committed to asserting the universal authority of the ways of life protected by them, and do not question the truth of value-pluralism, was the immediate impulse that made Berlin reflect upon this key problem. According to Gray it is possible to reconcile the pluralist standpoint with an authoritarian regime, which refutes the thesis of the necessary logical connection between pluralism and liberalism.

---

1. Berlin, 'Reply to Robert Kocis', 391.
2. Claude Galipeau, unpublished conversation with Berlin, 1 June 1988, 2.
3. In two conversations with Beata Polanowska-Sygulska in May 1995, and later in correspondence.

Berlin's reply to this argument boils down to the following thesis: a reconciliation of pluralism with particularistic monism assumes, somewhat implausibly, that representatives of such cultures adopt a liberal attitude with respect to the rest of the world; otherwise they would not be pluralists. In this sense, 'pluralism must entail liberalism'.[1] But this standpoint underwent an evolution. I quoted the following passage, obviously contrary to the above view, from Berlin's conversations with Ramin Jahanbegloo: 'I believe both in liberalism and in pluralism, but they are not logically connected.'[2] I also gave the example of Machiavelli, who, according to Berlin, was the first dualist, and thus the forerunner of pluralism, but who cannot possibly be recognised as a liberal. The case of Machiavelli demonstrates that the thesis of a necessary connection between pluralism and liberalism has been stated too strongly. Berlin's reply to the doubts I voiced was a modification of his earlier standpoint: the connection between pluralism and liberalism is not *logical* in character, but *psychological*.[3] In subsequent correspondence he elaborated this thought and supported it with theoretical argument.[4] The starting-point, contrary to his earlier position, was an acceptance of Gray's thesis: 'I think that Gray is perfectly right in saying that there is no logical nexus between pluralism and liberalism, though there are all kinds of other—in a way equally important—connections.'[5]

At the beginning of the analysis of these connections, Berlin outlines the image of the world as seen through a pluralist's eyes:

> To be a pluralist means that the choices of myself and my civilisation are not necessarily universal; there may be other civilisations, in the past or the present, which pursue values not compatible with those of my civilisation. If I am a pluralist, it means that I understand how people can come to accept these other values, whether because of their historical or geographical circumstances, or for whatever reason: the point is that I don't simply reject them as not mine and therefore nothing to me—as real relativism does—but I seek to understand what kind of world it is for those who don't share my beliefs, and how one can come to pursue values which are not mine.[6]

Thus it is characteristic of a pluralist to be able to understand different human aims and values, as well as other cultures. A typical reaction to the experi-

---

1. In conversation with Beata Polanowska-Sygulska, Oxford, 17 May 1995.
2. Jahanbegloo, *Conversations*, 44; cf. 82, 211, 225, 287 above.
3. In conversation with Beata Polanowska-Sygulska, Oxford, 24 May 1995, 226 above.
4. Letters of 18 February 1997; 19 April 1997; 28 June 1997 (84–8; 91–3; 99–101 above).
5. Letter of 19 April 1997, 91 above.
6. Letter of 18 February 1997, 84 above.

ence of strangeness is either indifference, or hostility; understanding exerts a moderating impact upon these reactions: 'If you are going abroad, you may find yourself in a strange foreign culture, but you don't necessarily reject or attack it—it is not yours, but you can put up with it, you can even understand how one might live that sort of life even though you yourself are not prepared to.'[1] Therefore the external sign of practising empathetic understanding is toleration: 'That state of mind [empathetic understanding] surely leads you to [. . .] toleration [. . .] toleration with limits, not indefinite toleration, toleration providing your culture is not in mortal danger—but still, toleration.'[2]

In Berlin's belief the idea of toleration is also at the heart of liberalism, for it maintains a close connection with the liberal institutions: 'toleration is a human right, a universal right as it were, or quasi-universal in my locution; if this is so, and only a liberal society can fully practice it, then that is a connection between them—it is not a logical connection, but a de facto one and none the worse for that'.[3]

Thus toleration plays the role of a bridge, linking pluralism and liberalism. While characterising the nature of the bond between the two standpoints, Berlin refers to his earlier assertion: 'Is there a psychological connection between pluralism and liberalism? Yes.'[4] He then reinforces this statement with a broader thought about the psychological dimension of human ends and values:

> It is a fact, discoverable by anthropological observation, that men seek different values—negative liberty, positive liberty, equality, justice, mercy, rational organisation, family life. Some of these clash, as we know, but the question is, why seek them at all, what makes them values? The answer to this is that everything is ultimately psychological—that that is how men are made, some differing from others, and so people choose values because they are so made; and if they clash, then they can compromise between them.[5]

The image that emerges from these quotations seems to differ to a considerable degree from the vision outlined by Gray. Berlin's liberalism is not a special form of life deriving its authority from local traditions. According to Berlin, liberal institutions are based on a pluralist ethical vision. Although this vision does not *entail* liberalism, the doctrines remain connected. If this

---

1. op. cit., 95.
2. ibid.
3. Letter of 19 April 1997, 93 above.
4. Letter of 18 February 1997, 87 above.
5. Letter of 28 June 1997, 99 above.

bond were to be characterised in anthropological categories, it would have to be described as a psychological dependence. The link which joins the standpoints is toleration.

IV

Among liberal pluralists, including Bernard Williams, Stuart Hampshire, Joseph Raz, Michael Walzer, William Galston and others, George Crowder occupies a special position. If any thinker could be labelled as a true heir to Berlin's legacy, it would certainly be him. In his *Liberalism and Value Pluralism* (2002) Crowder undertook what is definitely the most systematic and profound study of value-pluralism. Going beyond Berlin's views he made a powerful case for liberal pluralism. Henry Hardy has characterised the book as 'a really excellent and thorough synthesis of the argument so far which also makes numerous original contributions'.[1] Crowder's most recent work, *Isaiah Berlin: Liberty and Pluralism* (2004), was greeted by Hardy with even greater enthusiasm:

> George Crowder here performs the almost impossible feat of tidying up Isaiah Berlin's somewhat scattered, imprecise and inconsistent accounts of his views without oversimplification or misrepresentation. [. . .] But not only has Crowder given us a masterly exposition; he also brilliantly develops some of the vaguer clues left by Berlin, adding substantially to Berlin's intellectual legacy in a spirit entirely in keeping with his own work. It is as if an unfinished cathedral were completed by a new architect who intuited the vision of its original designer. Berlin would surely have applauded this exciting and original book, and learnt much from it.[2]

Crowder seriously tackles the issue of the pluralism–liberalism nexus. It is not possible to provide a comprehensive account of his investigations into the question here. Instead I shall briefly describe Crowder's response to antiliberal pluralists, and his masterly reconstruction of Berlin's arguments from pluralism to liberalism, and finally concentrate on his original contribution to the theory of value-pluralism.

1. Henry Hardy, description of George Crowder's *Liberalism and Value Pluralism*, http:// berlin.wolf.ox.ac.uk/, 'Publications about Isaiah Berlin', compiled by Henry Hardy (accessed 31 December 2005).
2. Henry Hardy, description of George Crowder's *Isaiah Berlin: Liberty and Pluralism* (Cambridge: Polity Press, 2004), ibid.

Crowder was once a severe critic of liberal pluralism. He has changed his views to become its keen adherent. Having undergone such an evolution, he questions not only his own former line of reasoning, but also the arguments of other anti-liberal pluralists. Countering Kekes's critique, Crowder points out that local social tradition is only one component of a person's conception of the good. Therefore a conservative, tradition-based approach proves to be too narrow to fit to a value-pluralist outlook. Analysing all three phases of Gray's anti-liberal argument ('subjectivist, 'particularist' and 'pragmatic'), Crowder also finds them unsatisfactory. Subjectivism excludes the possibility of reasoned choice; particularism suffers from over-narrowness, and pragmatism of the *modus vivendi* phase privileges either peace or self-interest, and so turns out to be closer to a monist than to a pluralist vision. Thus neither conservatism nor pragmatism can be reconciled with a pluralist point of view. Crowder also challenges Kekes's and Gray's approaches on yet another level. He denies their common assumption that reasoned choice under pluralism is relative to local contexts. According to Crowder there are universal principles implicit in value-pluralism itself. None the less, before he makes his own substantial contribution to the theory of pluralism, he offers a reconstruction of Berlin's pluralist case for liberalism.

In Crowder's interpretation, there are two main lines of reasoning from pluralism to liberalism implicit in Berlin's writings, namely the argument *from choice* and the *anti-Utopian* perspective. Unfortunately, both are unsuccessful. The first one hinges on the necessity of choice inherent in the human condition. If choice is unavoidable, then we should value freedom of choice, which is best respected in a liberal order. Crowder finds this argument logically flawed. It is worth quoting the appropriate passage: 'It is essentially an instance of the naturalistic fallacy, since it passes directly from the fact that choice is unavoidable to the value of freedom of choice. But the mere fact that choice is unavoidable does not make it (or the freedom with which to make it) valuable.'[1]

The second argument rests on the impossibility of political perfection implicit in the pluralist viewpoint, which requires an anti-Utopian approach to politics. Although this argument fares, in Crowder's view, better than the first one, it suffers from incompleteness, because liberalism is not the only political form meeting the anti-Utopian requirement. Conservatism and pragmatism also recognise the imperfectibility of the human condition. Crowder concludes that 'Berlin does not wholly succeed in explaining why pluralists

---

1. Crowder, *Isaiah Berlin: Liberty and Pluralism*, 144.

should be liberals.'[1] However, he shares Berlin's view that pluralism and liberalism can be reconciled; moreover, he maintains that pluralism implies a universalist and perfectionist kind of liberalism. This conclusion is the result of his extending Berlin's pluralist case for liberalism. It is by going beyond Berlin's views that the new architect aims at completing the unfinished cathedral. Does he succeed? Let us enquire into his original contribution.

In Crowder's interpretation, the pluralist outlook in ethics is based on the recognition of four attributes of values: the universality of certain generic values; plurality; incommensurability; and conflict. These formal attributes of value-pluralism imply five normative principles that are best respected within a liberal form of politics. Thus, they provide a universal argument for liberalism grounded in pluralism. The first two principles eliminate liberalism's political rivals:

1. Respect for generic universal values (rules out conservative or strong communitarian views)
2. Recognition of value incommensurability (rules out Utopian forms of politics such as classical Marxism and anarchism)

The next three principles amount to a positive, universal justification of liberalism:

3. Commitment to diversity, best satisfied under a liberal political framework, thanks to liberalism's 'approximate neutrality'
4. Acknowledgement of reasonable disagreement among conceptions of the good, again best recognised under liberalism
5. Practising the pluralist virtues: generosity, realism, attentiveness and flexibility, required by practical reasoning under pluralism; powerfully reinforced by close, or even overlapping liberal virtues: broadmindedness, moderation, respect for persons, and autonomy.

Crowder's contribution to value-pluralism, especially expressed in his treatise *Liberalism and Value Pluralism*, constitutes an ambitious attempt at reviving both liberal universalism and philosophical respect for the truth. I have confined myself merely to drawing a rough outline of the subtle theoretical construction relevant to the pluralism–liberalism nexus. Nevertheless, this brief sketch casts, surprisingly enough, a serious doubt on Crowder's line of reasoning. Let me quote several passages *in extenso*. In one context

---

1. ibid., 126.

Crowder claims that pluralism is 'a theory of the real nature of value'.[1] In another place, formulating the principle of commitment to diversity, he writes: 'To acknowledge the truth of value pluralism is to acknowledge a multiplicity of genuine goods, of diverse natures, not merely ethical mistakes with which it is nevertheless best not to interfere. It is to acknowledge a duty to promote those goods so far as possible: a duty to promote diversity.'[2]

So it is from the empirical *fact* of the plurality of values that Crowder draws the conclusion of the *value* of diversity, which imposes a duty of promoting diversity of goods and ways of life. It is hard to resist the temptation of confronting the above quotation with a famous passage from Hume's *A Treatise of Human Nature*:

> In every system of morality which I have hitherto met with, I have always remarked, that the author proceeds for some time in the ordinary way of reasoning, and establishes the being of a God, or makes observations concerning human affairs; when of a sudden I am surprised to find, that instead of the usual copulations of propositions, *is*, and *is not*, I meet with no proposition that is not connected with an *ought*, or an *ought not*. This change is imperceptible; but is, however, of the last consequence. For as this *ought*, or *ought not*, expresses some new relation or affirmation, it is necessary that it should be observed and explained; and at the same time that a reason should be given, for what seems altogether inconceivable, how this new relation can be a deduction from others, which are entirely different from it.[3]

Let us return again to Crowder and to the wording of his fourth principle: 'if pluralism *is* true, then we must accept that many (although not all) disagreements about the nature of the good life will be reasonable, and therefore that the State *ought to* accommodate such disagreements rather than attempt to eliminate them'.[4]

It is striking that the quoted passage contains the words *is* and *ought*. Although Crowder accuses Berlin of the naturalistic fallacy, he himself breaks Hume's law. It seems that only his fifth principle, i.e., the argument for liberalism based on the affinity or overlapping of pluralist and liberal virtues, is not grounded in deriving duty from fact. Crowder makes this explicit himself in his most recent book, *Isaiah Berlin: Liberty and Pluralism*: 'The argument avoids the naturalistic fallacy, because it passes not

---

1. Crowder, *Liberalism and Value Pluralism*, 162.

2. ibid., 137.

3. David Hume, *A Treatise of Human Nature* (London: J. M. Dent; New York: E. P. Dutton, 1960–1), 2: 177–8.

4. Crowder, *Liberalism and Value Pluralism*, 158 (my emphasis).

from necessity to value but from necessity to necessity. If pluralism is true, we cannot avoid hard choices, and if we are to cope well with these hard choices, we need to be autonomous.'[1]

It is striking that, although Crowder has not changed his views since 2002, when his treatise on pluralism was published, nowadays he formulates his theses in a milder way: the same components of value-pluralism no longer 'imply', but rather 'suggest' principles, give us 'good reasons' to recognise them, or 'tend in a liberal direction'. Could it be that Crowder is half aware of the weak point of his reasoning?

If we take into account the above objection, it seems right to recognise that the ambitious attempt to derive a universalist argument for liberalism from value-pluralism is unsuccessful. It is therefore worth returning to Berlin's final statement about the mutual relation between pluralism and liberalism, and his thesis of a weaker, non-logical but psychological connection. Such a vision also fits in with Crowder's fifth principle. Apart from Berlin, William Galston and Michael Walzer also draw attention to a psychological connection between a pluralist standpoint in ethics and a liberal position in political theory. Both authors stress the similarity of the temperaments of a pluralist and a liberal, and the common fundamental orientation which gives rise to the two attitudes:

> Many people (ordinary citizens as well as academics) are both value pluralist and political liberals and see these positions as mutually supportive. If they are mistaken about this, they must in some measure revise important theoretical and practical commitments.[2]

> I don't know anyone who believes in value pluralism who isn't a liberal, in sensibility, as well as conviction. [. . .] You have to look at the world in a receptive and generous way to see a pluralism of Berlin's sort, i.e., a pluralism that encompasses a variety of genuine but incommensurable values. And you also have to look at the world in a sceptical way, since the adherents of each of the different values are likely to rank them very high on a scale designed for just that purpose. And receptivity, generosity, and scepticism are, if not liberal values, then qualities of mind that make it possible to accept liberal values (or, better, that make it likely that liberal values will be accepted).[3]

Counter-examples provided by the history of ideas also seem to support the thesis of a weaker, psychological connection. The first thinker who broke

---

1. Crowder, *Isaiah Berlin: Liberty and Pluralism*, 164–5.
2. Galston, 'Value Pluralism and Liberal Political Theory', 769.
3. Walzer, 'Are there Limits to Liberalism?', 31.

with monism, Machiavelli, was not a liberal. Steven Lukes, with deep insight, provides two other instances that speak against the thesis that pluralism 'leads naturally to liberal conclusions':

> Berlin has cited Max Weber's 'Politics as a Vocation' as a classic statement of [pluralism], yet Weber's liberalism is far from unambiguous. Perhaps the most dramatic example of thoroughly value-pluralist or 'decisionist' anti-liberalism is the case of Carl Schmitt, the Nazi-symphathising legal theorist, for whom politics reduces to the opposition between friend and foe and whose hostility to liberal democracy is probably unequalled by any other major modern thinker.[1]

An adherent of the thesis that liberalism can be logically inferred from the pluralist standpoint in ethics would need to point out an inconsistency in the views of the above thinkers. Considering all the arguments, one is inclined to admit that Berlin's cautious thesis of a psychological connection between pluralism and liberalism gives an adequate account of the nature of the bond.

In the end, then, it looks as if the unfinished construction has not been successfully completed by the new architect. This may possibly be because the original designer, unlike his successor, did not aim at putting up anything as massive and solid as a cathedral. Or because the time of cathedrals is over . . .

Appendix

The above article was presented at the twenty-second World Congress of the International Society for Philosophy of Law and Social Philosophy in Granada, Spain, in May 2005. Before my departure for Granada I sent the text to Henry Hardy, who forwarded it to George Crowder. This gave rise to an informal exchange of messages. George Crowder commented on this piece, and also on my two 1995 conversations with Berlin, in several emails to Henry Hardy, who then forwarded them to me 'with bated breath'.

Among several points concerning this article, the key one amounted to the subverting of my main thesis. George Crowder kindly agreed that I might publish the passage in question:

> Beata's criticism of my 'diversity' argument—namely, that the argument violates Hume's law—seems to me to miss a crucial point. The starting-point for the argument is not the fact that plural things happen to have been

---

1. Lukes, *Liberals and Cannibals*, 94.

valued universally (IB's usual account of universals). If that was the starting-point, then indeed it wouldn't follow that any particular society ought to pursue more rather than fewer such ends. My starting-point is an understanding of universal ends as contributing objectively to human well-being (as in Aristotle, the natural law tradition, or Nussbaum). Pluralism enjoins us to take all of these ends equally seriously at a fundamental level. That's why a particular society ought, at least *prima facie*, to promote or allow more rather than fewer such ends—subject to considerations of coherence within any package of ends etc. This argument doesn't violate Hume's law, because it doesn't move from fact to value, but from value to value. The starting-point is not a claim of fact about what people happen to value, but a value judgement to the effect that certain generic goods contribute to human well-being. I have tried to say this in my existing publications, but maybe it didn't come through clearly enough.[1]

Henry Hardy bated his breath with full justification. This argument does undermine my line of reasoning. At first I thought of withdrawing the text from the emerging volume. But then I remembered that the arguments presented in my piece had already made one of the leading authorities on value-pluralism elaborate his position, which was more than I could possibly have hoped for. Instigating further discussion of Berlin's intellectual legacy was precisely what I aimed at when engaging myself in this project. Eventually, I decided to include the article.

While investigating the reasons for my mistaken interpretation of Crowder's pluralist case for liberalism, I went back to his books, mostly to *Liberalism and Value Pluralism.* Read together, the relevant excerpts from the book and the passage quoted above felt as if they had been written from somewhat different perspectives. There is indeed no doubt that the argument moving from value to value, as it is stated in the email comment, does not break Hume's law. Yet the wording of the following extract from the book by no means suggests that the starting-point is indeed value and not fact: 'To acknowledge the truth of value pluralism [. . .] is to acknowledge a duty to promote these goods.'[2] Indeed, one encounters in the book many references to Nussbaum's 'thick vague' conception of the good. The author labels such a theory of the good life as 'controversial', but as 'having a respectable philosophical pedigree'.[3] Yet it remains not quite clear what his own position is. One needs to study the notes thoroughly to find an indication that Crowder's own approach is different from Berlin's and has something in common with Nussbaum's:

---

1. Email to Henry Hardy, 29 May 2005.
2. Crowder, *Liberalism and Value Pluralism*, 137
3. ibid., 66.

Nussbaum's formulation of the objectivity required for value pluralism is probably too strong, since a life that lacked certain of the capabilities she lists may still, surely, count as recognisably 'human', and even a good life to some degree. All that is necessary from a pluralist point of view is that there are certain goods that *contribute* to human well-being universally and independently of particular beliefs, that is, that such goods make human lives go better than they would otherwise. On the other hand, Berlin's version of value objectivity is probably too weak for pluralist purposes. Berlin sees universal values as those goods that all human beings in fact value.[1]

This raises the question why a statement of this weight needs to be extracted from a footnote. Why wasn't it made in the main text and given the prominence which it deserves? Moreover, if the author's understanding of universal values is to be associated with that of 'Aristotle, the natural law tradition, or Nussbaum', then his commitment is open to all of the problems and questions raised by this philosophical tradition, especially as his is a universalist case for liberalism based on pluralist premises.

It seems that George Crowder's contribution to value pluralism does not in the end amount to finishing the old cathedral, but to putting up a new, semi-detached edifice. But the erection of the new building has not weakened the old construction. They are both standing firm, though each of them is exposed to its own risks, resulting from the particular architectural solution it has adopted.

When one starts with the Berlinian approach that universal values are those goods which 'a great many human beings in the vast majority of places and situations, at almost all times, do in fact hold in common',[2] one may justifiably arrive only at the weak conclusion reached by Berlin, that the nexus between pluralism and a liberal commitment to liberty is of a psychological nature. This resolution was labelled by Crowder, elsewhere, as 'feeble stuff'.[3] Yet in Berlin's case it is impossible for the stuff to be stronger. Moreover, there is nothing alarming in the emergence of differing standpoints within the pluralist movement. It would indeed be surprising if such diversity were perceived by pluralists as unsettling. In the end, as Berlin used to say, 'all the differences between philosophies and outlooks boil down to different conceptions of human nature'.[4]

Value-pluralism is the one idea of Berlin's which undoubtedly proved to be alive while I was preparing the manuscript. After having written my short reply to George Crowder's key remark, I sent the piece to Joshua Cherniss,

---

1. ibid., 73–4, note 1.
2. Jahanbegloo, *Conversations*, 37.
3. Email to Henry Hardy of 27 May 2005.
4. See 172 above.

who introduced another critical comment. I found it really substantial. It seems to me that it may mark the beginning of the next stage in the discussion of ethical pluralism. As I received Joshua's email just before submitting the manuscript, there was no time to address his comment. Despite this I include it here; its author kindly allowed me to do so. I hope that my two email correspondents will develop the statements they made in our private exchanges and give them a more permanent form. I very much hope that the discussion will go on. This is precisely what I aimed at in emptying the drawer that contained my Berlin materials.

> I think that this particular point hinges on an ambiguity in the use of the term 'value pluralism', which affects what the putative 'truth of value pluralism' means. The 'truth of value pluralism' could mean that value pluralism, as a theory about the nature of values—that is, a purely ethical theory, a statement about value—is true (or, to avoid fact/value confusion, valid [the distinction is derived from the work of the neo-Kantian philosopher Rickert, who held that truth applies to questions of fact, and validity to questions of value]). However, 'value pluralism' can be used to refer to, not an ethical theory, but a state of affairs, a state of reality. If this is what 'value pluralism' is taken to mean, then it seems to me that 'the truth of value pluralism' could be taken to mean 'the fact that people pursue a variety of different, valid values'. The former meaning seems to me not to violate Hume's law; the latter does. This ambiguity seems to me to be at the root of your initial criticism of the passages from George's book that you cite: you took him, I think, as making an argument about value pluralism as a fact about people and their values—so that 'the truth of value pluralism' means the fact of a plurality of human values—as opposed to making an argument about value pluralism as a *theory*—so that 'the truth of value pluralism' means the truth of the ethical theory that there exist a plurality of valid values that are important to leading a good human life etc. Now, it does seem to me that clearing up the difference between these two senses of 'value pluralism' doesn't quite get us out of the woods, since the theory of value pluralism, so far as I can see, involves referring to the reality/situation/fact of value pluralism, and offering a particular interpretation/evaluation of it. This being the case, while conclusions about values may not be derived simply from statements of fact, facts and values remain connected, and not utterly divorced. And, while some have argued that it is possible to accept Hume's critique of the naturalistic fallacy, and still hold to an objective notion of value, without recourse to some Platonic or other faith, I remain unconvinced and unquiet in my own mind as to whether this is true.[1]

---

1. Joshua Cherniss, email to Beata Polanowska-Sygulska, 15 September 2005.

Bibliography

Aron, Raymond. *An Essay on Freedom*. New York: World Publishing, 1970.

Baghramian, Maria, and Attracta Ingram, eds. *Pluralism: The Philosophy and Politics of Diversity*. London: Routledge, 2000.

Benn, Stanley I. 'Freedom and Persuasion'. *Australasian Journal of Philosophy* 45 (1967), 260–2.

Berlin, Isaiah. 'Rationality of Value Judgments'. In Carl J. Friedrich, ed., *Nomos VII: Rational Decision*. New York: Atherton, 1967.

———. *Concepts and Categories: Philosophical Essays* (1978), ed. Henry Hardy. Oxford: Oxford University Press, 1980.

———. 'Reply to Robert Kocis'. *Political Studies* 31 (1983), 388–93.

———. *The Crooked Timber of Humanity*, ed. Henry Hardy. London: John Murray, 1990.

———. *Dwie koncepcje wolnosci* [*Two Concepts of Liberty*]. Warsaw: Res Publica, 1991.

———.*The Proper Study of Mankind: An Anthology of Essays*, ed. Henry Hardy and Roger Hausheer. London: Chatto & Windus, 1997.

———. *The Power of Ideas*, ed. Henry Hardy. London: Chatto & Windus, 2000.

———. *Liberty*, ed. Henry Hardy. Oxford: Oxford University Press, 2002.

Berlin, Isaiah, and Bernard Williams. 'Pluralism and Liberalism: A Reply' [to George Crowder, 'Pluralism and Liberalism', *Political Studies* 42 (1994), 293–303]. *Political Studies* 42 (1994), 306–9.

Blokland, Hans. 'Berlin on Pluralism and Liberalism: A Defence'. *European Legacy* 4 (1999), 1–23.

Brogan, A. P. 'Objective Pluralism in the Theory of Value'. *International Journal of Ethics* 41 (1931), 287–95.

Cohen, G. A. 'Isaiah's Marx and Mine'. In Margalit and Margalit, *Isaiah Berlin*.

Cohen, Marshall. 'Berlin and the Liberal Tradition'. *Philosophical Quarterly* 10 (1980), 216–27.

301

Constant, Benjamin. 'The Liberty of the Ancients Compared with That of the Moderns'. In *Political Writings*, ed. Biancamaria Fontana. Cambridge: Cambridge University Press, 1988.

Crowder, George. 'Pluralism and Liberalism'. *Political Studies* 42 (1994), 303.

———. *Liberalism and Value Pluralism*. London: Continuum, 2002.

———. *Isaiah Berlin: Liberty and Pluralism*. Cambridge: Polity, 2004.

Dostoevsky, Fedor. *The Brothers Karamazov*, translated by David Magarshack. Harmondsworth, UK: Penguin Books, 1958.

Dworkin, Ronald. *Taking Rights Seriously*. London: Duckworth, 1978.

Dzur, Albert. 'Value Pluralism versus Political Liberalism?' *Social Theory and Practice* 24 (1998), 375–92.

Feinberg, Joel. *Social Philosophy*. Englewood Cliffs, NJ: Prentice-Hall, 1973.

Friedman, Jeffrey. 'Pluralism or Relativism?' *Critical Review* 11 (1997), 469–80.

Forster, E. M. 'Our Diversions', 3, 'The Doll Souse' (1924). In *Abinger Harvest*. London, 1936.

Fromm, Erich. *Fear of Freedom*. London: Routledge & Kegan Paul, 1960.

Galipeau, Claude. *Isaiah Berlin's Liberalism*. Oxford: Clarendon Press, 1994.

Gallie, W. B. 'Essentially Contested Concepts'. *Proceedings of the Aristotelian Society* 56 (1956), 167–98.

Galston, William. A. 'Value Pluralism and Liberal Political Theory'. *American Political Science Review* 93 (1999), 769–78.

———. *Liberal Pluralism: The Implications of Value Pluralism for Political Theory and Practice*. Cambridge: Cambridge University Press, 2002.

Gaus, Gerald F. 'Pluralistic Liberalism: Making Do without Public Reason?' In *Contemporary Theories of Liberalism*. London: Sage, 2003.

Gray, John. 'On Liberty, Liberalism and Essential Contestability'. *British Journal of Political Science* 8 (1978), 386–7

———. *Hayek on Liberty*. Oxford: Basil Blackwell, 1986.

———. *Liberalisms: Essays in Political Philosophy*. London: Routledge, 1991.

———. 'The Unavoidable Conflict'. *Times Literary Supplement*, 5 July 1991.

———. 'Constancy and Difference: Isaiah Berlin's Contribution to the Life of the Mind'. [English original of Dutch translation published in] *Nexus* 12 (1995), 5–15.

———. *Isaiah Berlin*. London: HarperCollins, 1995.

———. *Two Faces of Liberalism*. New York: New Press, 2000.

———. 'Where Pluralists and Liberals Part Company'. In Baghramian and Ingram, *Pluralism*.

Gray, John, and Bronislaw Wildstein. 'Zycie jest bardziej zlozone niz tradycyjna etyka (Rozmowa z Johnem Grayem)' ['Life is More Complex than Traditional Ethics (A Conversation with John Gray)']. In Bronislaw Wildstein, *Profile wieku* [*Profiles of the Century*]. Warsaw: Politeja, 2000.

Hampshire, Stuart. 'Nationalism'. In Margalit and Margalit, *Isaiah Berlin*.

Hardy, Henry. Description of George Crowder's *Liberalism and Value Pluralism*.

London: Continuum, 2002. http://berlin.wolf.ox.ac.uk/, 'Publications about Isaiah Berlin', compiled by Henry Hardy (accessed 31 December 2005).

————. Description of George Crowder's *Isaiah Berlin: Liberty and Pluralism.* Cambridge: Polity Press, 2004. http://berlin.wolf.ox.ac.uk/, 'Publications about Isaiah Berlin', compiled by Henry Hardy (accessed 31 December 2005).

Hayck, Friedrich A. *The Constitution of Liberty.* London: Routledge & Kegan Paul, 1960.

————. *Studies in Philosophy, Politics and Economics.* London: Routledge & Kegan Paul, 1967.

————. *Law, Legislation and Liberty.* London: Routledge & Kegan Paul, 1982.

Hegel, Georg W. F. *Phenomenology of Spirit*, translated by A. V. Miller. Oxford: Clarendon Press, 1977.

Herzen, Alexander. *Sobranie sochinenii v tridtsati tomakh* [*Collected Writings in Thirty Volumes*]. Moscow, 1954–66.

Hume, David. *A Treatise of Human Nature.* 2 vols. London: J. M. Dent; New York: E. P. Dutton, 1960–1.

Ignatieff, Michael. *Isaiah Berlin: A Life.* London: Chatto & Windus, 1998.

Jahanbegloo, Ramin. *Conversations with Isaiah Berlin.* London: Peter Halban, 1992.

Joas, Hans. 'Combining Value Pluralism and Moral Universalism: Isaiah Berlin and Beyond'. *Responsive Community* 9 (1999), 17–29.

Kateb, George. 'Notes on Pluralism'. *Social Research* 61 (1994), 511–37.

Katznelson, Ira. 'A Properly Defended Liberalism: On John Gray and the Filling of Political Life'. *Social Research* 61 (1994), 611–30.

Kaufman, Arnold S. 'Professor Berlin on Negative Freedom'. *Mind* 71 (1962), 241–3.

Kekes, John. *The Morality of Pluralism.* Princeton, NJ: Princeton University Press, 1993.

Kieslowski, Krzysztof, and Danuta Stok. *Autobiografia: O sobie* [*Autobiography: About Myself*]. Krakow: Znak, 1997.

Kocis, Robert A. 'Toward a Coherent Theory of Human Moral Development: Beyond Sir Isaiah Berlin's Vision of Human Nature'. *Political Studies* 31 (1983), 374–5.

Kolakowski, Leszek. 'Jeden z olbrzymow stulecia' ['One of the Giants of our Century']. *Gazeta Wyborcza*, 7 November 1997, 1.

Lamprecht, Sterling P. 'The Need for a Pluralistic Emphasis in Ethics'. *Journal of Philosophy, Psychology, and Scientific Methods* 17 (1920), 561–72.

Larmore, Charles E. 'Pluralism and Reasonable Disagreement'. *Social Philosophy and Policy* 11 (1994), 44–60.

Legutko, Ryszard. 'On Postmodern Liberal Conservatism'. *Critical Review* 8 (1994), 1–22.

————. 'O postmodernistycznym liberalnym konserwatyzmie' ['On Postmodern Liberal Conservatism']. In *O czasach chytrych i prawdach pozornych* [*On Sly Times and Sham Truths*]. Krakow: Stalky i Spolka, 1999.

————. 'O obiektywnym pluralizmie wartosci' ['On Objective Pluralism of Values']. In *Liberalizm u schylku XX wieku* [*Liberalism at the Close of the 20th Century*], ed. Justyna Miklaszewska. Krakow: Meritum, 1999.

Leontiev, Konstantin Nikolaevich. *Vostok, Rossia i Slavyanstvo* [*The East, Russia and Slavdom*]. Moskva: Respublika, 1996.

Lessnoff, Michael H. 'Isaiah Berlin: Monism and Pluralism'. In *Political Philosophers of the Twentieth Century*. Oxford: Blackwell, 1999.

Lukes, Steven. *Moral Conflict and Politics*. Oxford: Clarendon, 1991.

————. 'Pluralism Is not Enough'. *Times Literary Supplement*, 10 February 1995.

————. *Liberals and Cannibals: The Implications of Diversity*. London: Verso, 2003.

Lovelace, Richard. *Lucasta: The Poems of Richard Lovelace*. Chicago: Caxton, 1921.

MacCallum, Gerald, Jr. 'Negative and Positive Freedom'. *Philosophical Review* 76 (1967), 312–34.

Macfarlane, Leslie J. 'On Two Concepts of Liberty'. *Political Studies* 14 (1966), 77–81.

MacIntyre, Alasdair. *After Virtue*. London: Duckworth, 1985.

Mack, Arien, ed. *Liberty and Pluralism*. *Social Research* 66 (1999).

Macpherson, C. B. *Democratic Theory: Essays in Retrieval*. Oxford: Clarendon Press, 1973.

Magee, Bryan. *Popper*. London: Fontana/Collins, 1974.

————. 'Dialogue with Isaiah Berlin'. In *Men of Ideas: Some Creators of Contemporary Philosophy*. London: BBC, 1978.

Margalit, Edna, and Avishai Margalit, eds. *Isaiah Berlin: A Celebration*. London: Hogarth, 1991.

Marx, Karl, and Friedrich Engels, *Collected Works*. 50 vols. London: Lawrence & Wishart, 2004.

McCloskey, Henry J. 'A Critique of the Ideals of Liberty'. *Mind* 74 (1965), 483–6.

Mehta, Pratap B. Review of Gray, *Isaiah Berlin*. *American Political Science Review* 91 (1997), 722–4.

Merton, Thomas. *No Man Is an Island*. London: Hollis & Carter, 1955.

Nagel, Thomas. 'Pluralism and Coherence'. In *The Legacy of Isaiah Berlin*, ed. Ronald Dworkin, Mark Lilla and Robert B. Silvers. New York: New York Review of Books, 2001.

Nicholls, David. 'Positive Liberty'. *American Political Science Review* 56 (1962), 114–15.

Oppenheim, Felix. *Dimensions of Freedom: An Analysis*. New York: St Martin's Press, 1961.

Parekh, Bhikhu. 'Review Article: The Political Thought of Sir Isaiah Berlin'. *British Journal of Political Science* 12 (1982), 209–10.

Parent, William A. 'Some Recent Work on the Concept of Liberty'. *American Philosophical Quarterly* 11 (1974), 149–67.

Pelczynski, Zbigniew, and John Gray, eds. *Conceptions of Liberty in Political Philosophy.* London: Athlone, 1984.

Polanowska-Sygulska, Beata. 'Krytyka koncepcji wolnosci pozytywnej w ujeciu Isaiaha Berlina' ['Isaiah Berlin's Critique of the Positive Concept of Freedom']. *Studia Nauk Politycznych* 3 (1984), 49–65.

———. 'Give Them Soothing Pills'. *Oxford Magazine*, Noughth Week, Hilary Term, 1987, 3.

———. *Filozofia wolnosci Isaiaha Berlina* [*Isaiah Berlin's Philosophy of Freedom*]. Krakow: Znak, 1998.

———. 'Dwie twarze liberalizmu' ['Two Faces of Liberalism', review of John Gray, *Two Faces of Liberalism*]. *Przeglad Polityczny* 56 (2002), 150.

———. *Oblicza liberalizmu: Isaiah Berlin, John Gray, Steven Lukes, Joseph Raz w rozmowie z Beata Polanowska-Sygulska* [*Visages of Liberalism: Isaiah Berlin, John Gray, Steven Lukes, Joseph Raz in Conversation with Beata Polanowska-Sygulska*]. Krakow: Ksiegarnia Akademicka, 2003.

Popper, Karl. *Conjectures and Refutations: The Growth of Scientific Knowledge.* 4th ed. London: Routledge, 1972.

———. *The Poverty of Historicism.* London: Routledge & Kegan Paul, 1972.

———. 'Winch on Institutions and the Open Society'. In *The Philosophy of Karl Popper*, ed. Paul Schilpp. La Salle, Illinois: Library of Living Philosophers, 1974.

———. *Unended Quest: An Intellectual Biography.* Glasgow: Fontana/Collins, 1976.

———. *The Open Society and Its Enemies.* London: Routledge & Kegan Paul, 1984.

Rhees, Rush. *Without Answers.* London: Routledge & Kegan Paul, 1969.

Riley, Jonathan. 'Crooked Timber and Liberal Culture'. In Baghramian and Ingram, *Pluralism.*

———. 'Interpreting Isaiah Berlin's Liberalism'. *American Political Science Review* 95 (2001), 283–95.

———. 'Defending Cultural Pluralism within Liberal Limits'. *Political Theory* 30 (2002), 68–97.

Russell, Bertrand. *German Social Democracy: Six Lectures.* London: Longmans, Green, 1896.

———. *A History of Western Philosophy.* New York: Simon & Schuster, 1945.

Ryan, Alan. 'Freedom'. *Philosophy* 40 (1965), 108–11.

Sandel, Michael. 'Introduction'. In *Liberalism and Its Critics.* Oxford: Basil Blackwell, 1984.

Scheler, Max. *Vom Umsturz der Werte: Abhandlungen und Aufsätze* [*Gesammelte Werke*, vol. 3] [*On the Revolution in Values: Treatises and Articles* [*Collected Works*, vol. 3]]. Bern: Francke Verlag, 1955.

Steiner, Hillel. 'Individual Liberty'. *Proceedings of the Aristotelian Society* 75 (1974–5), 33–6.

Szacki, Jerzy. 'Sir Isaiah Berlin: historia idei a filozofia' ['Sir Isaiah Berlin: History of Ideas and Philosophy']. *Literatura na Swiecie* 179 No. 6 (1986), 195–207.

Taylor, Charles. 'What's Wrong with Negative Liberty'. In *The Idea of Freedom: Essays in Honour of Isaiah Berlin*, ed. Alan Ryan. Oxford: Oxford University Press, 1979.

————. 'Plurality of Goods'. In *The Legacy of Isaiah Berlin,* ed. Ronald Dworkin, Mark Lilla and Robert B. Silvers. New York: New York Review Books, 2001.

Waismann, Friedrich. 'Verifiability'. In *Logic and Language*, ed. Antony Flew. Oxford: Basil Blackwell, 1952.

Walzer, Michael. 'Are there Limits to Liberalism?' *New York Review of Books*, 19 October 1995, 28–31.

Watola, Judyta, and Dariusz Kortko. 'Czesto czulem sie jak kat (Rozmowa z Franciszkiem Kokotem)' ['I Often Felt Like a Hangman (A Conversation with Franciszek Kokot)']. *Magazyn Gazety Wyborczej*, 10 January 2002, 23–5.

Weinstock, Daniel. 'The Graying of Berlin'. *Critical Review* 11 (1997), 481–501.

Williams, Bernard. 'Conflicts of Values'. In *The Idea of Freedom: Essays in Honour of Isaiah Berlin*, ed. Alan Ryan. Oxford: Oxford University Press, 1979.

Wollheim, Richard. 'The Idea of a Common Human Nature'. In Margalit and Margalit, eds., *Isaiah Berlin*.

Index

Compiled by Douglas Matthews

Works by Isaiah Berlin (IB) and Beata Polanowska-Sygulska (BP-S) appear directly under their titles; works by others under their author's name.

Crooked Timber of Humanity, The (IB),
40n1, 69
Crowder, George: on liberal pluralism,
89–90, 267–9, 280–2, 286, 292–6,
297–300; on value pluralism,
269–70; on moral conflicts, 271,
276; Isaiah Berlin: Liberty and Pluralism, 292, 295; Liberalism and
Value Pluralism, 268, 292, 294, 299
cultural imperialism, 10

Danton, Georges Jacques, 181
deity: idea of, 226–7
democracy: and illiberalism, 88;
Schumpeter defines, 157
Descartes, René, 143, 147
desire: awakening of, 70
despotism: enlightened, 88; and historical theory, 180
determinism, 55, 120–1, 124
Diderot, Denis, 138, 143
dimensions (spatial), 125–6, 170
'Does Political Theory Still Exist?' (IB),
51, 228, 259n1
Dostoevsky, Fedor Mikhailovich, 117,
184; The Brothers Karamazov, 145
duty, 127
Dworkin, Ronald Myles: on idea of liberty, 63, 158, 173, 253–4, 260–1;
on equality, 260, 262, 281; on pluralism and moral conflict, 276;
Taking Rights Seriously, 260

Einstein, Albert, 186
Elders of Zion, 115
emotivism, 276
empathy with, 148
empirical categories, 169n2, 170, 227–9
empiricism: Hume and, 205; and experience, 222–3
Engels, Friedrich, 55, 133, 181
Epictetus, 122
Epicurus, 135

equality, 121, 260, 262, 281
essentialism, 52, 55–8, 60–2, 176–8,
255–7
essentially contestable concepts, 135–6
ethics: right and good in, 127; Wittgenstein on, 185; incommensurability
in, 226–7; pluralism in, 625–7
Euripides, 272
'European Unity and Its Vicissitudes'
(IB), 90n2, 125n2
existentialism, 144, 239

family resemblance, 41n1, 43, 193
Feinberg, Joel: Social Philosophy, 236n3
Fichte, Johann Gottlieb, 108, 135
Filozofia wolnosci Isaiaha Berlina
(BP-S; Isaiah Berlin's Philosophy
of Freedom), 48n2
Forster, Edward Morgan, 138
Four Essays on Liberty (IB), 34–5,
36n1, 37, 75, 79, 89
France: attitude to Germany, 118
Franck, César, 168
Frederick II (the Great), King of
Prussia, 88
free will, 55, 121, 205–6
freedom see liberty
French Revolution, 181–2, 210
Freud, Sigmund, 42, 181, 183, 186
'From Hope and Fear Set Free' (IB), 37
Fromm, Erich: Fear of Freedom, 153,
239

Galileo Galilei, 137, 140
Galipeau, Claude, 28, 67, 69, 288
Gallie, Walter Bryce: 'Essentially Con-
tested Concepts', 135n1
Galston, William A., 281, 292, 296, 626
Gaulle, Charles de, 188
genius, 135
Germany: attitude to France, 118
'Give Them Soothing Pills' (BP-S), 54n1
God: existence of, 39